The Expos  in Their Prime

MW01074445

The Expos
in Their Prime

*The Short-Lived Glory
of Montreal's Team, 1977–1984*

ALAIN USEREAU

McFarland & Company, Inc., Publishers
Jefferson, North Carolina, and London

All photographs are from the National Baseball Hall of Fame, Cooperstown, New York, unless otherwise noted.

LIBRARY OF CONGRESS CATALOGUING-IN-PUBLICATION DATA

Usereau, Alain.
The Expos in their prime : the short-lived glory of Montreal's team, 1977–1984 / Alain Usereau.
    p.   cm.
Includes bibliographical references and index.

ISBN 978-0-7864-7081-5
softcover : acid free paper ∞

1. Montreal Expos (Baseball team)—History.   I. Title.
GV875.M6U74 2013
796.357'640971428—dc23   2012040191

BRITISH LIBRARY CATALOGUING DATA ARE AVAILABLE

© 2013 Alain Usereau. All rights reserved

No part of this book may be reproduced or transmitted in any form or by any means, electronic or mechanical, including photocopying or recording, or by any information storage and retrieval system, without permission in writing from the publisher.

Front cover image: The 1979 Expos were the winningest in franchise history, with 95 victories. It was the start of a journey that would make the Expos the most popular sports team in Canada (National Baseball Hall of Fame Library Cooperstown, New York)

Manufactured in the United States of America

McFarland & Company, Inc., Publishers
  Box 611, Jefferson, North Carolina 28640
   www.mcfarlandpub.com

Table of Contents

Preface

The Montreal Expos and baseball were a big part of my life when I was in my teens. Baseball is still there but the Expos are not. The memories are still there, too, though; memories that I wanted to share with those who were also there and with those who want to discover what it was like to have a baseball team touch the hearts of sports fans in a country that was (and still is) crazy about a different sport — hockey, of course. This journey began in 2005 when a friend suggested that I begin working on a baseball book as a distraction in a very difficult time. Thank you, Pierre Fortier.

I'd like to thank as well all the people I interviewed for this book, a list of which you will find in the back. Big thanks also to the Bibliothèque Nationale du Québec, where I spent countless hours digging through all five daily newspapers that were published during the period covered, *La Presse*, *Journal de Montréal*, *Montréal-Matin*, *The Gazette* and *Montreal Star*. Unfortunately, two of them folded along the way (*Montréal-Matin* and *Montreal Star*), but they still provided me with lots of useful information.

Big thanks also to the whole community of the Society for American Baseball Research. They came through every single time I needed information in another city or in a publication I didn't have access to in Montreal. I can't be grateful enough to SABR members. The websites www.baseball-reference.com and www.retrosheet.org were invaluable when I wanted to get the record straight, to cross-check information, to get the right stats, etc. When play-by-play specifics are related in this book, you can be sure they were proofed through Retrosheet. Same with the players and teams stats through Baseball-reference.

I am grateful also to Daniel Bertrand and my French publisher, les Éditeurs Réunis, who first believed in the book in French (*L'Époque Glorieuse des Expos*, 2009) and allowed me to go ahead with this translation. And, lastly, thank you to the Expos of the late 1970s and early 1980s for those wonderful summer nights. You were part of my life then and for the last seven years, while working on this book, you were able to get me passionate about these teams once again!

1

Introduction

The story of the Montreal Expos is fascinating in many ways. When the team played its last game in September 2004, its departure from the city had been expected for quite some time. The fans had decided to do away with a team that wasn't given the chance to fight evenly with other teams, either by being forced to play so-called home games in Puerto Rico or being refused the privilege of calling up players from the minors in September 2003 as it was fighting to get into the playoffs (the Expos were tied for the wild card berth in late August). These two examples demonstrate how little management respected the fans and the players. Nonetheless, there were more than 30,000 fans on hand for a final salute on September 29, 2004, at Olympic Stadium when the Expos took on the Florida Marlins. Through Brad Wilkerson, Brian Schneider, Jamey Carroll, Livan Hernandez, Tomo Oka and Chad Cordero, the fans waved a final goodbye to Rusty Staub, Coco Laboy, Mack Jones, Bill Stoneman, Bob Bailey, Ron Hunt, Steve Rogers, Gary Carter, Andre Dawson, Tim Raines, Tim Wallach, Hubie Brooks, Pascual Perez, Dennis and Pedro Martinez, Marquis Grissom, Vladimir Guerrero and others.

The Expos never had it made from the moment Montreal was awarded a franchise in May 1968. John McHale and Charles Bronfman saved the team as it was on the verge of being moved before playing even one game. This start should not be surprising in retrospect; it's the perfect picture of the team's whole history. It wasn't long before the nickname "Nos Amours" ("Our True Love" would be a good English translation) stuck with the francophone fans, who truly embraced their new heroes at Jarry Park. A real love story developed between the team and the fans, the apex of which was the glory years from 1979 to 1981. Never again were the Expos so loved. Talented, charismatic, colorful, all qualities that were the perfect reflection of what Montreal fans were looking for. On and off the field the Expos of that era were a success which was never again duplicated. This passionate relationship between the fans and the team lasted three full seasons before unfulfilled (and maybe unrealistic) promises compromised it. Failed expectations created frustration and then resignation from 1982 to 1984.

There were reconciliation attempts, in 1987, 1989, from 1992 to 1994, in 1996 and 2003. But never again would the Expos be able to create the atmosphere that lived from 1979 to 1981. Some would say that the famed hockey team in Montreal, les Canadiens, always have the unconditional support of the whole city, even through the bad times. The relationship however is entirely different. The Canadiens are part of the family, and will always be welcomed. For the Expos, the relationship was based on passion from 1979 to 1981, a passion that was very difficult to sustain. In this book, you'll find out how it was built... and how it subsided, beginning the slow succession of events that sent the Expos to Washington.

1

1976: "Phase 2"

The 1976 season was tagged as the beginning of "Phase 2" by the Expos' brass. Up to then, Gene Mauch had been the only manager the Expos had known since their inception in 1969. However, as the team wanted to take a youthful direction, it was decided that Mauch was not the right man to lead a group of youngsters. Karl Kuehl, who knew the organization and its players inside out, was named the Expos' manager. He had led the Expos' AAA affiliate in 1974 and 1975,[1] so he knew the players who would be brought up to form the new nucleus of the team. However, the task at hand was huge. First, Kuehl succeeded a manager who had been very popular and had a very solid reputation, Gene Mauch. Second, Mauch had been able to get the most out of a very ordinary team in the years prior. Lastly, Kuehl was asked to manage a team that was young, full of promise, but too inexperienced to battle with the likes of the Pittsburgh Pirates and the Philadelphia Phillies in the National League East Division. The season was a disaster from the beginning to the end: 55 wins, 107 losses. The Expos finished last in runs scored and runs allowed.

Karl Kuehl lost all credibility in the second month of the season when Tim Foli publicly questioned his skills as manager in Philadelphia.[2] The hot-tempered Foli was suspended by Kuehl but the decision was overturned by the general manager, Jim Fanning. The Expos' ship, which was already sailing in troubled water, was practically without a captain thereafter. Also in May, veteran Steve Renko was traded to the Chicago Cubs. He was the last Expo still with the team to have played the initial season in 1969. Renko then ranted against Montreal, complaining about the climate, and the taxes, among other things. He went on to say a law should forbid the obligation the players have to play in Montreal.[3]

Larry Parrish, in his second season in the majors, would eventually lament the lack of experience in the clubhouse: "In 1975, Mauch was there. We had Fairly, Bob Bailey, some of the pitchers were older, Duke Snider was the hitting coach. They could help a young man through it a little bit. And in 1976, they got rid of Mauch, brought in Karl Kuehl, an inexperienced coaching staff, and they got rid of all the veteran ballplayers. I think, player-wise, Mike Jorgensen might have been the oldest player at that time and he was 26."[4]

Without any offense, pitching, spirit and direction, the team stockpiled defeats one after another. In early September, Kuehl was fired, replaced by Charlie Fox. After a few games, Fox decided to invite the media to attend a team meeting, where Barry Foote, Ellis Valentine and Parrish were the main recipients of Fox's diatribe, which was of course published in the media.[5] The papers could count on more interesting stuff, but that didn't help the team on the field. To crown that miserable season, Tim Foli went on strike the last game of the year. The reason: he wanted to voice his displeasure over the choice of Woodie Fryman as the team's player of the year, as selected by the Montreal chapter of the Baseball Writers Association of America.[6] Really, that was a year to forget!

The Expos couldn't however pick a better year for such a dismal showing. They weren't invisible by any means but they never were the number one attraction during that season, or even the number two or three for that matter. That spring, the Montreal Canadiens won back the Stanley Cup after a "slump" of two years. The Canadiens were so successful during that period that one would ask a friend, "Do you expect to go to the Stanley Cup rally today?" and a common reply would be "No, I'll go next year!" After hockey, the 1976 Summer Olympics were the main news topic for several weeks. And right after that, people began talking about the first real international hockey tournament to be held, The Canada Cup. For the first time, teams from around the world would meet in a single tournament. The Expos, however, as inconspicuous as they were in 1976, knew that the fans and the media wouldn't be that tolerant again. Management had to act, especially with the expected move to Olympic Stadium from tiny Jarry Park.

Shortly after the end of the nightmare of the 1976 season, John McHale announced a major reshuffle within the organization. Dick Williams was named the new manager. Williams was no stranger to Montreal as he was a coach there in 1971 under Gene Mauch. Charlie Fox, who had showed interest in the manager position, was named general manager, replacing Jim Fanning, who was put in charge of scouting and player development.

John McHale wanted a proven winner and he got someone who fit the bill. Williams had led Oakland to two World Series championships and Boston to one American League pennant. He had the reputation of being a no-nonsense manager who demanded (and usually got) the most out of his play-ers. His hiring also meant an almost complete overhaul in the coaching staff.

Ozzie Virgil was the only one to be retained. Jim Brewer, Mickey Vernon and Billy Gardner completed the quartet (there were only four coaches per team then).

Charlie Fox's nomination as the new GM came as a surprise. But the Expos had to make substantial changes. Jim Fanning conceded that he was not at ease in this new world, where players were represented by professional negotiators: "As close to John as I was, I think he always wanted me to have responsible jobs and he wanted another voice to talk to players, to talk to agents. And very frankly, I did not do very well in the agent area. And it was my fault because I guess I created a combative atmosphere between agents and myself."[7] As

Dick Williams was the manager who led the Expos on the field from eternal afterthought to serious contender. As different as one could be from executive John McHale, Williams nonetheless added some badly needed credibility to the Expos' organization.

for Fox, he had a little idea what he was dealing with — personnel-wise — after managing the team in the last month of the season.

Williams brought instant credibility and some stability, which were terribly lacking in Montreal in 1976. The arrival of Williams and the new coaches meant the organization was serious. But the hardest part had yet to come: strengthen the team on the field. The most-used players at each position didn't instil much fear in a pitcher's mind: the catcher was Barry Foote; infielders were Mike Jorgensen, Pete Mackanin, Tim Foli and Larry Parrish; main outfielders were Gary Carter, Ellis Valentine, Del Unser and Jerry White. Except for Foli and Unser, acquired via a mid-season trade in 1976, nobody had been a regular before. On the mound, Steve Rogers and Woodie Fryman couldn't do it all. Dale Murray led the league in appearances but his performances were below par compared with 1975. Don Stanhouse had an outstanding first half, before faltering down the stretch.[8]

The task at hand was huge for Charlie Fox. But he could count on outside help: for the first time in baseball history, free agents would be available for the taking. Before 1976, players were bound to their initial team for as long as management decided before either trading or releasing them. It had been that way since the end of the nineteenth century. There were attempts to contest that way of doing business, but with no success. The players thus had very little negotiation power. However, there were few special occasions where a player was able to shop himself around. In 1967, Ken Harrelson, a young slugger, was released by the Kansas City A's owner, Charles O. Finley. That led to many offers from other teams. He ended up getting a lucrative contract with the Boston Red Sox, with a substantial bonus (from $40,000 to $75,000, depending on the source).[9] After the 1974 season, Jim "Catfish" Hunter was free to negotiate after an arbiter established that Finley, him again, defaulted on contract terms, voiding Hunter's contract. Hunter had just won the Cy Young Award and three World Series championships with the Oakland A's. He had completed his fourth straight 20-win season. He finally signed for close to $3 million with the New York Yankees. The average salary then in the majors was around $40,000![10]

However, Harrelson and Hunter were exceptions rather than the norm. Players couldn't expect to be released at the prime of their career or be freed contractually due to some owner's negligence (or stubbornness!). But Hunter's case gave a very good indication of the player's real value on an open market. The Players Association, which was established in 1966, was beginning to make big strides on many issues, mainly the pension plan and the right to salary arbitration after two years. As for complete free agency, not much had been done but 1975 would change all that. Two players, Andy Messersmith, pitcher with Los Angeles, and Dave McNally, of the Expos, decided to play without a signed contract. According to the Basic Agreement, a team could renew a player's contract for a year without his consent. The Players Association decided to dispute whether the team could do that for one year and one year only, or perpetually, as contended by management. The arbitrator, Peter Seitz, the same one who sided with Jim Hunter against Charles O. Finley, again decided in favor of the players. Thus, McNally and Messersmith were free from any obligation towards their respective teams. It didn't mean much for McNally, as he had retired during the course of the 1975 season (but still wanted to pursue the case). Messersmith took full advantage of the opportunity to sign a $1 million three-year contract with the Atlanta Braves. The owners had no choice but to sit with the Players Association. An agreement was reached in July 1976, not without some disturbance through a lockout-dotted spring training. The players would at last have some freedom, according to some criteria that would be redefined several times along the way.

In this new context, Charlie Fox could hope to improve his team in a more substantial way than just waiting for his young players to mature. With owner Charles Bronfman's blessing (and money), Fox had no intention to be a mere spectator. A total of 24 players were available, including eight from the Oakland A's (and owner Charles O. Finley).[11]

In this first players auction ever, a draft was instituted: each player could not be chosen by more than 12 teams, plus the original one. These teams earned the privilege to talk to the players they selected. The first one to sign was reliever Bill Campbell, with the Boston Red Sox. As for the Expos, their needs were enormous! Pierre Ladouceur, of *La Presse*, one of the best baseball analysts among Montreal writers, pointed out the main priorities of the Expos: a second baseman, a right fielder, a left-handed reliever and a starting pitcher.[12]

The Expos targeted three players: second baseman Dave Cash and out-fielders Reggie Jackson and Gary Matthews.[13] In mid–November, Cash became the first free agent to sign with the Montreal Expos, for a five-year $1 million contract. He had spent the preceding three seasons with the Philadelphia Phillies, the NL East Division champions. He had also won a World Series with the Pittsburgh Pirates in 1971 and had the reputation of being a leader. Upon his arrival in Philadelphia, a franchise that had been moribund for some years. he was the one who coined the slogan "Yes we can!" His teammates and also the city embraced his enthusiastic demeanor.

Cash was introduced to the Montreal media in a press conference on November 18, 1976. However, the atmosphere was politically charged and had nothing to do with baseball.[14] Three days earlier, the province of Quebec had just elected the Parti Québécois, which wanted Quebec to separate from Canada and be recognized as a country. Shortly before the election, Expos owner Charles Bronfman, addressing the Allied Jewish Community, hinted that the team could move out of Montreal if the Parti Québécois was to be elected, in comments that were published by the *Montreal Star*.[15] Many people expected some explanation from Charles Bronfman at the Dave Cash press conference. To his credit, he wasted no time. He apologized publicly, adding that the Expos wouldn't leave Montreal and that he would never again be involved in politics.[16]

Back to baseball, most agreed that the addition of Cash would be benefi-cial to the Expos. Alan Richman, of the *Montreal Star*, disagreed strongly. He stressed Cash's shortcomings: no power, no plate discipline, a below-average arm. To Richman, these weaknesses shouldn't warrant a $1 million invest-ment.[17] For a second baseman, arm strength is not as important as being able to turn a double play. But the first two points brought up by Richman are extremely pertinent. The Expos however needed stability, leadership, rigor, all qualities Cash could undeniably add to the team.

After Dave Cash's case was settled, it was time for the pièce de résistance: Reggie Jackson. He was the most recognizable player among that first crop of free agents. He was spectacular, flamboyant, a showman, a winner of three World Series. He sought attention and thrived under it. From the get-go, the Expos seemed to be among the contenders for his services. *La Presse* believed (with good accuracy) that it would take $3 million to sign the star outfielder. The French daily reported that this $3 million would be a good financial investment: the additional revenues caused by Jackson's presence would justify his hiring at this price.[18] Charlie Fox had carte blanche but in this special case, higher-ranking team officials were also directly involved, among them owner Charles Bronfman, president John McHale, and financial controller Harry Renaud.[19] *The Gazette*, which was pretty much in the know with the organization and its leaders, even reported that the Expos' board allowed a special added budget of $4 million.[20] The Expos could also count on their new manager, Dick Williams, with whom Jackson won the World Series in Oakland. The two men, although very different, had lots of respect for one another.

But Jackson was the one holding the cards. Many teams were luring him and, of course, he took advantage of all the attention. The weekend following Cash's signing, everything was put into place in order to host Jackson and his entourage in Montreal. Olympic Stadium was to hold a press conference, where the Expos expected to play for the first time in April 1977. But things didn't really go as expected. Jackson's arrival was delayed due to customs issues, holding up the press conference for several hours. The day after, Saturday, November 20, Jackson and his cohort were Charles Bronfman's guests at his mansion. Montreal mayor Jean Drapeau was also among the invitees. Lots of money was to be discussed, so Bronfman's financial consultant Leo Kolber was also present. Talks were to resume on Sunday but Jackson left.[21] The Expos would never again be able to have direct contact with Jackson or his representatives. In the next few days, the papers would report that a small quantity of marijuana was discovered in Jackson's luggage at the airport.[22]

Nonetheless, the Expos still seemed to be in the hunt, along with San Diego, Baltimore, the Los Angeles Dodgers and the New York Yankees. San Diego Padres general manager Buzzie Bavasi strongly believed that the Expos were in the lead.[23] But Jackson needed all the attention he could get, on the biggest stage baseball could offer. On that criteria alone, nobody could match the Yankees. In late November, an agreement between Jackson and the Yankees was announced: "George Steinbrenner (owner) and Gabe Paul (general manager) showed me more guts than the others. That's what made the difference."[24] Charles Bronfman and John McHale didn't appreciate these comments, especially after investing $30,000 just trying to seduce Jackson.[25] His contract with the Yankees called for close to $3 million for five years. The Expos' offer was, in fact, superior, up to $5 million, according to Jackson's autobiography.[26]

After striking out with Jackson, the Expos turned their attention to Gary Matthews. But like Jackson, Matthews turned down a more lucrative offer from Montreal and signed instead with Atlanta. But Charlie Fox wasn't done by any means. The baseball winter meetings would offer him another occasion to try to reshuffle the team. Fox let it be known that Barry Foote and Gary Carter were available.[27] Carter had been playing in the outfield to accommodate Foote, but the Expos' minor league system was full of prospects in the outfield. Al Oliver, of the Pittsburgh Pirates, was targeted by Fox. Acknowledged as one of the game's purest hitters, Oliver was considered available as the Pirates were loaded with big hitters. But they wouldn't give him away. The Pirates wanted a catcher and two more players, preferably a starting pitcher and a regular position player.[28]

Fox was able to trigger only one deal during the meetings, sending first baseman Andre Thornton to Cleveland for veteran pitcher Jackie Brown. Thornton finished the 1976 season hitting below .200. His future, a very bright one, would be settled in Cleveland. Fox was able, though, to set the table for a trade with the Cincinnati Reds, who had just won the World Series. Tony Perez was available, as the Reds intended to make Dan Driessen their regular first baseman. The Expos and the Reds agreed on the players. But the Expos wanted to make sure they had Perez under contract for more than one year. Perez agreed to a three-year deal and thus became an Expo, along with left-handed reliever Will McEnaney. The Reds got in return veteran Woodie Fryman and reliever Dale Murray. Fryman had led the Expos with 13 wins, on a team that won only 55 games. Furthermore, Fryman would be closer to his Kentucky farm.

In the meantime, team president John McHale had to finalize the move to Olympic Stadium. An agreement had been reached shortly after the end of the 1976 season with the provincial government, led by the Liberal Party. The provincial authorities chose to delay the official signing until after the election. However, the Liberals lost the election to the Parti Québécois, which promptly rejected the agreement.[29] The Expos had to start from scratch again with new people, including the minister in charge of Olympic Stadium, Claude Charron.

Shortly after his appointment as minister, Charron invited the Expos' management to discuss the stadium's lease. John McHale was among the Expos' delegation. Charron, a huge baseball fan, began the meeting by blasting McHale and the Expos about their showing in the 1976 season! He also brought up the disastrous trade after 1974 that sent Ken Singleton and Mike

Torrez to Baltimore for Rich Coggins and Dave McNally. These two players combined didn't even play a complete season while Singleton and Torrez would have long and productive careers. Both players also had married girls from Quebec. In short, that meeting set the tone for what would be a long and arduous relationship between the Expos and the authorities in charge of Olympic Stadium, not only in 1976 but right until the Expos' departure for Washington.

Because of the uncertainty related to the stadium lease situation, the National League decided to take the 1978 All-Star Game away from Montreal. The situation was so tense that there were talks about beginning the 1977 season at Jarry Park or in another city with the blessing of the National League. John McHale was complaining that he was dealing with people who had no decision-making power. Harry Renaud would reminisce about that period, one of the most frustrating of his tenure as the Expos controller from 1969 to 1981: "Claude Charron tried to impose some things on the agreement that we had already reached with the Quebec government, so we couldn't accept those. And I remember having a revised lease proposal from them delivered to my house on Christmas eve that year in 1976 and we were given like four or five days to respond to it. So, the whole thing was very kind of bullyish and we finally said we're not gonna take this anymore. We didn't have to move from Jarry Park. We called the minister and announced we were going to stay at Jarry Park."[30]

An agreement would finally be reached, but only in mid–March. If one had to determine a winner, surprisingly, it would be the Expos! According to Gilles Blanchard, from *La Presse*, the new lease was more favorable to the team than the original one that was rejected by the Parti Québécois, an assessment that John McHale and Harry Renaud would agree on.[31] Even if incomplete (the mast wasn't even completed, let alone the roof!), Olympic Stadium would be at last the new home of the Montreal Expos. The main question remained: what kind of team would show up on the field?

2

1977: The Move to the Big O

When spring training began in February 1977, Dick Williams warned that many jobs were on the line, which was easily understandable with a team coming off a 107-loss season. Among the position players, Tony Perez (first base), Dave Cash (second base), Tim Foli (shortstop), youngster Ellis Valentine (right field) and pitchers Steve Rogers, Don Stanhouse and Will McEnaney seemed to be assured of a spot on the roster.[1] Barry Foote and Gary Carter were set to battle for the everyday job behind the plate. Larry Parrish had to prove he belonged, even though he had been the regular third baseman the preceding two seasons. Del Unser was the only experienced outfielder, but many prospects were showing promise, including Warren Cromartie, Bombo Rivera, Jerry White, Gary Roenicke and especially Andre Dawson, who crushed minor league pitching in 1976. In 114 games in Quebec and Denver combined (the Expos' AA and AAA affiliates), Dawson hit 28 home runs and drove in 73 runs, along with a .353 batting average and a slugging percentage of .658 in his first complete season in professional baseball. Even with all these prospects, management still had doubts, as they tried to get veterans like Rick Monday[2] and Bobby Murcer,[3] after missing out on the Reggie Jackson sweepstakes and coming up empty with Gary Matthews.

Dick Williams' main concern, however, was pitching. Many names were tossed around as targeted by general manager Charlie Fox but three of them seemed serious enough to warrant a closer look: Mike Torrez,[4] Vida Blue[5] and Ross Grimsley.[6]

Torrez had already played in Montreal and was married to a Quebec girl, Danielle Gagnon. He was traded after the 1974 season in what is still arguably the worst transaction in Expos history (Torrez and Ken Singleton to Baltimore for Rich Coggins and Dave McNally). Before spring training, Charlie Fox voiced his interest in bringing back both Torrez and Ken Singleton.[7]

Vida Blue had been one of the best left-handers in the American League since 1971. He had won a Cy Young Award, was named MVP, had won five

American League West Division titles and three World Series. The Oakland A's were left with ruins after the departure of several free agents, including Joe Rudi, Sal Bando, Bert Campaneris, Rollie Fingers, Joe Rudi and Don Baylor. It was obvious that Blue would be next. But he wouldn't come cheaply. Charles O. Finley told the Oakland media that the Expos were very active.[8] According so some sources, the Expos were ready to spend $1.5 million to get Blue.[9] It was very different to think that such a deal would have been approved by Commissioner Bowie Kuhn. In the middle of the 1976 season, Kuhn had voided such cash-for-player deals when Finley tried to sell Fingers and Rudi to the Boston Red Sox and Blue to the New York Yankees.

Grimsley was playing the last year of his contract with the Baltimore Orioles and would become a free agent after the 1977 season. The Orioles were looking for catchers. Barry Foote was mentioned several times in the papers.[10] What added to the speculation was the continual presence of super-scout Jim Russo around the Expos' training location in Daytona Beach.[11] But the player Russo was contemplating was not Barry Foote but rather a young athlete that he couldn't stop dreaming about: Ellis Valentine.[12] Charlie Fox was trying hard to get Williams some help on the mound, but to no avail.

During the second week of spring training, Dick Williams was already praising the play of Andre Dawson and Warren Cromartie.[13] The original plan was to play Dawson and Del Unser with Ellis Valentine in the outfield. But Cromartie had other ideas and, contrary to Dawson who was very quiet, he liked to be noticed. As for Dawson, he wanted to be noticed more for his play than for his mouth, but two incidents early in camp showed that he wouldn't be intimidated by anyone. As Dawson and the team were riding the bus in one of those long journeys that were commonplace in Florida, Tim Foli and Dave Cash had a serious verbal clash. To the surprise of many, Dawson told Foli to shut up.[14] Later in camp, Dawson wouldn't let Tony Perez prolong his turn in the batting cage.[15] Players have a set number of swings during batting practice, which is almost sacred. Perez wanted to take some more swings, but Dawson refused to let that go, even though he was a rookie and Perez was one of the most respected players not only with the Expos but throughout baseball. Dawson and Cromartie couldn't be more different. Dawson was a low-key, power hitting, five-tool player that every organization dreamed about. Cromartie was a trash-talk specialist who spread his line drives to all fields. But their performances on the field didn't give Dick Williams much of a choice; they would begin the season as the Expos' center and left fielders.[16]

As for the two remaining spots, Dick Williams didn't waste any time. With two weeks to go before the regular season, he knew that Gary Carter would go back to catching and that Larry Parrish would remain his regular third baseman.[17] Williams had thus set a line up that would be the envy of many teams in the coming years, especially with Carter, Parrish, Cromartie, Dawson and Valentine, all home-grown talent, nurtured and developed within the Expos' organization.

As for pitching, two left-handers got the manager's attention: Gerald Hannahs and Shane Rawley.[18] Hannahs won 20 games with Quebec in the Eastern League in 1976 and added two more victories with the Expos after a call-up in September. Rawley was really the biggest surprise of the camp. He was the last cut, but at 21 the Expos wanted to let him develop further in the minors.

Still looking for help with a few days left in camp, the Expos gave veteran Carl Morton a trial.[19] Morton had been with the Expos from 1969 to 1972. In 1970, he was the Rookie of the Year in the National League with 18 wins. In Atlanta from 1973 to 1975, he won more than 40 games. Morton was looking for a job and the Expos desperately needed reinforcements on the mound. But the experiment lasted only a few days before Morton would be back home. In fact, he would never pitch again in the majors. As for the Expos, Steve Rogers, Don Stanhouse, Gerald Hannahs and Jackie Brown would begin the season in a four-man starting rotation.[20]

The lack of depth in the pitching department was unanimously acknowledged by those who followed baseball. Still most observers believed the Expos would make a step forward. A year following a 55–107 season, very few chose the Expos to finish last in the National League East.[21] A new aggressive direction with general manager Charlie Fox and manager Dick Williams and the move to a new modern facility converged to give the team some renewed credibility.

The Montreal Expos began the 1977 season on April 9 in Philadelphia against the defending National League East champions, the Philadelphia Phillies.[22] That first game would be a very good indication of what the Expos' fans could expect from their team, not only for that season but also in the not-so-distant future. Behind 3–0 at the top of the sixth inning against left-hander Steve Carlton, one of the best in the business, the Expos scored four runs with three home runs from Ellis Valentine, Tony Perez and Gary Carter. Jackie Brown, who pitched five scoreless innings in relief of Steve Rogers, got the win. The following day, a three-run home run by Tony Perez in the eighth inning let the Expos secure a 9–8 victory. After two losses in Pittsburgh, the Expos flew to Montreal, getting ready for the first-ever baseball game played at Olympic Stadium.

Friday, April 15, was brisk, and after a ceremony including several former major leaguers born in Quebec, Don Stanhouse threw the first pitch at what was to be known as the Big O. Stanhouse, however, was on the mound for only two innings, long enough to allow three runs. Dave Cash got the historic first hit in the first inning. The first home run ever at Olympic Stadium was hit by Ellis Valentine. Ironically, he was also the last player to hit a home run at Jarry Park. That was the highest point of the game for the Expos as they lost, 7–2, to the Phillies and Steve Carlton. But the Expos went on a four-game winning streak against Philadelphia and Pittsburgh. The Pirates ended that streak with an 8–6 win. In a losing effort, Gary Carter hit three home runs off Jim Rooker.

The first month of the season was pretty satisfactory for the Expos as they compiled an 8–8 record. Aside from that surprising start, the attention was turned to the situation of shortstop Tim Foli.[23] His hot temper exasperated everyone around the team. Even the umpires warned Dick Williams during spring training that they wouldn't put up anymore with his constant bickering.[24] Foli was also part of the former regime from which the Expos wanted to separate themselves. In the meantime in San Francisco, the Giants had a shortstop, Chris Speier, who wanted out.[25] Charlie Fox had managed Speier in San Francisco and knew him well. But he first wanted to be sure that he would be under contract for some years before acquiring him. Finally, the trade was announced on April 27, straight up, Foli for Speier. Most beat writers applauded Foli's departure. His days had been numbered since his strike on the last day of the 1976 season. Serge Touchette, from *Le Journal de Montréal*, had been very harsh on Foli after his one-day strike in an article published in the form of an open letter, pointing out his egotistical temperament.[26]

The Expos began May as they had left April with five wins in the first seven games, a very good outcome considering that six of these games were played on the West Coast, where the team always had problems. After a 4–3 win against the Dodgers at the Big O on May 10, the Expos boasted a 13–10 record, four games out of first place. But the Expos returned to reality the hard way with 11 straight losses during which they allowed 79 runs! The starting pitchers were hit unmercifully, producing a 6.75 ERA. Worse: nine of those games were played at home. This losing streak showed everybody what was already known: the pitching staff needed some help. On May 21, as the Expos lost for the eleventh time in a row, a 21-inning affair against the San Diego Padres, Charlie Fox acquired veteran Stan Bahnsen from Oakland for Mike Jorgensen. Bahnsen already had more than 100 career victories, mostly with the Yankees and the Chicago White Sox. His best days were probably behind him, but his addition was most welcome, given the dire situation of pitching in Montreal. Jorgensen was another player who was quite unhappy with his situation with the Expos.[27]

Six days after Bahnsen's acquisition, Fox got another pitcher, Santo Alcala, from the Cincinnati Reds. The cost was, however, much higher than for Bahnsen: Shane Rawley, the revelation of spring training. Rawley would become a solid pitcher in the 1980s with Seattle, the Yankees and Philadelphia. Alcala had won 11 games in 15 decisions as a rookie in 1976. His win total was, though, misleading as his ERA was 4.70 in a year when the pitchers had the upper hand with a league ERA at 3.50.[28] The Reds offense, dubbed the Big Red Machine, provided Alcala with the needed support to get all those wins. But in his quest for better arms, Charlie Fox was blinded by the 11 wins. For his work and his effort in trying to improve the team, Fox was praised by Jerry Trudel, from the *Montréal-Matin*.[29] Trudel, it must be noted, was one of the harshest critics of John McHale, going as far as giving him the nickname "The Canon"!

To free up a spot for Alcala, the Expos sent down Gerald Hannahs to the minors. In his first five starts, he allowed three earned runs or less four times. Since then, in two starts, he lasted only three and a third innings, allowing seven earned runs. He would never pitch for the Expos again.

From May 15, catcher Barry Foote was used more often by Dick Williams. In the next 15 days, he would start 10 games.[30] Foote's use was of course at the detriment of Gary Carter, who was not happy with the situation. Publicly, Williams justified his decision by pointing out Carter's defensive deficiencies. Carter, who would always be aware of his own worth, replied that the Expos' record with Foote as the catcher was well below par (two wins in 10 games).[31] That comment was true, but not very kind to Foote. It wouldn't be the last time Carter would inadvertently ruffle some teammates with his comments. But Carter's defence had nothing to do with Williams' decision. The manager confided to Carter that the Expos wanted to show Foote to the other teams in order to trade him. He asked Carter to be patient and the latter got his job back for good in early June.[32] Foote then reiterated his demand for a trade. Upon the Expos' arrival in Houston from Cincinnati late on Sunday, June 12, Foote held a press conference at the airport.[33] Three days later, at the trading deadline, Foote was sent to Philadelphia along with Dan Warthen. The Expos got pitcher Wayne Twitchell and backup catcher Tim Blackwell. The Phillies had been seeking a new catcher for some weeks. As Twitchell would relate: "Bob Boone had torn cartilage in his knee that nobody knew about. The backup catcher was Tim McCarver, who I believe at the time was 38 or 39 years of age. They were going to be quite competitive. They needed an every-day catcher. We, as players, knew that Bob had a problem. He was still able to play but we had a team doctor who was with a medical center. I overheard him tell the trainer that, you never know, that cartilage rolls in and get caught, you can't walk or endure the pain and play through it. Tim McCarver couldn't catch every day. So the Phillies were shopping for a catcher from somewhere, the question was who they were going to trade to get the catcher."[34]

The pitchers swapped in that deal had also been in their team's doghouse. On May 25 against the Cubs, Warthen faced four batters, who all reached base via walks. The

Expos had given up in his case. He had been brilliant in 1975, with an ERA of 3.11, but was never able to duplicate that success thereafter. Twitchell, a rather big man, had had some success with the Phillies, especially in 1973 when he was selected for the All-Star Game. His season ended after a collision at first base with the Cubs' Billy Williams.[35] Twitchell injured a knee and was never able to regain either his strength or flexibility. Still, in 1976, in long relief, his ERA was only 1.75. Back to the rotation to begin the season in 1977, he lost his first five decisions. Twitchell was immediately inserted in the

Warren Cromartie was asked repeatedly to adjust to new roles and positions during his stay in Montreal. More often than not, Cromartie responded, even though he could anger some people with his acid tongue.

Expos' rotation and in his second start had a perfect game into the eighth inning against the Pirates, in Pittsburgh. He retired the first 22 batters before all hell broke loose. With the addition of Twitchell and Bahnsen, Steve Rogers, who was still the team's number one pitcher, had at least some support.

Offensively, the Expos got more and more respect. Veterans Dave Cash and Tony Perez brought the team exactly what was expected of them. But all eyes were turned towards the three young outfielders: Warren Cromartie, Andre Dawson and especially Ellis Valentine. The tall and handsome right fielder was selected to represent the Expos in the All-Star Game at Yankee Stadium. He possessed everything that could be asked from the ideal ballplayer: athleticism, speed, power and an arm deemed among the best in the game. Cromartie began the season doing what he had been showing in spring training: hitting line drives all over the place, no matter the pitcher or whether he was at home or away. Cromartie didn't lack confidence, but knew his deficiencies, especially in defense, and worked hard to improve his game.[36] In center field, Andre Dawson took a little more time in 1977 to really establish himself. He had only two home runs in the first two months of the season, for a paltry .236 average. Dick Williams never thought about sending him back to the minors.[37] The manager let him sit out some games in May, when he started only 11 games, in order to let Dawson relax a little and get back to letting his talent do the talking. Dawson got untracked from June on and never looked back again. These three outfielders, all under age 25, were the subjects of many articles throughout baseball.

After that 11-game losing streak, it took the Expos some time to go back to their early-season success. After a 12–16 month of June, they embarked on their best stretch of the 1977 season. From July 1 to July 23, they won 15 out of 20 games, which gave them a 45–47 record. That's the closest they would get to .500. In the middle of that streak, as the Expos were in Chicago, Dick Williams summoned Don Stanhouse to tell him that from that point on he would be his number one man in the bullpen.[38] Stanhouse didn't have a good season at that point. He was considered a fluke by the baseball establishment. When he was in Oakland, Williams oversaw Rollie Fingers' successful move from the rotation to the bullpen. Williams was hoping to do the same with Stanhouse. That decision was made easier by the team's bullpen struggles. Will McEnaney, who had problems adjusting to the city,[39] had problems also with opposing hitters. Joe Kerrigan and Canadian Bill Atkinson would give their heart out for the team, but Williams didn't seem to see either of them as the solution.

Third baseman Larry Parrish was still trying to hold his own as a bona fide major leaguer. At 23, he badly needed some sort of backing. His outside demeanour seemed lackadaisical (as was and still is the case for many third basemen) but he was really struggling inside. The fans, more attached to the exuberance of a Gary Carter or to the perpetual smile of Ellis Valentine, began booing Parrish to the point where his performances were affected. He even asked to be traded.[40] His batting average in the first three months was only .257 but more importantly his slugging percentage was .394 with only seven home runs, including three in the same game in St. Louis on May 29. Veteran Wayne Garrett finally got the nod from Dick Williams and got the most of his opportunity at the hot corner; he was named the Expos' player of month in July.

Also in July, the Expos expanded their executive ranks with the announcement of Roger D. Landry as vice president of marketing. Landry had already been working since May. He was back in Montreal after four years in New York where he had worked in the executive ranks at ITT (International Telephone and Telegraph). Expos owner Charles Bronfman personally recruited Landry by showing up unannounced at his home. His hiring was a big step towards big changes in the way the Expos did things. The move from Jarry Park to Olympic Stadium forced the Expos to change. Landry first determined how things were done from a marketing standpoint, then constructed a plan, which contained goals to be attained and ways to reach them, be they in sales, sponsorships, tickets or broadcasting.[41] His work would begin to pay off in 1978 and would keep paying off in the following years.

In August, Montreal lost a huge media and baseball personality with the sudden death of broadcaster Russ Taylor. Along with *La Presse* sportswriter Marcel Desjardins, he was the one who suggested in 1968 that Jarry Park could be a good place to host the new National League franchise. Montreal was very close to losing its team before it actually began playing. League president Warren Giles, accompanied by John McHale, went to the Jarry Park location. As a junior league game was being played, the small crowd welcomed the delegation with a standing ovation.[42] Whether this reception had any bearing on Warren Giles' decision is unknown (and quite honestly unlikely!). The president was however very pleased with Jarry Park, saying that it would be perfect if a major league stadium could be built in time, which was done even under one of the toughest winters of the time.

With the Expos out of the race for quite some time, the last two months of the 1977 season allowed Dick Williams to evaluate his players who gained some added experience during that time. On August 10, Wayne Garrett hurt his knee in the first game of a doubleheader against the Philadelphia Phillies.[43] His season was over, allowing Larry Parrish to get his job back at third base, which he wouldn't relinquish until the trade that sent him to Texas in 1982. On August 17, right after the game, Warren Cromartie and reserve outfielder Sam Mejias got into a fight in the clubhouse. Mejias was tired of Cromartie's needling. The altercation would have no sequel, even though both players showed a bruised lip (Mejias) and stitches above an eye (Cromartie).[44]

As is the case every September, some prospects were called up from the minors. Two pitchers were able to get noticed: Dan Schatzeder and Hal Dues. Schatzeder, a left-hander, was brought up to work with pitching coach Jim Brewer. He wasn't expected to be used much but ended up winning two out of three starts, including a shutout, with an ERA of 2.49. It was not the first time Schatzeder took full advantage of a small opportunity. He was drafted by the Expos after a single bullpen session! As he later recalled: "I had had some shoulder difficulties in my senior year in college. So what surprised me was how high I was drafted, in the third round. I think the Expos took a little bit of a chance drafting me. Red Murff came out to watch me throw, but he never saw me throw in a game. Red Murff was the scout who signed me. Red asked me to come out and throw and I threw for 10 minutes, just to a catcher, with no batter. And he must have liked what he saw. Because about a month later there was the draft and the Expos drafted me. But that was the only scout who saw me throw as far as I know. For nobody had ever seen me in a game."[45] Dues won his first start against the powerful Pirates, in Pittsburgh. As important to Dick Williams as his performance were his guts, determination and competitiveness.

The first season at Olympic Stadium could be considered a success, even with a 75–87 record, good for fifth in the National League East. It was a 20-game improvement from 1976. Gary Carter was the player of the year with a team-record 31 home runs. Tony Perez led the team with 91 RBIs, the eleventh straight season he had surpassed the 90-RBI plateau. Andre Dawson was named rookie of the year, finishing strong with 19 home runs, tying a team record for a rookie. He also stole 21 bases. Warren Cromartie finished third for the award, batting .282 with 41 doubles, one less than team-leader Dave Cash.

Individually, the Expos showed interesting stats offensively. They established team records for doubles, home runs and slugging percentage. They still managed to finish next to last in runs scored. How did they manage that? In 1977, the runs output increased by 10 percent overall comparing to 1976 and the number of home runs rose 45 percent, which meant that many teams saw their offensive stats increase substantially. But the team was still young and there was place for improvement. According to the offensive evaluator OPS+ as can be seen at the www.baseball-reference.com website, the Expos were in the middle of the pack offensively in the National League. If they were in the middle in overall output, how come they still finished next to last in runs scored? Two main reasons: too few walks and a below-par performance with runners in scoring position (.239 batting average).

Steve Rogers was easily the best pitcher, leading the team in almost all categories: wins, innings pitched, strikeouts, ERA, etc. His 17 wins were more than double the second-best total on the team. Don Stanhouse made Dick Williams look like a genius. As the number one reliever on the team, Stanhouse got 10 saves, won six games in eight decisions, and had a minuscule ERA of 1.35, contrasted with his 5.07 ERA as a starting pitcher (16 starts). Stanhouse could have put himself in trouble at the start of spring training, by missing a bus.[46] He loved Montreal and everything that the city had to offer and, being single, took plenty advantage of it. He was concerned, however, with the organization's reaction to his nightlife, according to Jean-Paul Sarault, from the *Montréal-Matin*.[47] John McHale and Jim Fanning told him so directly.[48] On the diamond, Stanhouse seemed to have found his niche as a reliever.

Overall on the mound, the Expos finished eighth with an ERA of 4.01. If the batters didn't seem to appreciate the value of a walk, the opponents took full advantage of Montreal's hurlers. Only Atlanta and San Diego allowed more free passes than did the Expos. They still managed to finish fourth in hits allowed per inning. The Expos were still a long way from being contenders, but improvements were noticeable. The fans seemed to appreciate the team, as attendance reached more than 1.4 million, double the year before.

Most observers agreed that the Expos were on the right path. The regular line-up seemed solid. Furthermore, the nucleus was still young and could only get better with Carter, Parrish, Cromartie, Dawson and Valentine. All these players had been signed and groomed by the Expos' organization. It was the first time the team could count on their farm system to such extent. The Expos would in fact continue to reap the benefits of their farm system right through the end of their journey in Montreal. A great deal of the credit belonged to John McHale and Jim Fanning for launching the player development system. Mel Didier was another individual who should earn accolades for his work, as he was responsible for scouting and developing players for the Expos from 1970 to 1975.

Mel Didier has always been associated with sports in some capacity, especially in baseball and football. After attending Louisiana State University, where he excelled in both sports, he first signed a contract with the Detroit Tigers' organization. He played only two years professionally, in 1947 and 1948, but during that time he came into contact with John McHale, a member of the Tigers' organization. After the 1948 season, McHale kept Didier, signing him first as a part-time scout. Before long, it became a full-time job. In the following years, Didier would follow McHale to Milwaukee, Atlanta and Montreal.

Didier wasn't sure what was awaiting him in Montreal. He never saw snow before his first visit to Montreal in January 1969 on a very cold winter day. In 1970, he was in charge of the draft and player development. He then took charge of the managers and coaches to make sure that the teaching and coaching from the lower levels of the minors up to AAA would be in line with the Expos' (and his) expectations. Walt Hriniak, Larry Bearnearth, Marcel Lachemann, Bob Gebhard and Karl Kuehl were among this group, all baseball men whose qualities have been acknowledged through the years.

When looking for talent, Didier had his preferences: big, strong athletes from high schools. Gary Carter and Ellis Valentine fit that mold perfectly.

Scout Bob Zuk had his say in drafting these two players in 1972. He established right from the first few times he saw Carter that he would be a catcher, even though he played everywhere, especially as a third baseman and pitcher. As for Valentine, he suffered a serious ankle injury not long before the draft and a screw had to be inserted in surgery. Afterwards, Zuk sought Dr. Frank Jobe who assured the scout that Valentine would be as good as new. The outfielder was drafted in the second round.

Didier was also responsible for the signing of Larry Parrish. Parrish was from a little town, Haines City, located in central Florida. Nobody was interested in him in 1971, so he enrolled at Seminole Community College. He played one year there, where he opened the eyes of numerous teams and scouts throughout the majors. He dominated the competition and got all the awards one could dream about. Parrish was in an ideal situation as nobody saw fit to claim him in the draft, so he was a free agent, free to negotiate with everybody! He was lured by many organizations but his father opted for the Expos, even though some teams made better offers, especially the Baltimore Orioles. As Parrish later recalled: "I was talking to like 14 different teams at that time. Mel Didier was from Louisiana, he was from a country background, sort of like my father. While the other guys were in three-piece suits, Mel was in slacks and a golf shirt and he told my dad, there weren't going to be any drugs as long as he ran the Expos. We got through with the talks that night and we were supposed to meet another team and my dad said, 'You're gonna sign with them!' He loved Mel Didier. You know, at that time, the Expos had a farm system, an expansion club from 1969 and this was 1972. I had actually played catcher in high school and in junior college that year I played right field, but Didier told me that if I signed with the Expos that I was going to play right field in the short-season club, but in the instructional league I would be moved to third base."[49] As was the case for Carter, the Expos had a plan for Parrish right from the get-go.

Even if Didier would rather sign high school athletes, that didn't mean he wouldn't be looking for talent elsewhere. Steve Rogers was drafted out of the University of Tulsa in the first round in 1971. Andre Dawson is another example, although one must admit the Expos got very fortunate on that one, as his name came up only in the eleventh round of the 1975 draft. Bill Atkinson was another pitcher who really didn't fit what Didier was looking for. "Very short stocky right-handed pitcher that we normally didn't sign but he had outstanding breaking ball," said Didier. Overall, Didier followed his plan until his departure in 1975, even if the Expos had to wait some years before reaping its first quality fruits. Player development and proper coaching were priorities that were placed higher than winning, according to Didier: "Pat Daugherty used to call me every day and say, Jesus, we got beat again.

We won 11 games, maybe 10 and lost 50. Cincinnati won 50 and lost 10, and they were all college. Cincinnati didn't have a single player going to the big leagues, and we had 11! We knew what we were doing because we would draft these young kids and we knew. We gave them three or four years and they would be as good as everybody and we would work their butts off. I'm telling you! Everyone of them can tell you that, coaches that I've hired, Lance Nichols, Gordie McKenzie, they all thought I was crazy because we had this highly organized thing but by the second year, they knew we were going in the right direction. They said, Mel, we will be partners. Anyway, we did some things that we were good at and the program stayed with the Expos for 10 or 15 years. They just used the program that we had set up and they just went on with it." In 1972, in the Florida East Coast Rookie League, the Cocoa Expos finished dead last in the four-team circuit with a 9–47 record, 17 games out of third place, last in batting, pitching and defense. Valentine, Carter and Dennis Blair were part of that team. Six other players made the majors on the other three teams and except for Randy Bass, who made his mark in Japan, nobody had a substantial career in baseball.

Didier left the Expos in 1975 for the Dodgers. It was a welcome change for Didier, who became involved with a Montreal woman who would become his wife, a situation he was not comfortable with.[50] Didier's legacy would be felt for a long time with the Expos.

GM Charlie Fox showed that he was a mover and shaker when needed. His goal was clear for 1978: strengthen the pitching department. In the free agent process in November, the Expos selected Ross Grimsley, then reliever Rawly Eastwick, Doc Medich, Terry Forster, Mike Torrez and Rich "Goose" Gossage.[51] The latter two were the most interesting pitchers available. Torrez had just won two games in the World Series, leading the Yankees to their first title since 1962. Gossage had spent 1977 with the Pittsburgh Pirates, where manager Chuck Tanner made him a reliever again, after being a starting pitcher in 1976. Gossage was the most intimidating reliever in the majors. But even if Torrez had pitched and succeeded in Montreal, and even if Gossage listed Montreal as one of his favorite cities,[52] team president John McHale wanted to target more financially affordable players. Torrez signed with the Boston Red Sox and Gossage with the Yankees.

During the winter meetings in early December, the Expos announced the signing of Ross Grimsley. They also acquired another lefty starter from Baltimore, Rudy May, along with pitcher Randy Miller and a minor leaguer, pitcher Bryn Smith. The Orioles received in return pitchers Don Stanhouse and Joe Kerrigan and outfielder Gary Roenicke. Roenicke was a first-round selection in 1973. But he was stuck behind Valentine, Dawson and Cromartie and there was no opening in sight for him. Stanhouse loved Montreal, too much to the desire of Expos management.[53] Stanhouse was also very unhappy after getting the latest contract offer after 1977,[54] a clear sign that the team wanted to buy some time before getting rid of him. An offer was made to Rawley Eastwick, who had been the number one reliever of the Cincinnati Reds when they won two World Series in 1975 and 1976. But he chose the New York Yankees, even though the Expos' offer was better.[55]

Two more players were added to the Expos' roster before spring training. In January, Tito Fuentes arrived from Detroit. In 1977, he established career marks for batting average (.309), hits (190) and runs (83). But the Tigers had another second baseman in the wings, Lou Whitaker, who would play the next 18 seasons in Detroit. Finally, Charlie Fox got lefty reliever Darold Knowles from Texas for cash. Knowles had played an important role with the Oakland A's in their three World Series championships, including two with current Expos manager Dick Williams.

For the first time in years, fans and baseball insiders expected the Expos to climb a notch higher in 1978. But they were up for a huge disappointment.

3

1978: The Year of Disappointment

In one year, the Expos went from being the laughingstock of baseball to a very respected organization and the future looked promising as spring training got closer. Every single year, either in Florida of Arizona, all teams boasted about their talented rookies, their experienced players, an improved lineup, etc. In short, optimism was the norm, exaggerated in many cases, whose real purpose was to sell tickets for the upcoming season. The Expos were no exception, but in 1978 there seemed to be legitimate reasons to really believe in this team.

For the first time in years, the lineup seemed set as seven position players were assured of their spots. Larry Parrish still had to show that he belonged. Towards the end of 1977, general manager Charlie Fox said Parrish's performance was his main disappointment that season.[1] Still, at the winter meetings, Williams was very cautious, saying that he believed Parrish had yet to reach his potential.[2] But Charlie Fox didn't want potential but rather immediate results. To protect himself, Tito Fuentes was acquired to add some depth at third base, even though he was first and foremost a second baseman by trade. Along with Williams, Parrish had the backing of coach Ozzie Virgil, whom he played for in the Venezuela Winter League. "You'll see a new Larry Parrish," said Virgil.[3] Parrish indeed crushed the league's pitching, hitting .362 with 14 home runs and leading the league with 54 RBIs. Virgil was so excited by Parrish's play that he woke up Charlie Fox in the middle of one night towards the end of the winter season to share his enthusiasm.[4]

After the 1977 season, Norm Sherry was added to the coaching staff. Sherry and Williams had been friends for a long time[5] and the former was available after being fired as manager of the Angels. Sherry's mandate was clear: work with Gary Carter on his defense. Sherry was a former catcher, signed originally by the Brooklyn Dodgers, who had the reputation to develop sound defensive backstoppers who weren't afraid to block the plate when necessary.

For once, starting pitching seemed to be on solid ground, with a quartet of veterans: Steve Rogers, Rudy May, Ross Grimsley and Wayne Twitchell. According to many observers, Rogers was one of the toughest right-handers in the National League. May and Grimsley had won 18 and 14 games, respectively, for Baltimore in 1977. Twitchell was able to earn six victories in 11 decisions after he became an Expo in June. Even though his ERA was an unspectacular 4.21, Twitchell ranked among the top 10 starting pitchers in the National League in hits allowed and strikeouts per nine innings.[6] He had been very impressed by the play of the three young outfielders, Cromartie, Dawson and Valentine, which was very different from having to deal day in and day out with Greg Luzinski in Philadelphia, whose physical qualities were better suited for a linebacker. Given what he had done in 1977, Twitchell was expected to make a solid contribution as a middle-of-the-rotation starting pitcher.

With higher expectations, Dick Williams, in his second year at the Expos' helm, decided to go back to his old ways. In 1977, he had been told by John McHale to take it easy with the youngsters in order to help them develop.[7] Gene Mauch was fired in 1975 exactly because McHale didn't believe he could lead a young team.[8] After the 1977 season, columnist Jerry Trudel, from the *Dimanche-Matin* newspaper, wrote that Williams had done a lot of observing during the season.[9] Williams had the reputation of being tough to play for. In his first days as a manager with Toronto in the International League in 1966, Williams was involved in an altercation with one of his own players, who was asking him whether or not he believed he had a future in baseball. Williams' negative reply triggered the scuffle.[10] With the Red Sox, Williams had his problems with superstar Carl Yastrzemski, which eventually led to Williams' firing. With the Oakland A's, the situation didn't warrant any hard feeling toward Williams, as everybody shared a mutual hatred for owner Charles Finley. In 1975, Williams was in the middle of a big brawl against the A's when he was the Angels' manager. Later that same year, he would get into a shouting match with Bill Melton, one of his own players. For 1978, Williams promised to be a lot less lenient than he was the year before.[11]

Spring training came and went without many surprises. When it became obvious that Larry Parrish would be back at third base, Tito Fuentes was let go. Fuentes had let it be known anyway that he had no interest in playing third base.[12] Another sign that the Expos were no longer in a desperate mood: Santo Alcala was sent to Seattle and Will McEnaney to Pittsburgh. Of the nine pitchers who began the 1977 season with the team, only two remained to begin the 1978 campaign: Steve Rogers and Canadian reliever Bill Atkinson.

The 1978 Montreal Expos were expected to legitimately contend with the best in the NL East. Bad luck and lack of experience delayed this prediction for a year. First row (left to right): Ellis Valentine, Ozzie Virgil, Jim Brewer, Dick Williams, Norm Sherry, Billy Gardner, Mickey Vernon, Larry Parrish, Wayne Twitchell; second row (left to right): Harvey Stone, Ross Grimsley, Andre Dawson, Tony Perez, Bob Reece, Hal Dues, Stan Bahnsen, Steve Rogers, Rudy May; third row (left to right): Rodger Brulotte, Darold Knowles, Del Unser, Pepe Frias, Bill Atkinson, Stan Papi, Gary Carter, Yvon Bélanger; fourth row (left to right): Sam Mejias, Wayne Garrett, Chris Speier, Fred Holdsworth, Jerry White, Dave Cash, Warren Cromartie, Daniel Plamondon, Dino Trubiano.

Hal Dues won a job on the pitching staff, the only rookie to do so. Dan Schatzeder was expected to make the team after his impressive showing in September 1977, but Fred Holdsworth was kept instead. The rookie southpaw was quite unhappy with the team's decision and Schatzeder let it be known to Dick Williams: "I expected to make the team. I would say I had an average spring training. We had traded for Rudy May and Grimsley was there. Fred Holdsworth was a right-hander pitcher who took a roster spot. Charlie Fox traded for him and Fred hurt his shoulder in spring training but was kept on the roster. I felt if I would have had a better spring training, I would have made the team. I still thought I would but they just called it the number's game. We had some players that were not in the formula the year before. Dick Williams sent me down, I was angry, I told him so, I said I deserved to be here and I don't think he expected that. You're supposed to go to the manager's office and say, 'Yes sir, I'll go down and work hard.' Jim Brewer was in the office also and he had the look, 'Dan, what are you doing?' I said I didn't deserve to go down, I belonged on this team and I was quite angry with Dick Williams at that time. And looking back on that year, he told me later on that year, 'You really showed me some courage, you really showed me some balls, doing that.' He really liked me standing up to him like that."[13]

The bench had some veterans, like Del Unser, Wayne Garrett and Pepe Frias. Jerry White, after a year back in the minors, made the team. Jose Morales, the pinch-hitter par excellence in the National League in 1976 but whose production had declined sharply in 1977, was sent to Minnesota.

The camp was not without distraction. The contractual situations of Cromartie, Dawson and Valentine made headlines through the whole month of March.[14] Nick Buoniconti, a former football star with the Miami Dolphins, was the agent for Cromartie and Dawson while George Kalafatis represented Valentine. Their situation was far from unique: everywhere players were trying to get more money after taking a look at what was offered to free agents. As for the three outfielders, the team's offers were under $100,000 for a year, which of course was far lower than what the agents and the players expected. The Expos believed that these players didn't have enough years of service to justify their demands. The players got more frustrated, even more so that they had no negotiating power. It got to the point where Charlie Fox personally threw out Nick Buoniconti from the team's premises in Daytona Beach![15] All three players finally agreed to a one-year contract, but not without some kind of resentment, especially Valentine who was the last to sign, a $75,000 contract in June.[16] But his sense of commitment was in doubt early in the season. In the first week of the season, Serge Touchette reported that Valentine was available. "Enough is enough," wrote Touchette, implying that those concerns went back some time ago.[17]

The biggest question mark was the bullpen. Nobody had any experience in closing games. Darold Knowles, even if he was a veteran who knew the ropes, didn't figure in Dick Williams' plans as the stopper. Stan Bahnsen showed some interest for the position during the winter[18] and it looked like he was the only viable option.

The Expos began their 1978 campaign in New York against the Mets, arguably the worst team in the National League East. The Expos managed to win only one game out of four at Shea Stadium, with Ross Grimsley preventing the Mets from sweeping the four-game series with a brilliant three-hit shutout in the last game. The Expos finally found their groove to finish April with a 11–8 record, tied for the lead in the NL East with the Philadelphia Phillies. Grimsley won his first four starts, including three complete games, with a 1.53 ERA. Not surprisingly, he was picked as the pitcher of the month in the National League. Grimsley didn't possess that explosive fastball and had to outthink and outbalance hitters with his assortment of off-speed pitches. Referring to his first win of the season in New York, a three-hit shutout, pitching coach Jim Brewer said: "I'd rather watch Grimsley pitch the way he did in that game than watching Sandy Koufax or Nolan Ryan."[19] Grimsley, however, warned the fans not to get too excited: "They shouldn't expect a 20-win season. I've always won between 12 and 15 games." He was in for a big surprise!

After winning three out of four games in May, the Expos encountered some adversity in their first long road trip of the season, with only four victories in 14 games, a stretch that would push the team below .500 at 18–19 on May 21. The offense was mostly to blame: they were able to score more than three runs only three times in those two weeks. The roster underwent a couple of changes in the meantime. Schatzeder was called back, for good. The Expos also acquired reliever Mike Garman from the Los Angeles Dodgers for two minor league pitchers, Gerald Hannahs and Canadian Larry Landreth. Bahnsen was leading the team with five saves and had blown only one lead but Williams was obviously looking for a better alternative.

The day Garman became an Expo on May 20 was a historic one at Olympic Stadium. On a beautiful Saturday afternoon, Willie Stargell launched a fastball from Wayne Twitchell far into the upper deck in right field. Contrary to many baseball venues, the upper deck in Olympic Stadium was way back instead of lurching over the lower sections. The seat where Stargell's ball landed was painted in yellow. Most observers agreed that it was (and would be) the longest distance a ball had ever been hit in Montreal. As for Twitchell, that game was a good reflection on a season that was going the wrong way. Never a control pitcher, his problems got worse and he just couldn't avoid the hitters' bats as his strikeout rate was dwindling. According to Twitchell, his problems were due to health issues unrelated to baseball: "We lived in Ste-Adèle (close to Chris Speier, some 30 miles north of Montreal). In 1978, the public water system was out of a little lake, and my wife and I and her sister, who drove up from Georgia, had all contracted a parasite that attacked the intestines. It caused a diarrhea-type problem. The trainer for the Expos gave me something, I don't remember. Something that was supposed to help me. For a long time, I was getting weaker and weaker. I think I completed a game against the Phillies, against Steve Carlton, in fact. I think Montreal won 7–1, 7–2, or something like that. But I was so tired after the game, I couldn't even get out of my chair in the locker room. That was a week or two into this. That's when I was physically experiencing a real downturn. One time, we were in Houston, flying to Atlanta after the game. I was sitting in the back with Ellis Valentine, we had dinner, I drank one beer, I went to the bathroom in the back of the aircraft and the next thing I knew, I was lying across the seats because Dave Cash and a couple of guys had picked me up off the floor.

I had passed out." It would take only a couple of weeks after getting back to Portland before Twitchell would overcome his problems.[20]

With an 18–19 record, lots of people were wondering if that was a déjà vu, when the Expos went into a tailspin in the middle of May in 1977. The Expos, however, responded with 13 wins in 18 games, which led to a 31–24 record, one game and a half behind the Chicago Cubs, who took over first place in the East. The pitchers allowed three runs or less in 14 of these 18 games. Inevitably, the Expos were no more an afterthought and the team was beginning to raise eyebrows. Opposing pitchers were wary of a lineup that instilled respect, even if it was only because the Expos had some physical bodies. Coincidence or not, the players were hit by pitches five times in one week from May 24 to May 30, which was more than usual. It may have been purely anecdotal but there was one player who didn't believe so: Ellis Valentine. On May 31, the Cubs were at Olympic Stadium. In the first inning against Dennis Lamp, Valentine hit a three-run home run. The right fielder seemed to be on his way after a rough start in the first few weeks of the season. In the fifth inning, as the Expos led, 5–0, Valentine came to bat against Lamp when all hell broke loose. As Valentine recalls: "Lamp was pitching me inside, but he never shook his catcher off. I figured these pitches were called by the catcher (Dave Rader). I then warned him that I would jump on him if the next pitch was inside."[21] The next pitch was indeed inside, which triggered an all-out brawl. Wayne Twitchell took care of Dave Kingman, another huge man (both were among the biggest players the majors). Valentine was the only one ejected. The Expos, even with two outs, scored four more runs in the fifth against the division-leading Cubs. After the game, Rader acknowledged the calling of inside pitches: "When a player tells you that he doesn't like inside pitches, what do you think I'm going to call?"[22]

On June 6 nothing special was expected as the Expos hosted the San Diego Padres. But the fans were able to enjoy one of the most entertaining shows ever at Olympic Stadium, thanks to a power outage. It took a few minutes to get some light back, but it was not enough to resume play on the field. The players then decided to take matters into their own hands with a little spectacle they would not forget. The Padres' Derrel Thomas began by throwing some balls over the outfield fence. He won a little contest with Ellis Valentine but when the Expos' outfielder asked for a rematch, Thomas just declined. Some players began throwing an imaginary ball through the diamond in what amounted to an excellent demonstration of improvisation. Valentine played his part to the fullest. He began to have a reputation as someone not tough enough to play through injuries. So Valentine fell to the ground after what appeared to be a very painful leg injury as he was taking a throw at first base, so painful in fact that he had to be removed on a stretcher. San Diego's shortstop, rookie Ozzie Smith, made the acrobatic moves he would become famous for some years thereafter. Veteran pitcher Gaylord Perry added his touch when he showed up on the mound with a bucket full of water, where he dipped some balls. Umpire Bruce Froemming, after some thorough inspection, found nothing wrong with Perry, whose reputation for throwing a wet one was second to none. The show was appreciated by the fans, to the point where John McHale said: "I've never seen such an example of that kind of connection between the players and the fans in my whole career."[23]

The Expos looked for real in 1978. On June 9, their winning streak reached five with a 10–9 triumph over the Los Angeles Dodgers in one of the most spectacular games of the year at Olympic Stadium. The Dodgers took a 5–0 lead but the Expos came back with four runs in the third inning and six more in the fourth. Larry Parrish's grand slam appeared to be the coup de grâce, but the bullpen made it a lot more interesting than Dick Williams would have wanted. After one out in the ninth, Mike Garman, who became the number one reliever when he joined the Expos from the Dodgers, walked two men, followed by a one-run double. At 10–7, Darold Knowles was brought in but he loaded the bases with another walk, putting the tying run on base, Dave Lopes, one of the best baserunners in the league. Bill Russell then hit a single to right to drive in two runs. The runner on second was waved in to the plate, but right fielder Ellis Valentine decided to throw to third. Valentine, who had arguably the best arm in the majors, nailed Lopes with a terrific relay. Knowles got the next batter to seal the 10–9 win.[24]

The Expos fans had another reason to celebrate that day: Woodie Fryman, a crowd favorite during his two years with the Expos in 1975 and 1976, was acquired from the Chicago Cubs for a player to be named later. The Expos needed a fifth starter, an issue that was exacerbated by Wayne Twitchell's problems. With Fryman's arrival, the Expos had to let someone go, and that someone happened to be Jerry White, who was sent to the minors. White would be the player-to-be-named-later for Fryman. White's departure annoyed Dick Williams and some people wondered why he was the player sent down, instead of Sam Mejias.[25]

As for Fryman, this was his last chance after a rough year and a half in Cincinnati and Chicago. His trade from Montreal to Cincinnati, even though it was a lot closer to his Kentucky farm, proved disastrous for both Fryman and the Reds: "I thought it would work out better too. That organization to me was one of the best. I didn't want to burn bridges when I left. I asked to be traded, I wasn't satisfied then. They said they wouldn't do it. I said, if you don't trade me, I will just retire. They didn't think I would do that. Sparky Anderson told me to my face, you can't turn down the money. I said, Sparky, I never did have a whole lot of money so it's not money as far as I'm concerned.

He said, we won't trade you. I said, well, I'm leaving today. So I went home and stayed and they traded me that winter. It's just one of those things. I wasn't happy there though. I thought it would be real nice for me because it was just an hour and a half from home. But it didn't turn out that way. Like I said, I don't burn bridges. I like to tell you I just didn't like the organization. I said the players, they had good talent there, good people, good ballplayers, and I wished them the best. That was the best thing for me to leave, to be honest with you. And I think that's the best thing that ever happened to me when they traded me that winter. They traded me to the Cubs and then traded me back to the Expos and that's the best thing that ever happened to me. It added three or four years in the big leagues."[26]

The Expos got some help for Gary Carter from Houston with veteran catcher Ed Herrmann. Rookie Bob Reece was Carter's backup, due mainly to his success in the winter leagues,[27] but the Expos wanted someone with more experience. Charlie Fox said he tried to contact Earl Williams, who was looking for a job and whose mother even paid for an ad in the *New York Times* to make sure that every team knew Williams was available. The Expos' GM was unable to locate him and instead had to settle with Ed Herrmann.

The Expos hit the wall on June 10 and never recovered in 1978. After two spectacular victories over the Dodgers that drew more than 20,000 fans each on Thursday and Friday, more than 40,000 people packed Olympic Stadium for the third game of the four-games series. The Dodgers had always been a good draw in Montreal, as lots of fans were still attached to the old Montreal Royals of the International League, a Dodgers farm team. The Expos were leading, 4–3, in the ninth inning but Mike Garman blew the game, giving up a two-run double to Dusty Baker. On Sunday, more than 48,000 spectators came to seen the new darling of the Expos, Ross Grimsley, whose record was 10–2 and ranked among the leaders in most pitching categories. Grimsley's day of work didn't last long, as he couldn't even finish the second inning, allowing six runs, five earned, on six hits as the Expos lost, 11–4. These two losses set the tone for the next three weeks, up to the All-Star Game break. The Expos couldn't even stage a two-game winning streak in a stretch that saw the team win only ten games out of thirty-one.

On June 29, the Expos had to play an exhibition game against their Canadian counterpart in the American League, the Toronto Blue Jays, for the Pearson Cup, named after former Prime Minister Lester B. Pearson, who was a huge baseball fan. The profits were used to help baseball in Canada, but the players would have rather taken a day off instead of playing a meaningless game that garnered very little interest anyway. On the last play of the game, reliever Bill Atkinson injured himself while sliding home with the winning run. He would be sent back to the minors not long thereafter. As if things weren't tense enough due to the uninspiring play of the team, while in Philadelphia for the last series before the All-Star Game break, the Expos had to spent some extra time in the bus because the driver couldn't find the right road. Del Unser, who had played in Philadelphia, had to intervene in order to get the bus to its destination. Dick Williams, who was already fuming over his team's latest performances, let it be known that he didn't appreciate spending time on a lost bus.[28] The manager made some important decisions, adding Dan Schatzeder and Hal Dues to the starting rotation. The only bullpen help he got came from the minors with the call-up of Gerry Pirtle, who would finally get his chance in the majors after several years in the minors.

At the All-Star break, the Expos record stood at 42 wins, 45 losses, and 8 games and a half behind the Phillies, the NL East leaders. For the first time in the team's history, two players were picked for the All-Star Game, held that year in San Diego, pitchers Ross Grimsley and Steve Rogers. Grimsley didn't pitch but Rogers blanked the American League in two innings of work. Both had 11 wins at that point. Grimsley had a spectacular start but had had some problems in the preceding weeks. Rogers was as regular as one could be, never allowing more than three runs in any start so far.

If one would like to point out where the Expos' problems were, the first three games after the break were a perfect example of what was going wrong. The day after a shutout against Houston at Olympic Stadium, thanks to Ross Grimsley, the Expos got swept in a doubleheader, both losses in extra innings. In the first game, Mike Garman and Darold Knowles were unable to save the game after a very good performance from Rudy May. In the second game, Gerry Pirte gave the game away by issuing three walks in the tenth inning, including one with the bases loaded. To his defense, Pirtle, who was mainly used in short relief, was in his third inning of work. Up to that point, he had been impressive with no runs allowed in his first 11 and two thirds innings.[29]

The team was not playing up to expectations and as is usually the case in such situations, the tension was more and more palpable. Before the July 20 game against Atlanta in Montreal, Charlie Fox came down to the clubhouse to talk to Chris Speier, who was mired in a huge slump with only two hits in 26 at-bats. Speier knew Fox from their days in San Francisco: "There was probably a lot of frustration. I remember Charlie coming in. You have to know Charlie Fox, very old-school guy, he talks, screams and raves. That's how Charlie was and he came down. At that time I wasn't doing very well, and he came down to the clubhouse, telling me to step it up a little bit. I got a little upset about it. That was Charlie."[30] The tone of the exchange got heated and louder, though, and Steve Rogers, who was the Players Association representative with the Expos, intervened and asked Fox to leave the clubhouse. When Fox finished with Speier, he turned his attention to Rogers, who recalled: "They were just screaming to one another and all I said was Charlie, that's just exactly what we don't need in here. We don't need that yelling. That was funny because as soon as he quit with Speier, he charged me and he's screaming at me. I don't remember what it was. He started bumping me with his chest like he was an umpire. And I go: 'Charlie, don't provoke me, don't be doing that, get away from me.' And he bumped me and I put my hand on his chest to push him away, and because I put my hand on him, he swung and he hit me in the jaw. A couple of guys got in between before he left. What is funny about it, there was already a meeting set for the next day about my contract with Charles Bronfman and John McHale, and Charlie Fox was going to be there. Dick Moss, my agent, was in town and the next day, I can tell you what, it was already going to be that way, but we didn't really have too many problems with some of the final details, which worked out to our satisfaction."[31] The new contract was, in fact, replacing an existing agreement. Roger D. Landry, the new VP marketing, abhorred these renegotiations and thought a contract should be respected until the end by both sides, to which John McHale retorted: "It's easier to find a VP marketing than a number one starting pitcher!"[32]

Whether or not Fox's intervention had any bearings on Speier is unknown. However, Speier came out of his slump in grand fashion. That same night against the Atlanta Braves, Speier hit for the cycle in a 7–3 victory. The team's resurgence was short-lived as the Expos embarked on a seven-game losing streak, that for all intents and purposes ended any hope the team had to finish the season with at least a .500 record. The most demoralizing defeat of the season happened in the middle of that streak in the Astrodome, in Houston. The Expos were leading, 5–0, in the bottom of the ninth. Galveston, Texas, native Hal Dues, who was pitching in front of numerous family members and friends, battled for six innings, shutting out the Astros even though he allowed ten hits and three walks as 11 runners were stranded on base. But the Astros scored six times against Mike Garman, Darold Knowles and Gerry Pirtle to win the game. In spite of that losing streak, veteran Darold Knowles, who knew a thing or two about championship teams (he won three World Series with Oakland), told André Rousseau, from the *Journal de Montréal*, that the team was really close to become a very competitive one.[33] The Expos in the meantime acquired a veteran utilityman who would play an important role the following season, Tommy Hutton. He was with the Blue Jays but didn't see much playing time and wanted out to play in the National League.

The Expos put an end to the losing streak in Atlanta on July 28, thanks to a solid outing from starting pitcher Dan Schatzeder, who allowed only one run on three hits in seven and a third inning. The Expos returned to their old habits the following day, wasting a 5–0 lead. But on Sunday, July 30, in what amounted to a day of collective release, the Expos demolished Atlanta, 19–0, in the most lopsided win in the team's history. The offense took charge with 28 hits, including eight home runs and a then major league record for total bases. Larry Parrish hit three home runs and Andre Dawson got two of his own in the same inning, the third. Even veteran pitcher Woodie Fryman took part in that offensive outburst with two hits, including a double, one run and one RBI. Fryman pitched the whole game for the shutout, even though it was scorching hot and very humid. It was reported that he lost more than ten pounds during the game![34]

In the following days, the papers published a story about a scuffle that had happened before that game between Warren Cromartie and Ellis Valentine. According to Cromartie's biography, the two players had an altercation, but rather in May. In his version, Cromartie related that he had complained to the hotel about the level of noise in a room that was obviously too close for comfort. The room was occupied by Valentine. The big right fielder confronted Cromartie and it didn't take long before the two went at it in the clubhouse.[35] Questioned whether there might have had two different incidents, Cromartie stayed with his biography's story as for the date of the incident.[36] One thing is certain though: the level of frustration within the team was very high. One year later, Tony Perez would confide to a reporter from the Los Angeles Times that at least six or seven fights occurred within the team in 1978.[37] Manager Dick Williams had his share when he was leading Oakland but he could care less then because the team was winning the World Series.

In early August, pitcher Scott Sanderson was called up from Denver, in the American Association. At first glance, Sanderson's record didn't warrant such a promotion, as his ERA was 6.06. But Sanderson would point out that Denver was an unusual place to play with the ball carrying much longer than usual. Also, a very bad outing inflated artificially his ERA.[38] He was inserted right away into the starting rotation, thanks to an injury to Rudy May.

On August 9, an incident which would have repercussions for the rest of the month involved Mike Garman. As the Mets were punishing the Expos, Garman was asked to warm up, which he refused, saying that he was tired. Even if he had been used only two times in the preceding eight days, he pitched in 16 games in July, including 11 times in 14 days in the preceding two weeks. After a verbal altercation with pitching coach Jim Brewer, Garman saw himself demoted to the manager's doghouse, as he wasn't asked to warm up even once in the next two weeks.[39] He would get back his number one reliever spot in September.

Gerry Pirtle, after a promising first impression, just couldn't get batters out anymore, which culminated in a horrible outing on August 27 in San

Francisco in the second game of a doubleheader. Pirtle was summoned to start the bottom of the sixth inning as the Expos were already trailing the Giants, 4–0. That was the only inning Pirtle would pitch, allowing seven runs and seven hits. None of runs were earned, however, thanks to an error by Gerry Pirtle!

In a season that was going nowhere, two more pieces of bad news hit the team at the end of August. Steve Rogers and Hal Dues would miss the rest of the season and would undergo surgery on their right elbows.

With the Expos out of the picture as far as the East Division race was concerned, that was a good occasion to test some youngsters, especially on the mound. Bob James and David Palmer would thus earn an audition. These two right-handers couldn't be more different. James was a first-round pick in 1976. His fastball was electric but his control was rather spotty to say the least. In September 1978, he just turned 20. Palmer was drafted also in 1976, but in the twenty-first round. He had attended an Expos trial in Montreal at Jarry Park some years before, driving from Glens Falls, New York. He climbed the organization ladder rather quickly for a low-rounder. In 1978, he began the season with West Palm Beach, in the Florida State League, where he established a league record with 37 consecutive innings without a walk. His control and poise obviously got the team's attention.

Bob James got a start on September 7 in Montreal against the New York Mets. Before the game, James was seen swinging a bat in the clubhouse. Manager Dick Williams couldn't help but warn his young pitcher: "Young man, you gotta have to go at least one inning to hit, so don't get ahead of yourself." As it turned out, James never got the chance to use the bat. He was extremely nervous to the point where his knees were shaking, by his own admission.[40] He pitched only one inning, facing eight hitters and allowing four runs on two hits and three walks. After the game, Williams would tell the writers that the decision to start James was not his but rather one that came from higher-ranked officials.[41] Palmer got a start in Philadelphia after several bullpen appearances. He got the loss as the Phillies tagged him for three runs and five hits in four innings. He would have a respectable 2.79 ERA in September.

One player whose standing was not at the highest level with Williams was Ellis Valentine. On September 19, it finally came to a clash. The Expos, going through the motions with no incentive, were hosting the Phillies. For Valentine, there was no personal satisfaction in playing a meaningless game. In the fourth inning against Dick Ruthven, Valentine made solid contact with the ball, believing it was destined to go over the fence for a home run. He was jogging nonchalantly when the ball caromed off the wall and he barely made it to second base for a double. Within moments, Valentine was picked off second. He didn't go back to take his right field spot in the fifth inning as Williams replaced him with Sam Mejias. The following day, Williams announced that Valentine was suspended for two games.[42] Two weeks prior to that incident, Valentine had been fined twice, for showing up late and then not at all at the pregame warm-ups.[43] He would also miss the last weekend of the season against the St. Louis Cardinals because of an injury to his heel. The fuse was getting shorter by the day for Valentine.

The Expos ended their local season on Sunday, September 24 when Scott Sanderson shut out the Pittsburgh Pirates, 4–0, on three singles. The Pirates had their regular lineup, with redoubtable Willie Stargell and Dave Parker leading the way, as they were desperately trying to catch the Phillies on top of the NL East (the Phillies would prevail on the next-to-last day of the season). Sanderson was drafted only the year before out of Vanderbilt University. In 1975, he had taken part in the Intercontinental Cup tournament held in Montreal. The sight of him warming up in the bullpen was a sign that the other teams had better get some runs soon before he took the mound.[44] At last, after years of producing position players out of their farm system, mainly outfielders, the first real crop of quality pitchers was beginning to show up at the big league level. Hal Dues and Dan Schatzeder were the first two of that generation, soon to be followed by Scott Sanderson, David Palmer and Bob James.

The Expos finished the 1978 season with a 76–86 record, in fourth place in the NL East Division, a huge disappointment, considering that many observers were absolutely convinced that the team not only would play over .500 but that they would also fight for the top spot. Brodie Snyder, from the *Montreal Gazette*, even intended to write a book about that elusive year when the Expos would fight for the title (he would get his wishes soon enough!). Some players pointed out the overall negativity surrounding the team. "Too many players are unhappy," said shortstop Chris Speier.[45] A good case is that of second baseman Dave Cash, whose averaged dipped to only .252, more than 30 points lower than the year before. Cash, however, had problems with Dick Williams' decision to favor utilityman Pepe Frias for defensive purposes.[46] In 1978, Cash was substituted for a total of 61 times. Rudy May, who had to battle injuries throughout the season, asked to be traded after his car had been vandalized.[47] Darold Knowles didn't look for excuses, saying that the players had only themselves to blame.[48] Ross Grimsley, after winning his twentieth game on the last day of the season, added: "With less talent, Baltimore won over 90 games in the last two seasons."[49]

But the overall picture was not as bleak as it appeared. They scored more runs than they allowed, which should have amounted theoretically to a record of 84–78, as shown on www.baseball-reference.com.[50] It was fairly common to believe that close games were tests of grit and character. Thanks to research by Bill James, whose numerous analyses would help fans understand the game better, we would know more in years to come that close games are too often a residue of luck to be as reliable as people believed. In fact, a team's record in games when the margins are wide is a better indicator of team's real strength and value. In 1978, in games with margins of three or more runs, the Expos had a record of 36 wins against 32 losses, the third best record in the NL East, behind Philadelphia and Pittsburgh, the powerhouses in the division. Even if the Expos had only one more win in 1978 than 1977, they made a huge step forward, contrary to the general belief of the time.

Despite the team's disappointing record, many players distinguished themselves. Ross Grimsley became the first Expos' pitcher to reach 20 wins. During the season, Grimsley was repeatedly accused of throwing a wet one.[51] In his autobiography, *The Gamer*, catcher Gary Carter wrote that Grimsley would put Vaseline on the ball, which of course was and is totally forbidden. Carter wrote that in one instance he was unable to grip the ball properly as he was trying to get a runner at second. The ball ended up in center field.[52] In an interview, Grimsley refused to acknowledge Carter and the accusation. "I won't admit to anything," he first replied with a big laugh. He was, however, quick to add: "But anything you can do to get the upper hand on the opponent, you will do!"[53]

One of the most improved players in the league was Warren Cromartie. In 1977, runners ran at will when the ball was hit to left field. Cromartie worked hard with teammate Del Unser to get better.[54] Cromartie ended up leading the league with Ellis Valentine in assists with 24, a total that has not yet been surpassed since in the National League. Cromartie showed as well that he wouldn't be easily satisfied regarding his own performance. Dick Williams offered him the chance to sit the last game of the season to protect his .300 average. Cromartie refused and finished at .297, but earned the respect of his manager.[55]

At last, Larry Parrish showed he was a bone fide regular third baseman. He established career bests in virtually all important offensive categories, improving defensively at the same time. The defensive qualities of Ellis Valentine were acknowledged by a Gold Glove. His 24 assists led the league, even when everybody knew that he had a cannon for an arm. Andre Dawson struggled some offensively but his play in center field improved dramatically. His 17 assists were fourth best in the league, giving the trio of outfielders more than 60 assists for the season!

All in all, the team's foundation seemed on solid ground. Some say that great teams have to learn to lose before winning. In 1978, the Expos could certainly attest to that.

On the management level, new marketing guru Roger D. Landry was

Ross Grimsley (middle, flanked by Bill Lee, left, and Steve Rogers) was the first and only 20-game winner in the history of the Expos. He was gone less than two years later when he was unable to duplicate his success.

able to implement in 1978 most of the ideas he spent the 1977 season working on, which he put in writing for the team's first real marketing plan. The employees were, of course, asked to contribute in a way that was a big change from what had been done before.

In his plan, Roger D. Landry never wanted to put the emphasis on the players, a surprising concept since they were the product he was trying to sell. Landry acknowledged that his approach was quite unusual in the baseball world: "I was reproached by Major League Baseball for not marketing the players. Commissioner Bowie Kuhn told me: You must sell the sport! To which I replied: Mr. Kuhn, I'll tell you something. If my marketing campaign is concentrated on Gary Carter and some other players, if they get hurt or traded, my campaign becomes obsolete! I'm going to sell the sure thing and the sure thing is that there's a game scheduled on the 18th and the 22nd. Whether or not you help me, that's the way it's gonna be! The complaint was made by Steve Rogers, who was the players' representative with the Players Association. He was arguing that I didn't market the players. My reply is still good today. I don't know whether Rogers will pitch a good game or not or if he's gonna have an arm injury. All I know for sure is that we're playing on the 18th! But overall, I was well accepted in the baseball circle. My boss was not completely enamored, neither was Kuhn, but they still backed me. Had the Olympic Stadium been empty, I don't think I would have had the same accolades."

To his credit, Landry knew he had the benefit of having good teams that were spectacular. "During my years with the Expos, I always had exciting teams. They weren't always winning, but they were entertaining, with spectacular players and we had young players. For the Expos, that was very important. We saw them mature before our eyes. We saw Gary Carter grow as a major leaguer. Warren Cromartie, Ellis Valentine, Tim Wallach. They were all part of the family. There was an automatic sense of belonging. That was the key for us. Win or lose, they were part of the family."

But what about winning? Isn't that what professional sport is all about? Doesn't winning draw crowds? Again, Roger D. Landry stayed the course: "When you go to the theatre for a play, you go there with the hope that you're going to be entertained to the point where you end up saying: 'I just saw something extraordinary tonight!' In my case, I didn't need to tell the fans whether it would be good or not, you know in advance they can win or lose. I had nothing to do with the outcome of the game. What I knew was that the fans would spend a nice evening with the hope that the team would win. To me, winning was a plus. I never saw winning or losing as the focal point of my plan, because the fan knows the team can win or lose, we didn't need to tell him. If we lost, I told myself that they would maybe come back the following day with the hope that we would win. I never saw the results on the field as directly linked to the attendance."

Landry and his marketing team worked to make the team more easily accessible, with services like Expotel, where people could reserve their tickets in advance by phone (that was well before the Internet!), by selling tickets to groups, and by selling group of games (as opposed to single games) as season tickets. It was not always easy for Landry to sell his plan, which was much more focused on business rather than on the baseball side. In fact, one his promotions backfired in 1978 and he had to defend himself alone in New York in the commissioner's office. Every Sunday, one could get a bingo card in the *Dimanche-Matin*, a French weekly published every Sunday. With that card, fans could play bingo between innings during Expos games at Olympic Stadium on Mondays, a traditional day for bingo aficionados in Quebec during the winter. At first, John McHale was very reluctant to go along, saying that the promotion would never be accepted by the commissioner, because of its gambling nature. Major League Baseball has been very cold on gambling since 1920 when it became public knowledge that players from the Chicago White

Sox conspired to throw the World Series to Cincinnati. Commissioner Kuhn went as far as banning Willie Mays and Mickey Mantle from any baseball duties when these two great Hall of Famers were hired by casinos.[56] Landry defended himself, telling John McHale: "Bingo in not a chance game, everybody plays bingo. We'll cross the river when we reach it. But now, I go on with the bingo." It didn't take long before Bowie Kuhn summoned Roger D. Landry. As it was Landry's idea, McHale told Landry to defend himself on his own. "I went there before the commissioner and his aides to explain in detail how it was done. We know in advance the winning combination. We just don't know who's got the winning card. It was limited, there's no chance involved. When my argument really didn't seem to impress them, I said: 'Listen! In Quebec, bingos are held in church basements, managed by the church's institutions, especially the Catholics. That's what helps them pay the bills. The church approves bingos! There's no way Major League Baseball will prevent me from holding this Quebec and Canada tradition. Gentlemen, I rest my case!' I will always remember the moment Tom Villante (who was deputy commissioner) turned to Bowie Kuhn and said: 'Well, after such a speech, we'll make an exception. Bingos will be allowed in Montreal.' When I came back to Montreal, John McHale inquired about the meeting. I told him: 'From next Monday on, you're gonna play bingo as well!'"

Roger D. Landry also took charge of the broadcast department and many changes were made, especially regarding the television rights. Before Landry's arrival, the Expos sold their rights directly to the broadcaster, a straight deal. Landry changed that, as the Expos first affiliated themselves with a major sponsor, in this case the O'Keefe Brewery. Then, the Expos would sell their rights, which included the sponsorship. The Expos were thus able to get money from both television and sponsors.

With that big an overhaul, one would expect some stumbles along the way, like the introduction of Souki, the first mascot in the team's history. Souki was owner Charles Bronfman's idea, who wanted a futuristic character that would remind fans of the blockbuster movie *Star Wars*. Landry didn't agree at all with the idea. "Souki was already planned when I was hired. That's not what I wanted but as everything had been set, I told them: Go ahead but it just won't work. It's not what we are! It was a complete disaster, children were scared of it, the crowd was booing, it was terrible." He suggested a mascot of his own, which he had to argue strongly to convince Charles Bronfman, who said, "OK, but it'd better be good, or you'll hear from me!" Landry mandated a New York firm to conceive a character with specific instruction, a character that became Youppi. According to Landry, "Youppi represents, in his soul and spirit, what I am. There's a little of Cyrano de Bergerac, some Falstaff, the Rubidon character who comes out of the tavern on Friday night, everything that's ingrained in Quebecers. It became a huge success and I'm very proud of it." Today, Youppi is the last living legacy of the Expos, as the mascot of the Montreal Canadiens of the National Hockey League.[57]

Landry's work didn't help the Expos much on the field, as they managed to win only one more game than the year before, even though they were better than their record indicated. The disappointment was so huge though that Charles Bronfman seriously contemplated selling the team after ten years as the owner.[58] Jerry Trudel, a *Dimanche-Matin* columnist, was the harshest critic among the writers.[59] On October 18, John McHale announced that he would be the general manager, replacing Charlie Fox, who would stay in the organization, mainly as a professional scout. McHale explained that Fox wasn't very flexible. The incident with Steve Rogers during the season was a major reason for Fox's demotion. "You can't go down in the clubhouse sparring and punching your number one pitcher. No matter what he says, you had to take it. Rogers was not the most lovable guy in the world when he was a part of the Players Association. The feeling was building up but you have to divorce yourself from your feelings about people and general manage the club."[60] Darold Knowles also had issues with Charlie Fox during negotiations for a new contract. The Expos were interested in keeping him, but talks turned sour to the point where it became a matter of principle for Knowles. "It was not a matter of money," said Knowles. When McHale tried to get him back, it was too late as Knowles had decided to become a free agent.[61]

In his two years as general manager of the Expos, Fox had to fill huge needs, especially in the pitching department. In spite of the way he ran things, Fox left with a much better team than when he arrived in October 1976.

By assuming both the presidency and the role of general manager, McHale became the lone person in charge, for better or worse. He was largely responsible for the Expos' birth in 1968. Ten years later, he had to take his team a step forward as the fans, used to see the Montreal Canadiens piling up Stanley Cups and the Canadian Football League's Montreal Alouettes filling Olympic Stadium, were getting more and more impatient. Charles Bronfman's patience had limits as well. McHale had no choice but to make sure there would be no repeat of 1978.

As was the case in both 1976 with Dave Cash and in 1977 with Ross Grimsley, the Expos wanted to use the free agent market to get some help in relief and/or to get some depth on the bench. Pinch-hitting in 1978 was horrible, with a batting average of .164. They only hit two home runs and both were hit by two regulars who had been benched for a day, Ellis Valentine and Andre Dawson. In the free agent draft, the Expos first picked reliever Mike Marshall, then Derrell Thomas and Elias Sosa.[62] Under manager Gene Mauch, Marshall became one of the most durable relievers ever with the Expos, especially from 1971 to 1973. Not an easy man to get along with, he alienated not only beat writers but management as well. Bob Bailey would say about his former teammate: "He was a different kind of person. It took some effort to get along with him but he is a very decent human being. You had to put forth some effort."[63] After the 1973 season, Marshall was traded to the Los Angeles Dodgers for outfielder Willie Davis. After pitching 179 innings in 92 games in 1973, Marshall pushed himself further in 1974 with 208 innings in 106 games, contributing to the team's winning the National League pennant! Marshall, who was a kinesiology specialist, maintained that a pitcher could throw every day with good conditioning. In 1978, he was looking for a job before landing the closer spot in May for the Minnesota Twins, led by his old manager Gene Mauch. Marshall stabilized the bullpen, with 10 wins, 21 saves and a 2.45 ERA, all that without spring training. Derrell Thomas was considered a super-substitute who could play everywhere but catcher and pitcher. Sosa was a veteran who could pitch often and efficiently. In 1978, he played with Oakland, his fifth team in five years. He was an interesting option for the Expos but they focused their energy towards Marshall.

Reserve catcher Duffy Dyer became the team's first addition before the winter meetings. In December, McHale added some depth by acquiring Ken Macha from the Pittsburgh Pirates in the Rule V draft. Macha had some success offensively in the minors. He led the Eastern League in hitting in 1974, beating Warren Cromartie. Veteran first baseman Tony Solaita was then bought from the California Angels. Solaita was solid defensively and could provide some power from the left side. On December 7, McHale got lefty starter Bill Lee from the Boston Red Sox for utilityman Stan Papi. Lee was available after numerous run-ins with manager Don Zimmer. A week later, the Expos got back outfielder Jerry White along with infielder Rodney Scott from the Chicago Cubs, for Sam Mejias. As was the case for Lee, Scott had some problems with his manager, Herman Franks. That wouldn't be the last time these two players would be linked together. But whatever the problems they might have had, one thing was certain: the Expos added two strong personalities with Lee and Scott. When Lee visited Montreal, the newspapers sports sections were filled with stories about the pitcher nicknamed Spaceman.[64] The Expos tried to keep outfielder Del Unser with a two-year offer, but the veteran opted to go to Philadelphia.

One case had yet to be settled: Mike Marshall. The veteran pitcher wanted to take his time but one after another, teams just decided to go another way. In early January, only two teams remained in the race for Mike Marshall, the Expos and the Twins. Even with a better offer from the Expos, Marshall decided to stay with in Minnesota. *The Gazette* reported that Marshall's family wasn't excited about returning to Montreal, because of the reaction of some fans when his wife attended games at Jarry Park.[65] Nancy Marshall, then Mike Marshall's wife, would confirm that information in her book (*Home Games*) co-written with the wife of another non-conformist, Bobbie Bouton (Jim's wife).[66] Marshall refuted all these allegations, stating that Gene Mauch was the reason he wanted to stay in Minnesota. He also said that he didn't really get along well with Expos manager Dick Williams, when both were in Montreal in 1971, Williams as a coach and Marshall as the closer. As for the negotiations, Marshall pointed out that Calvin Griffith was the one responsible for not closing the deal earlier.[67]

After the failure of the Marshall plan, the Expos turned to Plan B: Elias Sosa. According to reports, he was recommended by Jack McKeon, Whitey Lockman and Felipe Alou.[68] Sosa agreed to a multi-year contract. The shopping was over and John McHale had a whole month to get ready for what would be the most important training camp in the team's history, as it was now or never for the Expos.

4

1979: They Arrived at Last!

In his annual winter media tour in Quebec, manager Dick Williams reiterated that he would enforce some discipline rules more strictly,[1] repeating a vow he had made before the 1978 season. There was no doubt it was a warning to Ellis Valentine. The talented outfielder was fined twice and suspended another time during a tumultuous September. Still to the fans, Valentine was by far the most popular player on the team, according to local poll.[2] He led the team with 25 home runs and was overall the best position player on the team in 1978.[3] But the expectations were higher, much higher. John McHale believed that Valentine should have put up numbers that equalled those of another big right fielder, Dave Parker, who had just been named the Most Valuable Player in the National League. In *The Sporting News*, Valentine's mother, Bertine, said that her son had never been so happy and that he was comfortable in Montreal. "Nothing will prevent him from being a superstar," she said.[4]

For the first time, the Expos hired a physical education specialist for spring training. Ed Enos was attached to Concordia University in Montreal in the Physical Education Department. In 1974, he went to Soviet Union to study the training methods of its athletes. Among the other North American participants was Fred Shero, head coach of the Philadelphia Flyers, who had just won their first of two consecutive Stanley Cups, and Pierre Pagé, then head coach of Dalhousie University in Nova Scotia, who went on to coach the Calgary Flames and Quebec Nordiques. Paul Arsenault, head coach of the Concordia Stingers hockey team, was also among the contingent. Pagé had already included in his program a stretching technique called "proprioceptive neuromuscular facilitation," which was established by Dalhousie professor Larry Holt. Seeing the positive results of the technique in the Concordia hockey team, Enos offered his services to the Expos.[5]

The 1979 spring training was the first with John McHale as general manager. In 1978 he witnessed all the negative attention created by the turbulent contract negotiations involving Cromartie, Dawson and Valentine. In order to avoid all unnecessary distractions, all three players were signed before the first day of camp.[6] In fact, Rodney Scott's case was the only one unsettled in late February. In arbitration, Scott won as he was asking for $75,000, $20,000 more than the Expos' offer.[7]

The pressure was on very early, not only for the players but for management as well. Ian McDonald, the beat writer from *The Gazette*, stated that the Expos could be on the move to Birmingham, Washington or New Orleans if there was a repeat of the 1978 campaign.[8] Columnist Yves Létourneau, from *La Presse*, wrote that Dick Williams had to deliver.[9]

In the first days of camp, John McHale held a team meeting where he stressed the players' commitment to the team. He wanted to neglect absolutely nothing, promising that he would do anything to favor the players' and the team's progression.[10] On the field, Dick Williams was quick to praise David Palmer and Rodney Scott.[11] At the start of spring training, Williams told Palmer that he liked to have a dark horse among his pitchers, somebody who was not really expected to make the team. In 1978, Hal Dues was thrown in the mix. In other words, in 1979, it was Palmer's job to lose.[12] Palmer was a pitcher who was not afraid to throw strikes, which sat well with Williams. As for Scott, Williams liked his speed and his flair on the basepaths. At third base, for once, at least since Williams took over as manager, Larry Parrish didn't have to fight for his job. He was more confident than ever, showing up with much more muscle than the year before.[13] He came to Daytona Beach earlier than the other position players, taking ground balls on a daily basis. He had missed the last week of 1978 due to a knee injury that occurred in a home plate collision. After surgery, he followed a strengthening program for his legs, which he also applied to his upper body.[14]

As is the case for almost every team, the Expos' training camp was not without some injuries, the most important being Chris Speier's.[15] The shortstop wrenched his back while training during the winter. He had to be held back from playing in the Grapefruit League. Woodie Fryman also had problems with "Arthur," the name he gave to his arthritic left elbow. Trainer Yvon Bélanger was able to dislodge a bone chip, allowing Fryman to keep pitching. Fryman would say that Bélanger allowed him to prolong his career many years.[16]

In the first week of March, Valentine's lackadaisical ways were the subject of an article by Serge Touchette. According to the *Journal de Montréal* writer, Valentine was playing with fire the way he behaved himself.[17] In some ways, Valentine was ahead of his 1978 pace as his nonchalance was then criticized not until April.

Bill Lee got some ink as well for some off-the-field stuff only he could get into. The commissioner's office got hold of a story in which Bill Lee allegedly pretended to use marijuana. In an interview with a journalist from the Boston area, Lee said that he had been using for more than eleven years. A representative of Bowie Kuhn traveled to Daytona Beach for an inquiry. When asked if he had been misquoted, Lee said that he spread marijuana on pancakes, citing numerous health benefits, including immunizing him against toxic emissions from vehicles. He was fined $250. Lee instead sent a $251 check to a charity organization in Alaska as chosen by his wife. The fine was eventually rescinded to be replaced by a simple reprimand.[18] As for McHale, as baseball conservative as one could be, he didn't seem to care much about his pitcher's misadventures: "When I got the man, I made up my mind that I wasn't going to overreact to the outrageous things that he says."[19]

On the field, what was supposed to be a quiet camp turned out quite interesting, thanks to the play of Rodney Scott. In mid–March, Williams said that Scott would play regularly.[20] In the meantime, rookie second baseman Tony Bernazard was quite impressive. Jean Aucoin, beat writer from *La Presse*, wrote that Dave Cash was losing his job.[21] According to Ian McDonald, Rodney Scott and Tony Bernazard could be the middle infield combination at the start of the season, replacing Speier and Cash.[22] Speier had yet to play a game because of his back problems. Cash was struggling offensively and given Williams' appreciation (or lack thereof) of his defense, he was clearly on the hot seat. Even though his leadership qualities had been praised upon his arrival, Cash's value as a hitter was vastly overrated throughout his career. As stated by Allan Richman when he became the first free agent to sign with the Expos in November 1976,[23] Cash had no power and rarely would he draw walks. In order to be useful offensively, Cash had to get his average up to .300 at the very least to compensate. For such a player, the on-base percentage, a way better tool to evaluate a player, is far more important than the batting average. Thus, because of Scott's play and Cash's shortcomings, the former won the second-base job after hitting .333, along with better defensive play and some hustle on the bases.[24] Some players were, however, not very pleased with that decision, especially among the blacks on the team.[25] Scott even told Cash that he wanted Speier's job, not his.[26] Cash and Speier both struggled mightily in camp, hitting .174 and .118, respectively.[27] But Williams wasn't concerned about some players' grumblings, a trait he carried throughout his managerial career.

The rest of the lineup offered no real surprise. Pepe Frias, who had the most seniority with the Expos, was sold to the Atlanta Braves. Jim Mason would be the main middle infield utilityman. Tony Bernazard was sent to the minors, but was named the best rookie of the camp.[28] Tommy Hutton became the de facto captain of the bench, as he launched the "BUS Squad." As Hutton later remembered: "Daytona Beach is a long way away from most of the other spring training sites. I think the closest was Houston in Cocoa Beach, which is one hour away. But every other trip was a long bus trip. And on the longer trips, the Carters and the Valentines, the star players, didn't make a lot of those trips, if you know what I mean. So it was the Jerry Whites, the Ken Machas, me, the Duffy Dyers who made those long trips. One day, I was sitting around, I don't know how it came up, I just thought, they ought to call us the BUS squad, cause we're always on this bus. And then I put the acronym to it, B-U-S, most of us weren't high-paid players, we were all under-rated and none of us were superstars, so were the Broke Underrated Superstars."[29]

On the mound, the housecleaning had begun even before the start of training camp as the Expos let Wayne Twitchell go. Mike Garman was also cut towards the end of camp, opening the door for David Palmer. Bob James, who was among the last cuts, was also able to raise some eyebrows.[30] With his imposing physique and his blazing fastball, James drew some comparisons with Rich "Goose" Gossage.[31] James was a lot less nervous than when he was called up for the first time in September and his control seemed a lot better. Many saw James, nicknamed the "Canadian Goose," as the next closer.[32] Stan Bahnsen asked to be traded, as was his right as a veteran.[33] The Expos had until March 15 to oblige, or else Bahnsen could have elected to become a free agent. Bahnsen was not really happy to be used in long relief, an unappreciated job with almost no reward. But given the few openings in mid–March as most camps were in full gear, Bahnsen decided to stay with the Expos.

A training camp involving the Expos wouldn't have been complete without the annual visit of Babette Bardot, an infamous stripper from Quebec, who boasted being a cousin of her more famous namesake, Brigitte Bardot. In Daytona, a game between the Astros and the Expos was delayed after the commotion caused by Bardot's arrival, as players from both teams took a glance (or two) at the big-breasted stripper. Astros pitcher Joe Niekro could barely concentrate on the mound.[34] Dick Williams wasn't impressed either with his own players' lack of attention on the field. "The fans weren't the only ones looking in the stands," he said.[35] Even Bill Virdon, as serious as a man could be, couldn't help but smirk when asked if he ever witnessed a game delayed in that manner. "We don't see that very often!" he merely replied.[36]

The Montreal Expos launched their 1979 season in Pittsburgh. The Pirates had finished second in the preceding three seasons, each time behind the Philadelphia Phillies. They were still led by Willie Stargell. But their pitching staff seemed more solid and deep, especially their bullpen. Charlie Fox, one of the Expos' professional scouts, was very impressed by the Pirates in training camp.[37]

The 1979 Expos were the winningest team in franchise history, with 95 victories. It was the start of a journey that would make the Expos the most popular sports team in Canada. Seated: Frank Albertson, Rodney Scott, Dino Trubiano; first row (left to right): Tony Perez, Vern Rapp, Felipe Alou, Norm Sherry, Dick Williams, Ozzie Virgil, Jim Brewer, Pat Mullin, Rusty Staub; second row (left to right): Gene Kirby, Harvey Stone, Elias Sosa, Steve Rogers, Gary Carter, Bill Lee, Ken Macha, Dave Cash, Woodie Fryman, René Lavigueur, Yvon Bélanger; third row (left to right): Chris Speier, Warren Cromartie, Jerry White, David Palmer, Bill Atkinson, Tommy Hutton, Tony Bernazard, Tim Raines, John Tamargo, Dan Schatzeder; fourth row (left to right): Stan Bahnsen, Bill Gullickson, Randy Bass, Ross Grimsley, Andre Dawson, Scott Sanderson, Dale Murray, Larry Parrish, Bob Pate, Rudy May.

Steve Rogers was tabbed as the starting pitcher for the first game. There was some doubt whether he would be ready. Rogers was left on his own after his right elbow surgery, as nobody gave him a rehabilitation program to follow. He was very fortunate to live not far from pitching coach Jim Brewer, who suggested to him a program to follow.[38]

The first three games of the season set the tone for the season as far as the Expos and Pirates were concerned. All three games were decided by only one run, the Expos winning two out of three. On April 7, the Expos won the first one, 3–2, in 10 innings, thanks to two Pirates errors. The Pirates won, 7–6, the day after when the Expos returned the favor with two defensive miscues in the ninth inning. The Expos came back with a 5–4 win. During that three-game series, Dave Parker charged Gary Carter, a collision involving two big men totalling close to 500 pounds. Carter didn't appreciate Parker's course and some angry words were exchanged.[39] In the following two-game series in New York against the Mets, swept by the Expos, Carter had another run-in, this time with John Stearns. That one turned more physical as a brawl ensued.[40] It looked like the Expos would not be content to see the parade. They really wanted to be part of it.

After a successful four-wins-in-five-games road trip, the Expos opened their local season on April 14 hosting the Chicago Cubs before more than 35,000 fans as Ross Grimsley and Elias Sosa combined for a 3–0 shutout. The Expos won three of their next four games on home turf before losing three in a row at Wrigley Field. Undaunted, the Expos came back with a seven-game winning streak in Montreal against the West Coast teams (San Diego, San Francisco and Los Angeles). The Expos' record then stood at 15–5. Never in their history had the Expos been ten games over .500!

In a span of a few days, Ellis Valentine showed why he was such a popular player in Montreal and also why he could be his own worst enemy. On April 22 against the Cubs, Valentine pushed replacement umpire Steve Fields, which got the outfielder a three-game suspension.[41] The regular umpires were on strike and players were getting more and more critical of the quality of umpiring, even though most preferred to refrain from commenting. As for Valentine, nobody had any idea what he was doing during his suspension as he never showed up at Olympic Stadium. Not that he was missed: the Expos won all three games and Jerry White, who patrolled right field during the suspension, drove in six runs.[42] When the suspension came to an end, Williams, not sure in what condition his outfielder would be, opted to not write Valentine on his starting lineup, a decision made easier by White's latest performance and the fact that the offense didn't need help at that point as they had scored 29 runs in three games. In the bottom of the fourth inning, the Expos were trailing the San Francisco Giants when they got two men aboard with one out. Williams then sent Valentine to hit for starting pitcher Ross Grimsley. *Journal de Montréal*'s reporter Serge Touchette witnessed the spectacle : "It was at Olympic Stadium against Vida Blue. Valentine had been criticized heavily all week long, because of his lack of seriousness. But the fans just loved him. He came out of the dugout from the farthest point from home plate. He was walking slowly, stretching himself nonchalantly to the batter's box. Fans were giving him a standing ovation! In the press box, we told ourselves, he's crazy, it has no sense, he hasn't shown up in a week. Valentine, he went out, laughing with his bat in the air! He got set and hit a three-run home run! The Stadium exploded with applause! In that era, standing ovations were quite frequent but that was a memorable moment. In the press box, we were just stunned!"[43]

After the successful stay at the Big O, the Expos went on their longest road trip of the season to San Diego, San Francisco, Los Angeles, St. Louis and Philadelphia. The Expos won four out of seven games in San Diego and San Francisco but were swept in the three-game series against the Dodgers. The Expos lost two more games in St. Louis before Tony Solaita gave the Expos some life with a game-tying ninth-inning home run in a game that would be completed (and won by the Expos) in June due to suspension by a curfew.

In the second game of the Dodgers series, Ellis Valentine showed up late and Dick Williams didn't play him.[44] It was the third time in 1979 that Valentine was reprimanded for breaking a team rule.[45] *Montreal Star* columnist Fred Roberts wrote: "It's up to Ellis if he wants to be part of the team."[46] It looked as if nobody wanted to take the responsibility for how the Expos should have managed Valentine. Manager Dick Williams said that it was up to general manager John McHale to deal with Valentine while McHale said Williams had the authority to do so.[47] Valentine was not the only cause of tension as the Expos and especially McHale were concerned whether the team was going through the same spiral that had led to the tumbling of the past two seasons. After a game in St. Louis on May 15, McHale even second-guessed Williams, who chose to pitch to weak-hitting Mike Phillips in a scoreless game in the ninth inning when the pitcher was due up next.[48] Phillips ended up hitting a game-winning single.

The team landed in Philadelphia, the last leg of that five-city road trip, on the night of May 18, with a 20–13 record, four games back of the Phillies. Against all odds, the Expos swept the Phillies, thanks to an offense that scored 25 runs in three games. The hitting outburst was most welcome as no starting pitcher (Grimsley, Rogers and Lee) threw more than five innings in any of these three games. The Phillies were playing without many regulars, like Greg Luzinski, Garry Maddox and Manny Trillo. But the Expos had the reputation of not taking advantage of that kind of situation, especially when it counted the most. The sweep was a big relief, especially at the tail end of that long trip on the road.

Back to Montreal only one game back from first place, the Expos got three wins in five games against Pittsburgh and St. Louis before playing the Phillies, again, this time at Olympic Stadium. Steve Rogers, Bill Lee and Scott Sanderson were slated to start for Montreal against Dick Ruthven, Nino Espinosa and Larry Christenson. Both teams were tied for the NL East lead. The Expos were getting more attention as more than 32,000 fans showed up for the first game on Tuesday, May 29. Steve Rogers began with his second consecutive shutout, leading the way to a 7–0 win. Rogers was the recipient of a two-minute standing ovation when he came to bat in the bottom of the eighth inning.[49] On Wednesday, on national television, Gary Carter drove in the only two runs of the game with a home run in the second inning in a 2–0 victory. Bill Lee, with his unbuttoned shirt and a huge beard (he hadn't shaved since 1978), stymied the Phillies. The start of the last game on Thursday afternoon was delayed because thousands of people were still buying tickets at the last second.[50] Warren Cromartie drove in the only run of the game with a sacrifice fly in the first inning. The Phillies threatened in the top of the eighth. After one out, Tim McCarver hit a single and was replaced by pinch-runner Garry Maddox. Maddox was a fast runner but wasn't considered as big a threat as Dave Lopes or Omar Moreno. Still, most people expected Maddox to run since starting pitcher Scott Sanderson had a slow windup. But Gary Carter's throw to second was right on target, eliminating Maddox. That play earned Carter another standing ovation[51] and really cut all energy the Phillies might have had. The Expos, after winning six straight games against the Phillies, were in sole possession of first place. The Phillies wouldn't recover and went on to lose six of their eight next games, a sequence that saw the team slide to fourth place. The Expos on the other hand had at last proven that they were to be considered seriously for the NL title. As Scott Sanderson later said: "That series I think helped everyone on the team feel we did have a championship-calibre team. And if there was anyone doubting it before, it was erased during that series." Steve Rogers agreed: "It was a real sign that we had arrived. We were legitimate."[52]

After years of promises, Gary Carter had finally arrived, both offensively and defensively, thanks to the hard work with coach Norm Sherry: "The physical thing about him, he was big and strong. When we started working, I thought he had a good chance to be good, because when I told him things, he would start doing them and eventually started to get them done. And so whatever the coach did, I said, the coach is only as good as your pupil. If you're showing him things and he's doing it, then he's gonna be good and you're gonna be a good coach. But most of the work, the physical part, how you want to catch the ball, move your feet, see the ball, I did it in stages. Like I said the first thing we'll learn to do is this and the second thing is this. I didn't try to do it all at once, to avoid confusing somebody. We took all spring in 1978 to get to the point. We didn't do as much throwing as we did the next spring. But during the season, yes, you see things and you say, look we want to do this and that. And don't do it that way, the other way. And also, trying to give inside things on how to work with pitchers. But he did understand what we were trying to do and I give him credit because he did all these things and pretty quickly became a very good catcher."[53]

After the sweep of the Phillies, the Expos lost seven times in nine games as they were swept in both Houston and Cincinnati. But in 1979, all they Expos needed was a good infusion of home games to get them right on track and they got plenty with 12 games against Atlanta, Houston, Cincinnati and Philadelphia (again). They won each one of these series, which led to nine wins. They almost blew it in the first game as Rodney Scott drew a bases-loaded walk for the winning run in the bottom of the eleventh inning. But Scott, instead of going to first base, began walking directly to the dugout. To him, the game was over, which was the case ... but not before he touched first base to officially force the run from third base, which he was reminded of by his teammates. Scott took his time, giving the term walk its whole significance, before finally setting foot on first base.[54] That win was one more occasion for Dick Williams to praise his second baseman. In his autobiography *No More Mr. Nice Guy*, Dick Williams wrote that Scott was among his all-time favorites.[55]

At first glance, one must wonder what's to like about Rodney Scott. His stats were far from spectacular (his batting average would never surpass .238 with the Expos). But Scott was able to work the pitchers. He would lead the free-swinging Expos in walks all three years he was a regular from 1979 to 1981. But his presence was felt mostly on the basepaths. Montreal would see many proficient basestealers in the Expos' uniform, runners like Tim Raines, Marquis Grissom, Otis Nixon or Ron LeFlore. But nobody had the pure instincts of Rodney Scott. He could anticipate the opponent's moves like few players could and he had the capacity to completely unravel a team's defense. "He had a real impudent side. He would challenge the other team. I never saw a guy take such wide leads off first base. Usually, runners would take a few feet but Scott would take double! He would look the pitcher in the eyes. Raines and LeFlore were great basestealers but Scott was the one who really could unnerve a defense the most. He would drive the opponent crazy. He would be on second with arms folded and without anybody noticing he would slide into third, without even a throw from the catcher. He would completely destabilize the other team. The way he ran on the bases was exceptional," said Serge Touchette.[56] Norm Sherry added: "I'll tell you something. They talk about Maury Wills and all these guys stealing bases. This guy steals bases easier than anybody that I ever saw! I don't know how many times a catcher would throw the ball back to the pitcher and he would steal the base. He was quick, had perfect timing and he could really upset the other team."[57] What was Scott's secret? "To steal bases is an art. You have to learn the pitchers, the fielders, all these kinds of things that come into play. I was trying to catch the guys off guard, you know. Doing something you don't normally do or whatever. I think you steal bases off the pitchers. Catchers have to wait for the ball. I think it's more instinct than anything. The key to these plays is looking at the ball. Where the ball is, you gotta be watching the ball."[58] John McHale said that Scott had a kind of sixth sense: "He was an unusual guy. I would go on a road trip with the team, but nobody knew I would go and then join the team because I didn't want the players to think I was watching and putting pressure on them. Rodney Scott could spot me in the ballpark no matter where I was. He almost had a cat-like intuition. There would be 50,000 people in the St. Louis ballpark and he would spot me."[59]

There was no doubt that Scott brought some life to the team. He was not alone, though, to contribute to a livelier atmosphere. Ross Grimsley was far more at ease with the Expos than he was with Cincinnati, where he hated the strict discipline enforced by that organization.[60] Grimsley had to wear his hair short there, with no beard or moustache. With the Expos, Grimsley could be himself, as he let his curly hair grow to his shoulders, along with a moustache. Bill Lee, of course, was at ease in these surroundings. The way the Expos carried themselves didn't go unnoticed in some particular circles. Within a few months, feature articles on Dick Williams, Ross Grimsley and Bill Lee would be published in the magazines *Gallery*, *Genesis* and *Penthouse*, publications mostly reknowned for their pictures than for their writing.[61]

From June 24, the Expos won three games in St. Louis before splitting series in Pittsburgh and Chicago. The team was prepared to close the pre All-Star Game schedule at home, where they had won 26 games out of 32. They kept it going against the Dodgers with three wins in four games but reality struck hard thereafter as San Francisco left the Big O with a sweep and the Expos could do no better than a split in four games against the lowly Padres. Nevertheless, at the All-Star Game, the Expos held the top spot in the NL East Division with 50 wins and 35 losses, two games and a half in front of the Chicago Cubs, who those years made a habit of competing for the first few months before crumbling. Philadelphia was trying to hang on despite a depleted pitching staff, three games from the lead while the Pirates were fourth, four games back. Three Expos players were chosen to go to the All-Star Game in Seattle, Steve Rogers, Gary Carter and Larry Parrish, the latter picked to replace Dave Concepcion.[62]

Rogers' comeback from his elbow surgery was nothing short of spectacular. He hadn't missed a turn in a rotation that had been intact since the beginning of the season, with Rogers, Ross Grimsley, Scott Sanderson, Bill Lee and Dan Schatzeder. Lee and Rogers, with nine victories apiece, were the most consistent of the group. Grimsley recorded eight wins, but struggled at times as shown by an ERA over 5.00. Sanderson's stats were better but he was going through some growing pains in his first season in the big leagues. Dan Schatzeder was the fifth starter (there were many days off and he was used less often than the others) and did a creditable job with a 2.45 ERA. The bullpen, the biggest question mark entering the season, became an exclamation point, with Elias Sosa leading the way. He was backed mainly by Stan Bahnsen and Woodie Fryman. Bahnsen was injury-free for the first time in three years and it took him a year to adjust to being used in relief, which he had never done before 1978.[63] Rudy May and David Palmer were used mostly in mop-up roles, which didn't sit well with the veteran May, who was playing his option year. Palmer, a rookie, was silently hoping he would get a chance to pitch more often.

Whether or not physical education specialist Ed Enos had any bearing on the players conditioning could not be properly assessed, but one thing was certain: the team didn't suffer any injuries during the first part of the season as nobody spent any amount of time on the disabled list. Consequently, the non-regulars had very few occasions to be used. For example, Dave Cash didn't start a single game and had only 23 at-bats until mid–July.[64] Worse for him, when Rodney Scott would become the first player to miss games because of an injury, the Expos not only recalled Tony Bernazard from their AAA affiliate in Denver but they also used him at second base.[65]

The picture wouldn't be complete without a story or two about Ellis Valentine. He missed five games at the end June because of a hip injury and also missed an appointment with a physician in St. Louis.[66] Valentine was more distant towards the media members. According to Mike Boone, from the *Montreal Star*, even though the Expos seemed in good position, the water was boiling within: "The Expos have a player who doesn't play (Cash), a pitcher who rarely pitches (May) and a right fielder who's unhappy (Valentine). Something's got to give!"[67] On July 8, Jerry Trudel, from the *Dimanche-Matin*, a Sunday weekly, wrote an open letter to Ellis Valentine, imploring him to show his enormous talent.[68] But even with all that tension, the team didn't go through a major crisis for one reason: it was winning and winning big for the first time.

Another tense situation was the relationship between manager Dick Williams and his star pitcher Steve Rogers. From his first year at the helm of the team, Williams wanted him to be more aggressive on the mound.[69] On July 12, Rogers gave his skipper some ammunition, as if he needed any. As the Expos were playing San Francisco at Olympic Stadium, in the bottom of the fourth inning, Montreal was trailing, 2–1, but had the bases loaded with one out and Rogers coming to bat. The count was three balls and no strikes. In such situations, generally speaking, most batters would take the next pitch, even more so if he's the pitcher. But irrationally, Rogers tried to bunt and when he did, the result was an inning-ending double play. In his book, Williams wrote that it was the most stupid play he had ever seen and that he didn't even care to ask Rogers his reasoning behind that strategy.[70]

The Expos began the second half of the season on the West Coast in Los Angeles. The team lost its first two games but that was overshadowed by the return on July 20 of the first bone fide hero to wear an Expos uniform: Rusty Staub. He had been the face of the franchise in his three years with the team from 1969 to 1971 and had been enormously popular with the fans. He was traded in spring 1972 to the New York Mets for Tim Foli, Ken Singleton and

Mike Jorgensen, a transaction that really shook up Staub, who had been nick-named "Le Grand Orange." In 1979, Staub was available thanks to a contract squabble with the Detroit Tigers.[71] The Expos didn't lose a player as it was a straight cash deal. However, one player had to be cut and it happened to be Tony Solaita, who was a better defensive first baseman and had more power than Staub at that point of their respective careers. Solaita was in fact the biggest power threat from the bench. He had hit 16 and 14 home runs with Kansas City and California in part-time roles in different seasons earlier in his career. He was also one the few Expos players to show some discipline at the plate. From a strict baseball standpoint, it was hard to understand how the Expos got better, especially when it looked as if there was no place to play Staub on a regular basis. In fact, one writer, Michael Farber, from *The Gazette*, questioned the real motives behind the move: "Was the Staub deal just for business?"[72] The question had some merits. In fact, John McHale admitted implicitly that it was part of the equation: "He was available, he had been popular and he was still a good hitter. We thought that having him on our bench would give us a little extra and win a few more games, that's all."[73] As for Solaita, he would finish the season with Toronto before beginning a suc-cessful stint in Japan, during which he hit an average of 39 home runs per season in his four years in the Land of the Rising Sun. Staub began his second tenure with the Expos in Los Angeles on July 21, getting a hit before being pulled thanks to an injury as he was trying to catch a ball. Staub had yet to put on a glove in 1979 as he had been used as a designated hitter in Detroit.

While the team was playing the Dodgers, Mike Littwin wrote a lengthy feature about the Expos in the *Los Angeles Times*.[74] To him, the Expos were bringing a breath of fresh air to a sport that was extremely conservative and whose athletes were less and less cooperative with the media. Tony Perez stated that there was no harmony on the team the year before (how winning can change things!) and that it became a chore just to show up at the ballpark. When players would complain about their lack of media exposure due to playing in Montreal, Perez told them that winning would cure all that, that nobody wanted to cover losers. Perez, the uncontested leader on the team, said that he really began to believe in the Expos in late June after a trip in St. Louis, Pittsburgh and Chicago: "We had three chances to fall on our face and we ended up winning six games out of ten."

But Littwin's opinion about the Expos was not shared by everybody, especially Dodgers manager Tommy Lasorda. "Look at them," he said as he watched the Expos warming up, some without either a cap or a team shirt. "How can they show up on the field that way? It's a disgrace!"[75] The eccentric Bill Lee decided to prove Lasorda right. He showed up without a cap, with a shirt untucked, assorted socks, diving left and right on the diamond so that when he was over with his warm-up, he looked more like a tramp than a baseball player.[76] To add insult to injury, Lee got his tenth win of the season in the last game of the series against the Dodgers, allowing only two runs in seven innings. The Expos came back home from California with a .500 record on the trip with four wins and four losses. From July 27 on, the race would pick up some steam in the National League East.

A four-game series against the Pittsburgh Pirates was awaiting the Expos on their return to Olympic Stadium. The Pirates started their 1979 season modestly but added some important ingredients along the way. They first acquired Tim Foli in April from the New York Mets for Frank Taveras in a straight swap of shortstops. Taveras was a speedster but quite erratic defensively and limited offensively. Foli, even though his range was limited, was sound defensively and had calmed down somewhat from his crazy ways of some years before. Then on June 29, the Pirates acquired two-time batting champion Bill Madlock from the San Francisco Giants for three pitchers, Ed Whitson, Fred Breining and Al Holland. Madlock not only added some punch to an offense that was relying too much on aging Willie Stargell and Dave Parker, but his arrival allowed Phil Garner to move back to second baseman, where he was more comfortable, relegating Rennie Stennett to utility status.

As they landed in Montreal, the Pirates were in third place, but only two games and a half behind the Expos. But the Pirates' visit, starting with a doubleheader, was not the only reason fans were awaiting en masse for that series. Rusty Staub would make his return in front of adoring fans and thus on Friday, July 27, 1979, everything was in place for the biggest crowd so far in Olympic Stadium history for a baseball game as 59,260 people showed up. Staub was used as a pinch-hitter in the first game and from the moment he set foot on the field, he got one of the most enduring standing ovations ever given to a player in the history of the team.[77] With two men on and two out, Staub hit a fly out against tough lefty Grant Jackson. The atmosphere was festive but the Pirates refused to collaborate, as they won both games, 5–4 and 9–1. On Saturday, Dave Parker set the tone with a two-run home run in the first inning against Dan Schatzeder in a 5–3 win. The Expos avoided a sweep on Sunday thanks to a four-run first inning on an RBI single by Staub and a three-run triple by Andre Dawson. Steve Rogers threw a complete game in that 5–3 win. The Expos were still leading the division but the more experienced Pirates made a real statement.

The Expos certainly felt some kind of pressure and two meetings were held during that series, one called by Dick Williams and the other by the players themselves.[78] Williams wasn't one to call meetings left and right and in fact was not very akin to talking to his players, whether individually or as a group. In the players-only meeting, veterans Tony Perez and Duffy Dyer, who had experience in pressure situation after winning World Series, addressed their teammates as did Rusty Staub. Warren Cromartie, who was rarely without words, and Larry Parrish were the most vocal among the young guns.[79] Parrish had really matured in the last year and a half and it showed in his demeanor and of course on his overall play. He was tremendously demanding of himself and would play with numerous injuries throughout his career without searching for excuses when it could have been the easy way out. In March, after an exhibition game where he made some defensive mistakes, he stayed on the field to take numerous grounders.[80] Jean Aucoin, from *La Presse*, pointed out that Parrish was showing the qualities of a real leader.[81]

For the first time in 1979, Dick Williams decided to remove Scott Sanderson from his starting rotation, which meant that David Palmer and Rudy May would at last be given a chance to pitch more as the upcoming schedule was quite heavy with three doubleheaders in twelve days. Sanderson was unable to go more than five innings in his last four starts and worse for him, was hurt when hit by a pitch on a bunt attempt in mid–July. Palmer was in fact a little lucky to still be with the team. As he was seldom used, there was talk that he might be sent to the minors to let him pitch but Dick Williams insisted that he stayed in Montreal. As Sanderson later recalled: "Jim Brewer, the late Jim Brewer who was an outstanding pitching coach, came up to me and said that they had a meeting and they wanted to send me down but Dick said to stick with me a little bit longer. So the next time I pitch, I'd be pitching for my job. I said, I understand that, I just need to pitch. I went days and days and days again without pitching. And I don't remember the exact numbers but I know we were in Atlanta, I came on in relief and struck out a couple of guys. Came in relief the next night and pitched two innings and struck out four guys. And then two nights later, I pitched one inning in Cincinnati and struck out the side. And then Brewer said, 'I guess you can stay.'"[82] Rudy May was another matter though. He asked twice to be traded and even thought about leaving the team.[83] He just wanted to pitch, which he hadn't done a lot so far.

A second doubleheader in four days was awaiting the Expos, this time against the St. Louis Cards. St. Louis prevailed in the first game against Bill Lee but Palmer closed the door in the second game in a 5–1 win. The day after, Rudy May bettered Palmer, hurling a brilliant 5–0 shutout against the Cards. Larry Parrish hit his 15th home run in that game, a career high with almost two full months to play. This long home stretch ended with four wins in six games against the rapidly fading Cubs and the lowly Mets. Wayne Twitchell, wearing a Mets uniform, was booed heavily in his return to Montreal after trying to explain his 1978 problems with the quality of the water where he lived at the time.[84] But despite that 6–3 sequence, the Expos lost first place as the Pirates won five times in three days. On August 5, the Expos fell to second place, a half game behind Pittsburgh. The Expos went on to Philadelphia, facing a team they had dominated so far. But the Phillies reversed the roles, winning all three games with only Steve Rogers pitching more than four innings among the starting pitchers. But Rogers was being hit harder since the All-Star break as his arm was tiring. At the end of July, his ERA stood at a solid 2.45 and he had already thrown five shutouts. To his own admission, he had almost nothing left in his arm after coming back from an injury.[85] He had already pitched more than 200 innings. He would be almost useless in the last two months of the season as he would skip turns. He finished the season with an ERA of 3.00.

After the sweep in Philadelphia, the Expos' skid reached four games in New York before David Palmer got the team back on track with another solid performance in the second game of another doubleheader, pitching eight and two-thirds innings, allowing five runs, all of them in the bottom of the ninth. In the first game, Ross Grimsley was again hit hard, lasting only one-third of an inning during which the Mets tagged him for six runs, all earned. That performance earned Grimsley a ticket for the bullpen as his ERA reached 5.33.[86] The day after, Dan Schatzeder, the most consistent starter in August, beat the Mets. As the team was in New York, Tony Bernazard was sent to the minors, despite having an on-base percentage of .500, thanks to 15 walks in 13 games. But the Expos had won only six of these 13 games, which made it easier to put Chris Speier back at shortstop, where Rodney Scott was playing as Bernazard was patrolling second base. John Tamargo was recalled from Denver to take Bernazard's spot on the roster. Tamargo, a catcher, carried a solid bat. After New York, the Expos avoided being swept in Houston thanks to a combined effort by Schatzeder and Scott Sanderson. With a 3–6 record during that road trip, the Expos found themselves on August 16 four games behind the Pirates, who had won their last six. That gap would be the widest separating these two teams until the last day of the season.[87]

Back in Montreal where they were very dominant, the Expos swept the Braves, thanks to the brilliance of the pitchers. David Palmer, again, threw a complete-game shutout in the first game, his fifth win in seven decisions. In less than a month, he went from an afterthought to the most reliable pitcher on a solid pitching staff. Palmer's journey to the majors was quite an unusual one as was his pitching repertoire. "He had an unusual assortment of pitches. He was a very strong competitor. At one time, he was probably as good as any pitcher we had in baseball that year. He was awfully good," said John McHale.[88] Galen Cisco, who would become his pitching coach, also had praise for Palmer: "You talk about a competitor and that guy was a competitor. He not only was a competitor but he had a fastball that moved like crazy, the kind of fastball you'd like to teach but you can't teach it. He had a curveball from hell, if you know what I mean. It was over the top, a straight downer, and he was a smart pitcher. He had a palmball for a changeup and it was also a very good pitch."[89] Palmer admitted after his career that his competitive fire was always there: "Yes! Maybe too much. I've always been that way! I've always wanted to win at anything I did. I hated to lose, I didn't like to lose. I just loved to compete."[90]

Throwing strikes was never a problem for Palmer. But when one is drafted in the 21st round as was the case for Palmer, there is not much opportunity to show what one can do. After his first half-season in the pro in a rookie league in Lethbridge, Alberta, during which he lost his five decisions with an astronomical ERA of 7.20, let's say that he was on short leash. "I was the worst pitcher in the league in Lethbridge. That winter, I went home and someone told me to I needed to hold the fingers together to get the ball to move a little bit. So I taped my fingers and held a baseball all winter. When I went to spring training, I was beginning to wonder whether I would make the team or not, because of the spring that I had or the record I had the year before. So one night, before I was going to pitch, our hotel was next a mall. So I was at the mall with other guys playing video games. What I was playing was racing cars where you had to shift. When I shifted down my fingernail on my index finger got caught and was ripped off. And because I was wondering whether I would even make the team or not, I had to pitch the next day even if my index finger hurt. So what I did was I put my index finger off the ball, and kind of set off my little finger a little bit. So I wouldn't have any pressure on it. From that day on, I started throwing a cut fastball. I never threw hard, but I had very good control and good curveball. So when I began throwing that cut fastball, I started getting a lot of hitters out." So years before Mariano Rivera, David Palmer was getting people out with that now famous pitch.

His break came during a bullpen session with catcher Bobby Ramos, who was part of the organization and would become a major league coach for many years. The session was attended by several members of the organization. "Felipe Alou was there, Larry Bearnearth was there, a minor league pitching instructor at the time, and I believe Jim Fanning also was there, who was the minor leagues director. When I got them throwing on the side, Bobby Ramos came down to me with those guys there and asked me which game I was going to pitch. I said I wasn't even on the roster, I'm not even on the team. He looked at those guys and said, he's got the best stuff out there. He needs to pitch. So that was a big help from Bobby."

In 1978, Palmer started the season in West Palm Beach in the Florida

State League where he was absolutely dominant. He was promoted to Memphis during the season, being reacquainted with manager Felipe Alou, who had been with Palmer at West Palm Beach the year before. "I grew up in New York (state) so I was a Yankee fan and saw Felipe when he played for the Yankees. When he played for them, they played at Shea Stadium and I saw him get his 2000th hit. I knew the Alou brothers obviously. So, to play for somebody who had been in the major leagues for 16 years and when you're a young kid and you're around anybody who did play in the major leagues, you're in such awe of them. Wow he was in the show. I got to play for Felipe Alou for two years, and also my first two years in Montreal, he was the first-base coach. So I spent four years with Felipe Alou."

Palmer would go as far as saying that he owed his career to Felipe Alou. "He gave me the ball. When Gullickson and Sanderson signed in 1977, you know number one and number three draft choices, obviously they were right. They stayed over 20 years apiece in the big leagues. And Bob James, a number one draft choice, so when you have two number one draft choices and a number three draft choice and a number 21 draft choice, the other guys are going to have the ball. Felipe Alou had, I don't know how would you call it, major league experience whatever, he told them that I was a good pitcher and that I needed to pitch. So he believed in me and he gave me the ball. And the same thing in 1978 when I pitched for him in Memphis. At the end of the year, they called up Bob James to the big leagues. And I had a very good year between West Palm and Memphis and I didn't get called up. And Felipe said, trust me, you'll go, you're gonna be there. He was in my corner, he gave me the ball and gave me a chance to pitch."[91] Yes Palmer got some breaks but to his credit he took full advantage of it and eventually became the most trustworthy pitcher Dick Williams relied upon.

Approaching September, the Expos had only a dozen scheduled games remaining against Western Division opponents before entering the last stretch against their own division foes. The Expos won only once in three games in Cincinnati and could play only once in Atlanta, a game they won, as the weather was just too bad to allow any baseball at Fulton County Stadium. On August 26, they were back at home and after a loss against Houston, they embarked on a spectacular ten-game winning streak, including sweeps against Cincinnati, New York and Chicago, cutting the Pirates' lead to only one game after the September 6 games. That day, Palmer got yet another win, 1–0, at Wrigley Field, thanks to an opposite-field ninth-inning homer from Gary Carter, usually a dead pull hitter.

Coincidentally (or not), the Expos got back to their winning ways with the return of Dave Cash in the regular lineup. Before August 27, he had started only once, even though he had been able to maintain a batting average over

.400 in a very limited role. Rodney Scott was moved to shortstop to accommodate Cash, which left Chris Speier out of the equation. Speier never could recover from missing most of training camp in 1979. Cash had been waiting for a chance, even though he never thought in his worst nightmares that it would take almost five months before he got his second starting assignment of the season. He almost never complained (there were some mild comments about his unhappiness but nothing to trigger any major controversy), but he admitted that it was a very tough time for him, especially since he didn't expect to lose his job: "My first reaction was one of surprise. I didn't think that you're going to lose your job in spring training after being a starter for a number of years. But that's a manager's prerogative. If he feels that someone else should start, that's up to the manager. My job at that time was to do whatever I can to help the ballclub win. I was employed by the Montreal Expos. I was getting paid, so there really wasn't any bitching to be done. We wanted to keep the team that we had together and we didn't want any distraction. We were going into that season with an opportunity to win. We did have a good club and we just didn't want any outside distraction so I just became another member of the team." Easier said than done of course, which Cash was ready to admit: "It wasn't easy. It really wasn't easy and a tough pill to swallow. But there again, there is no 'I' in team and it takes 25 guys to win a championship. I played a number of seasons and I knew before long, it happens in every baseball season, somebody gets hurt once in a while and you get the opportunity to play. If you noticed what happened, they didn't have injuries but I got an opportunity to play, especially going down the stretch. I think I proved what I was made of and I think because I didn't cause any waves or any commotion, I think it kept us focused on the season and the job herein."[92]

Steve Rogers' elbow problems exasperated Dick Williams. In a column penned by Réjean Tremblay, from *La Presse*, Williams' opinion about Rogers couldn't be clearer: "He's not in the same league as Bill Lee or Catfish Hunter. He's not the winner he could be."[93] Williams' take on Rogers would never change and the relationship between both would be mild, at best.

On September 1, the Expos called up some players, not to take a look at them for the future, as was their custom, but rather to get some help for the final stretch run in their race for the NL East title. Ken Macha, who had been sent to the minors in late July, was back from Denver. Bill Atkinson was also called up and reliever Dale Murray was acquired from the New York Mets. Murray had spent two years and a half with the Expos from 1974 to 1976 with some success. But he had never been able to repeat his success since leaving Montreal. "When you come from a little town in Texas, New York is maybe not the ideal place," confided the tall righty. He admitted that the trade to

Cincinnati after the 1976 season was a shock. He knew the Expos' organization well and was at ease with players he grew up with professionally.[94] Six more players would join the team in the following two weeks, Tony Bernazard, Randy Bass, Bob Pate, Tim Raines, Bob James and Bill Gullickson. Among them, only Raines would have an impact and it would be strictly as a pinch-runner.

After a loss put an end to the 10-game winning streak, the Expos embarked on another streak, winning seven in a row for a total of 17 wins in 18 games. That sequence ended with a loss against the St. Louis Cardinals in the second game of a doubleheader at Olympic Stadium. Both teams split another doubleheader the day after, so that on September 16 the Expos were tied with the Pirates for the lead. Moreover, the Pirates were the next visitors at Olympic Stadium for a short two-game series.

The interest for the Expos had never been so high, not only in Montreal but also in the province and in the whole country. Scalpers were selling tickets seven times their face value.[95] The television ratings were at their highest. In other provinces, fans were upset over the CBC decision to keep broadcasting the Toronto Blue Jays, who were on their way to their third straight 100-loss season.[96] Radio broadcasts were followed like never before, both in French and English.[97] The interest was so high that the competition had to react. So, the radio broadcast that was competing against the French Expos broadcast decided to send someone to follow the Pittsburgh Pirates, who did report on air every half inning.[98] "We had to do something because everybody was listening to CKAC. That was the only thing to do," remembered Radiomutuel sports director Pierre Durivage.[99] Wayne Parrish was a young reporter for the *Montreal Star*, coming over from British Columbia. He remembered how the craze invaded the whole city: "You could get on the subway in downtown Montreal and there was that incredible sense of palpable excitement as you got closer to the Olympic Stadium. Even when you cover games, you go out quite early but even on those occasions, when we would be out there a couple of hours or more before the game, when you took the subway, there was just the sense that with each subway stop, something was growing toward a crescendo which would be reached at Olympic Stadium."[100]

The stage was set for a summit between the two best teams in the division. More than 50,000 people showed up for both games in a overcharged atmosphere as the Expos got long and loud ovations before each game. But as was the case when Rusty Staub made his return in July, the Pirates spoiled the party, winning both times. In the first game, sophomore Don Robinson threw a six-hitter in a 2–1 win. Bill Lee and Bruce Kison were the second-game starting pitchers. Lee was counted on to limit left-handed sluggers Willie Stargell and Dave Parker. With Kison, the Expos were facing what they dreaded most: a tough righty coming a little from the side who wasn't afraid to throw inside. The Pirates scored three times in a first inning that seemed endless as the Expos committed two errors, combined with four Pirates hits. The Expos came back with two runs in the third and tied the score in the sixth on a one-run single from Larry Parrish. Both teams remained tied until the 11th inning. Due to two long rain delays, it was almost 2 A.M. when Dale Murray started the 11th inning for the Expos. Mike Easler led off with a single. Then, Pirates manager Chuck Tanner asked umpire Andy Olsen to check Dale Murray for a foreign substance or something illegal.[101] Willie Stargell was the next batter and broke the impasse with a two-run home run from which the Expos didn't recover. Did Tanner's scheme contribute to the final outcome? Dale Murray laughed later at that notion, pointing out that he had two strikes on Stargell when he hit the ball out and that he had handled him well up to that point.[102] It was indeed the first home run by Stargell against Murray. The Pirates left thus Montreal with a two-game lead with less than two weeks to go. But another big series was awaiting these two teams, this time in Pittsburgh.

The Expos didn't have time to dwell on what happened because they had to go to New York to play two straight doubleheaders in Shea Stadium. Dick Williams had no choice but to pitch seldom-used Ross Grimsley, Scott Sanderson and Rudy May. Along with Dan Schatzeder, they all responded with brilliant performances, collectively allowing only four earned runs in 30 innings as the Expos won all four games. In the meantime, the Pirates lost twice in three games in Philadelphia, giving the division lead back to the Expos. On Friday, September 21, the Expos' game in Philadelphia was postponed, so another doubleheader was scheduled on Saturday. The Pirates lost that night, giving the Expos a one-game lead. The Expos managed to win two games out of three in Philadelphia, so that on Sunday night the team had a half-game lead over the Pirates. Pittsburgh and Montreal were then ready for a crucial four-game duel, beginning on Monday with another doubleheader, the fourth within a week for the Expos.

Against Bert Blyleven, arguably the best Pirates starting pitcher, the Expos got two runs from the get-go, thanks to a two-run single by Gary Carter. Blyleven however closed the door thereafter. Dan Schatzeder seemed in control as he had retired the last 13 batters when he walked Dave Parker in the sixth inning. Bill Robinson was the next batter, a tough customer for the lefty.[103] Schatzeder threw him his signature pitch, a knuckle-curve akin to that of Burt Hooton. But Robinson got hold of the ball and tied the game with a home run. After another walk, veteran Stan Bahnsen was summoned to the mound. One hit and two errors later the inning ended with the Pirates adding another run, paving the way to a 5–2 win.

In the second game, the score was tied at two when Rudy May filled the bases with one out. Bahnsen was again called from the bullpen, but an error by Dave Cash opened the floodgates that led to four Pirates runs, while only one was earned. The Expos however had some life left. In fact, the rest of the game belonged to Dick Williams. After one out in the eighth inning, veterans Rusty Staub and Duffy Dyer drew walks from Joe Coleman. Chuck Tanner then asked for Kent Tekulve, a pitcher the Expos always had trouble hitting. After a second out, Larry Parrish reduced the deficit to two runs with a single. Speedster Tim Raines was sent in to run for Parrish. It was the fifth time Raines was used since his call-up from Memphis in the Southern League, each time as a pinch-runner. Rodney Scott was due to bat. But even though Scott was a Williams protégé, the manager was looking for a guy who could drive the ball, not a Punch-and-Judy hitter who did all the little things that helped his team win. Williams knew more and sent John Tamargo and respond he did: a double that drove in two runs to tie the game, 5–5. In the bottom of the eighth, to the surprise of almost everyone, the new pitcher was Ross Grimsley, who hadn't been used much since his demotion to the bullpen in early August. In 1978, Grimsley had been extremely affable and available to the media but in 1979, he had really shut himself out. One could read on his locker, "STAY AWAY. THAT MEANS YOU!" Beat writer Ian McDonald was nonetheless able to talk to him. Grimsley acknowledged that he had not been as consistent as the year before, but refused to take solely the blame for not being as efficient as expected. He added that he didn't want to disrupt the team as it was in the middle of the NL East race.[104] But on that Monday night, Grimsley had to face the top of the lineup and he was up to the task as he retired Omar Moreno, Tim Foli and lastly, Dave Parker on strikes. In the top of the ninth, Staub and Dyer got on base after two outs with a single and a walk, respectively, before Ellis Valentine at last gave the Expos a 7–6 lead. Grimsley went back to the mound to try to finish the job. He first gave a walk to Rennie Stennett. The next batter was the always dangerous Willie Stargell, who broke the Expos' fans hearts the week before with his extra-inning home run. Stargell was the Pirates' inspirational leader, the man his teammates relied on when the game was on the line. He distributed little stars to worthy players, no matter their contribution to the team's success. He made "We Are Family," a hit song from the group Sister Sledge, the team's official anthem.[105] Given that the stakes were as high as they could get, at first glance, the confrontation seemed largely in favor of the Pirates. But for whatever reason, Stargell could never hit Grimsley. Up to that point, Stargell had been limited to six hits in 32 official at-bats for a meager .188 batting average with 10 strikeouts. Stargell had never hit a long ball against the curly lefty and got absolutely no walks![106] On this night, again, Grimsley, with his slow and slower pitches, prevailed as he induced Stargell to hit into a double play. Dick Williams had won his bet but had no intention to push his luck further with Grimsley. Redoubtable Bill Madlock was up next but there was no way he was going to face the lefty. Elias Sosa got the save when Madlock hit into a game-ending grounder to the shortstop. If there was ever a case when a manager won a game, that second game of the doubleheader clearly belonged to Dick Williams.

The status quo prevailed after the doubleheader and since the Expos were on the road and were still leading the division, and given how they were able to come back and win the second game, they should have been happy with the overall outcome. However, they suffered a huge loss when Gary Carter suffered a thumb injury in the second game. The diagnosis: a fracture and a severe strain.[107] Carter, who had become one of the best catchers in the game, would not be back in 1979.

The Expos needed one win in the next two games to maintain their lead. But the Pirates prevailed, winning both games unequivocally, 10–4 and 10–1. Another chapter of the tumultuous relation between Dick Williams and Steve Rogers was written during that series in Pittsburgh. Ted Blackman, from *The Gazette*, wrote a story about an incident that happened in the very first days of spring training, an incident related by Rogers with the team in Pittsburgh. Rogers was talking with coach Norm Sherry about his arm after his surgery. Rogers told him that his elbow was fine but that his shoulder was killing him, to which Dick Williams, who was nearby, replied: "If you can't pitch, I will get somebody else to pitch." Rogers didn't expect the story to go out. Williams would say that he'd like to have his best pitcher on the mound against the Pirates, but had to go with Rogers.[108]

As Rogers and Williams were battling each other via the media, Montreal lost what once was an institution among the Anglophone society. *The Montreal Star* decided to stop publishing, for good. It was the second daily newspaper to fold within a year in Montreal, after the French *Montréal-Matin* in December 1978. Two writers from the *Star* were in Pittsburgh when the announcement was made, Wayne Parrish and Mike Boone. When asked what their plan was that night, their answer left no doubt: "I don't know about you guys but for us, we're gonna go out and get drunk!"[109]

On Thursday, the Expos were one game and a half behind the Pirates and they still had hope as they were heading to Atlanta to play yet another doubleheader, this time in Atlanta, a make-up for the two games they couldn't play in late August. But the weather was no more cooperative than it was a month before and even though they tried to play, the conditions were just brutal.[110] The Expos would have to play the games after the last scheduled game only if it meant anything in the standings for the top spot of the NL

East. Still, the Expos got a half-game back after the Pirates lost, 9–5, against St. Louis. The Pirates didn't have to travel and wouldn't have to do so for the next series either against the Cubs, contrary to the Expos who, within a little more than 24 hours, had to fly from Pittsburgh to Atlanta to Montreal to finish the season against Philadelphia.

The Expos only had to match the Pirates during the last weekend of the season in order to give themselves a chance. In the first game against the Phillies, two young guns were on the mound, David Palmer for the Expos against Dickie Noles. Both pitchers excelled, Palmer allowing two runs in ten innings, his only mistake being a two-run home run by Mike Schmidt. Noles limited the Expos to two runs as well in nine innings. In the 11th inning, the Phillies, helped by two defensive miscues, scored once to win, 3–2. The Pirates had the upper hand over the Cubs, 6–1, to increase their lead to two games over the Expos. The margin of error was getting increasingly small.

On Saturday, Bill Lee and Randy Lerch, two lefties, were the starting pitchers. The Expos, thanks to RBIs by Andre Dawson and John Tamargo, took the lead in the first inning. The score remained 2–0 until the eighth inning. The Phillies scored once then and added another run in the ninth to even the score, 2–2. But in the bottom of the ninth, Dave Cash drove in pinch-runner Tim Raines with the winning run while in Pittsburgh, the Pirates lost, 7–6, in 13 innings against the Cubs. The margin was back to one game with one last day to go.

The Expos could still decide their own fate but they had to deal with Steve Carlton. Steve Rogers, who had been very inconsistent when used at all since August, was the Expos' starter. Throughout his career, Carlton had only had limited success against Montreal[111] but that afternoon, he was as dominant as ever. He led the Expos to three singles. Only three balls were hit in the outfield in the whole game. Rogers wasn't that bad, with eight innings and two runs allowed but Carlton was just too much for anybody that day. The Pirated finally nailed the Expos' coffin with a 5–3 victory to squash Montreal fans' hopes to see the Expos in the postseason for the first time. The Pirates went on to win the National League pennant and eventually the World Series. Willie Stargell was named MVP in both series.

The disappointment among Expos fans was heart-breaking but at last the team had finally arrived in their eleventh season. Jim Fanning and most people around the Expos were confident that they had the basis of a solid ballclub even before the 1979 season: "It was a matter of when we were going to win it. We knew that, I mean it was going to happen."[112] The Expos of 1979 were able to recreate the atmosphere of freshness that characterized the first few years of the franchise. Fans then identified themselves with Rusty Staub, Coco Laboy, Mack Jones, John Boccabella, Claude Raymond, Bill Stoneman and others. In 1979, the heroes were Larry Parrish, Gary Carter, Andre Dawson, Ellis Valentine and all the grown-ups from the Expos' farm system. With an attendance of 2.1 million, the Expos shattered their old record by 50 percent. The new mascot, Youppi, Roger D. Landry's creation, was an instant success with fans, who were immersed in a festive atmosphere right at the entrance to Olympic Stadium, thanks to a band akin to a Bavarian group. Music was played there from the opening of the gates until the last fan departed the premises. The Expos' popularity on both radio and television contradicted some skeptical prognosis from people directly involved! Jacques Doucet, the French voice of the Expos for almost their entire history, said that even the big boss of the radio network that was broadcasting the games didn't believe it would be a success. He couldn't help but concede that he was wrong after noticing that most of his neighbors in his vacation house around a lake were listening to ballgames on their radio.[113]

Not surprisingly, on the field players, coaches and executives were praised everywhere. Réjean Tremblay, from *La Presse*, wrote that that group of people was worthy of discovering them.[114] According to Tony Perez, the Pirates were not better than the Expos but that the experience made the difference. He underscored also that the Expos had to play eight doubleheaders in September.[115] The Expos however were not the only team to cope with a crazy schedule in September, especially in the Northeast of the continent, thanks to inclement weather through the summer. In fact, four of these doubleheaders were played on the road and a fifth in Atlanta was never played. Many wished Olympic Stadium would have had a roof over the field, as was expected throughout. Perez may have had a point as the Expos committed 12 errors in their last seven games. But the face-to-face confrontations with the Pirates were what really hurt the Expos the most. Montreal won only one of these six games. In his autobiography, Andre Dawson admitted that even though the Expos had more talent, the more experienced Pirates reacted a lot better under the pressure of the race.[116]

Individually, Larry Parrish deserved the bigger praise, especially in the latter part of the season. From June, he hit 29 of his 30 home runs with 71 RBIs and a batting average of .317, adding many clutch hits in the last stretch. He was named without surprise as the team's player of the year. A testament to his will to win at all cost, without regard to his own stats, he hit seventh in the lineup the whole season and he even laid down seven sacrifice bunts during the season, an unusually high number for a 30-home run hitter.

Of the three outfielders, Andre Dawson showed the best progression, hiking his batting average 23 points to .275. But like his outfield comrades, he was swinging at too many pitches which curtailed his on-base percentage. Left fielder Warren Cromartie had only 39 walks, including 19 intentional.

That total was the highest of the three outfielders! As for Ellis Valentine, even though his numbers were solid, people displayed disappointment towards his play and attitude. In his mid-season evaluation, Serge Touchette wrote that Dave Parker would be the second-best right fielder in baseball if Valentine wanted to give his all.[117] Jerry Trudel believed that Valentine had to go.[118]

On the mound, six pitchers finished in double figures in win, with Bill Lee the leader with 16. Steve Rogers had 13 while Dan Schatzeder, David Palmer, Ross Grimsley and Rudy May all ended at 10. Rogers was among the league leaders in several categories and Schatzeder was third in ERA. In the bullpen, Elias Sosa fulfilled his mandate with nine wins, 18 saves and a spectacular 1.98 ERA. Woodie Fryman and Stan Bahnsen were efficient, if not spectacular, mostly in back-up roles.

Dick Williams was rewarded for the team's season by Associated Press as the Manager of the Year. Steve Rogers and Warren Cromartie, though, didn't believe Williams deserved that kind of credit. According to Rogers, the players had to play in spite of bad communication and the negative influence created by Williams: "Gene Mauch once said that managers don't win games but can lose ones and I think so as well. Communication is important on a team but that aspect was lacking in 1979. We had to forget all that negativity in order to play."[119] Cromartie merely said that the role of the manager is overrated. Veteran Stan Bahnsen had a different take, even though he didn't agree with the way had had been used: "We lack maturity when it comes to the manager. The players just don't understand that he has a job to do. Personally, I didn't like some of his decisions but the bottom line is he's had success." Williams' reaction was typical of his character: "As long as we win, I don't care much about what they had to say."[120] He would add later that he didn't want to react on comments coming from players who had bad seasons.[121]

Even before the fourth annual free agent draft, the Expos lost an important member of their coaching staff. Jim Brewer decided to call it quit for family reasons.[122] Many times "family reasons" is the expression used to hide the real motives behind the decision. But Brewer really had enough of all the travel. Some pitchers would keep working with him, but on an informal basis.[123] Jim Brewer was tremendously respected by pitchers. He was the one who counselled Steve Rogers after his elbow surgery a year before.[124] He had just retired in 1976, so he could easily relate to the modern-day pitchers. He also had a first-hand knowledge of hitters in both leagues. Dan Schatzeder remembered a lesson he got early on from his pitching coach: "He was not only a player's coach, lot of coaches are so worried about their jobs or what the management think of them and thinks more about management instead the players, Jim Brewer was a player's coach and he was the pitcher's coach.

He was not afraid to tell the catcher, Gary Carter or Tim Blackwell or whoever is catching, that's what we need to do, it would be better working together in doing this. He was always in your corner. But if you messed up, he was not afraid to tell you. One time, after a game in New York, I did not pitch well against the Mets, and I sat on the bench, Dick Williams took me out of the game and I had a kind of pouting look at my face like, 'Oh boy poor me!' Jim Brewer looked over to me and said, 'Schatzie, don't you ever feel sorry for yourself because nobody is going to feel sorry for yourself, especially the other team. Now get that look off your face, learn from your mistakes and bounce back. Because in the big leagues, if you can't bounce back, it can be a long season.' I thought that's the biggest thing I learned from him. The longest your slump is, the harder it is to get out. Good players have short slumps. And after two bad games you better get your act together. So he was very honest with me and, like I said, he was like a father."[125]

Contrary to the first three years of the free agent draft, the Expos had no intention to sign an impact player. Dave Cash, Ross Grimsley and Elias Sosa were important additions that filled huge needs. This time, the Expos needed more to fine-tune a team that looked on the rise. Pitcher Bruce Kison was the first player chosen by Montreal. Among the other players picked was fireballer Nolan Ryan. But his price was deemed too prohibitive for the Expos and the only reason why the Expos added him on his list was out of favor to Expos scout Red Murff, who first signed Ryan and had remained close to him.[126]

The Expos expected to lose Rudy May but tried to keep Tony Perez. But even with an offer that matched that of the Boston Red Sox, Perez elected to leave the Expos to go to Boston. The contract was for three years at around $1 million. But Perez just couldn't accept the way Dick Williams used him towards the end of the season when he would be benched against tough right-ies, including twice in the fabled four-game series in Pittsburgh in the last week of the season. Perez loved the three years he spent in Montreal; he was the first Hall of Famer to speak some words in French in his induction speech.[127]

Dave Cash was next to go as he was traded away to San Diego for infielder Bill Almon and first baseman-outfielder Dan Briggs. Perez and Cash were both added during the winter of 1976 to add some credibility to a team that desperately needed some. Their departure meant that the team had matured enough to fly on its own wings. Cash wanted to leave anyway and never really accepted how he was used so sparingly in 1979. He was especially disappointed to not have played the last game of the season against the Phillies and Steve Carlton, a pitcher against whom he had had some success, as attested by his .301 lifetime batting average against the tall lefty.[128]

With Perez going to the American League, most assumed that Rusty Staub would become the regular first baseman in 1980, which would at the same time balance a lineup that was predominantly right-handed. In the winter meetings in December, the Expos signed veteran lefty Fred Norman, who was expected to replace Rudy May on the roster. The next move was a little surprising when Rowland Office was announced as a new Expo. The Expos were already loaded in the outfield and also had Jerry White whom Dick Williams called "the best fourth outfielder in the majors." Office had played an average of 120 games since 1974 with the Atlanta Braves. With the Expos, he became the fifth outfielder, with Cromartie, Dawson and Valentine the mainstays.

More importantly, the Expos acquired speedster Ron LeFlore from the Detroit Tigers for Dan Schatzeder. "The Canadiens have Lafleur, the Expos now have LeFlore," announced president and general manager John McHale.[129] Guy Lafleur was the Montreal Canadiens' superstar and had just led the hockey team to four straight Stanley Cup titles. LeFlore filled a huge void as the perfect leadoff hitter, a role that hadn't really been fulfilled since the days of Ron Hunt, who played in Montreal from 1970 to 1974. LeFlore had stolen 146 bases in the preceding two seasons and his batting average surpassed .300 in three of his last four seasons. LeFlore's story was quite unusual as he was recruited in a prison in Michigan, where he was serving a sentence for armed robbery. It didn't take him long to climb the ladder from the minors to the majors. His story was the subject of both a movie and a book.[130] In 1976, he got a hit in 30 straight games, which got him a berth on the American League squad in the All-Star Game. He had become available partly because he was on his way to become a free agent after the 1980 season. Also Tigers' manager Sparky Anderson was fed up with his lack of discipline, as he was said to be late several times for games.[131]

With six bona fide major league outfielders under contract, one didn't have to think long before figuring out that there was something brewing from the inside: Ellis Valentine was available. The problem however was that nobody wanted to pay the price the Expos thought he was worth. John McHale was adamant that he wanted the equivalent in talent. But even if his talent was widely acknowledged, nobody wanted to give something significant for a player whose reputation had become well known. McHale on the other hand didn't want to risk seeing Valentine blossom with another team without getting something in return. In short, if Valentine was to blossom, it would have to be with the Expos.

The Expos tried to acquire another lefty hitter during the winter meetings: Al Oliver. His name had been mentioned for some years with the Expos. Serge Touchette even reported that a trade was in place to bring Oliver to

Montreal for Steve Rogers. But Rangers' owner Brad Corbett was the one who nixed the deal, according to Touchette.[132] Corbett apparently had promised Oliver that he wouldn't be traded.[133] Eddie Robinson, who was the Rangers' general manager at the time, denied later in an interview any such intervention from his owner, even though he acknowledged that both men were working closely.[134] But Touchette maintained that a member of the Expos' organization told him the trade was agreed on. Some weeks later, respected New York writer Dick Young wrote in *The Sporting News* that Brad Corbett had voided another deal involving Oliver, this time with the Chicago White Sox.[135]

To close the year, the Expos got another prestigious award from the *Canadian Press*. The baseball team was picked as the team of the year in a poll of sports editors through the country.[136] There were less than two months to go before the start of spring training. Never before were the fans so eager to get news from the Expos in Florida!

5

1980: Close But No Cigar

Thanks to the success of 1979, spring training in 1980 had a totally different atmosphere than in any other year in the team's history up to that point. Fans, who were accustomed to unfulfilled promises and some years of futility, had every reason to be realistically optimistic for the future. It was no more a matter of justifying some potential but rather to consolidate what was built over the years, with 1979 as a point of reference.

Generally speaking, one doesn't change a winning formula. But in sports, changes are inevitable, even more so in baseball since the advent of free agency. The Expos were still young, so the core of the team was still some years away from exercising the right to leave on their own. The most important players to replace were free agents Tony Perez and Rudy May and pitcher Dan Schatzeder who was traded away to Detroit. Perez's place would be the most difficult to fill, because of his experience and leadership. Larry Parrish, who would manage in the majors and minors after his playing career, would still hold him up as an example: "I still talk to the hitters about stuff Tony told me. I remember, one thing in particular, a guy at third, less than two outs, I kept trying to hit a fly ball to score the runner. I tried to alter my swing and the last place you want to hit it is a ground ball to third. I was up there and trying to hit a fly ball and I would pop it up in the infield and if they threw me an off-speed pitch or a breaking ball, I tried to lift it and all I did was turn it over and hit a one-hopper to third base and didn't score the guy. I can remember really struggling at that point. And when we got Tony Perez, I said, 'Playing against you in Cincinnati, you were such a good RBI guy. What are you trying to do?' He said, 'I don't have to change my swing. I don't care where the runners are. The job is to beat the guy on the mound. I try to stay with the same swing and all I try to do is hit the ball hard in left center or right center. And if I do that, the rest will take care for itself.' He made the game easier, he didn't try to do more, alter your swing. He just stayed with what you're normally doing. He certainly took the pressure off of you. Your job every time you walk up there is to battle with the pitcher. And if you beat him, you'll get the RBIs. Tony Perez to me was a very big addition to our club out there."[1] Parrish was in fact the most likely to take charge in the same way Perez did in a quiet manner. His leadership qualities were talked about around the league and Tim Burke, from *The Gazette*, wrote during training camp that Parrish was the real leader on this team.[2]

So to most observers around the team, Parrish was the perfect guy to succeed Perez off the field. But on the field, someone had to fill his shoes at first base and in mid–February Dick Williams said that Rusty Staub would be the regular.[3] Staub, a lefty batter, was expected to balance a predominantly right-handed lineup. In the last three years, the only threat from the left side was Warren Cromartie, which was why he got 19 intentional walks in 1979, even though he was not the fearsome hitter that Dawson, Valentine or Carter were. Staub had an excellent reputation as a run producer, as did Perez. He drove in 121 runs in 1978 with Detroit. He also got his share of walks, contrary to the young Expos. According to Michel Lajeunesse, from *Canadian Press*, Staub was one of the toughest hitters with two strikes against him when he was at his peak.[4] Some questions were raised as to whether Staub could play first but spring training was held for some reasons, including … training! The task wouldn't be easy as Staub was primarily an outfielder. But he intended not to make a fool of himself.

With Staub apparently set at first, there was no real openings as Carter, Scott, Speier, Parrish, LeFlore, Dawson and Valentine were all assured of their regular jobs. Warren Cromartie, who seemed to be the odd man out, still saw himself in a fight with Staub for the first base job, even after Williams said the latter was his man.[5]

On the mound, it wouldn't be easy to get over the loss of left-handers Dan Schatzeder and Rudy May. They combined for 20 wins and 250 innings in 1979 and their ERA was among the best in the league. Scott Sanderson and Ross Grimsley were expected to take some of the slack. Sanderson had been inconsistent in 1979 while Grimsley really struggled. Both were dropped from the rotation during the season and a comeback from both of them would certainly help compensate for the departure of both lefties.

The biggest shoes to fill however were those of pitching coach Jim Brewer, who had been extremely popular. The new coach was not a neophyte, however. Galen Cisco had been the Kansas City Royals' pitching coach from 1970 to 1979, with a squad that won three straight Western Division titles in the American League from 1976 to 1978. Each time, the team's pitching had been among the best in the league. But after they were ousted by the Yankees all three times in the American League Championship Series, Cisco was let go after a disappointing 1979 campaign, along with the whole coaching staff, including manager Whitey Herzog. Cisco was thus available and since Dick Williams knew him, it didn't take long to reach an agreement. Cisco told how they began working together years before their Expos connection: "The Mets released me from Jacksonville (in 1966) when we were playing Toronto, which was Boston's AAA team. Dick Williams was the manager and Norm Sherry was the pitching coach. After I got my release that afternoon, I was sitting in the stands when Norm Sherry came out and said, 'What do you do?' I said, 'I am looking for a job.' He said, 'What do you mean you're looking for a job?' I said, 'I just got released from Jacksonville and I got to start looking for a job.' He said, 'Just a minute.' He went inside to talk to Dick Williams and Dick came out and said, 'Are you looking for a job?' I said, 'Yes I am.' He said, 'Let me tell you something. I'm short of pitchers. If you wait until tomorrow, I'd like to call Boston tonight after the game and tomorrow, if there is an agreement, we would like for you to pitch over here.' So to make a long story short, two days later, I signed with the Red Sox. I had known Dick as a player. He had played with Boston. I had known him a little bit before that but that was the contact when I really got to know him."[6]

For the second straight year, Rodney Scott and the Expos had to go through arbitration to settle their salary dispute. This time, the Expos prevailed as their offer of $125,000 was retained. Scott was asking for $185,000.[7] No other contract squabble was reported, as was the case the year before.

Another chapter in the arduous Steve Rogers-Dick Williams relationships was written in the second week of March. After an exhibition game, Rogers was furious over the way his manager used him, complaining that he had been left in to pitch for too long and that careers could be ruined that way. Rogers again criticized Williams' lack of communication. The day after, Rogers, Williams and pitching coach Galen Cisco ironed out their differences.[8]

As was the case in spring 1979, Stan Bahnsen again threatened to become a free agent in the middle of the camp. But contrary to the year before, the veteran right-hander had some leverage. In 1979, his ERA was a respectable 3.15 and he finally adapted to his new role as a long reliever. John McHale agreed to up his salary for fear of losing a very valuable asset in the bullpen.[9]

The first important decisions came in mid–March. The first player to be let go was backup catcher Duffy Dyer. His departure was far from unanimous among management. John McHale wanted him on the team but Dick Williams wanted to go another way, preferring John Tamargo's bat.[10] David Palmer was a rookie in 1979 and appreciated what Dyer could bring to a young pitching staff: "Duffy Dyer caught me in a few of my earlier starts. He was just a great back-up catcher because he was on the '69 Mets when they won the World Series. He was with the Pirates before that. He told me, 'When

I call a pitch, you throw it. If I want it in the dirt, you throw it in the dirt. If you shake me off, I'm coming out there.' I said, 'Yes sir!' So I had total confidence in him and we did real well together." Palmer believe the Expos might have underestimated Dyer's real value to the team. "Right, because he was one of the few guys on our team that had won a World Series. So when you have somebody who had won a World Series on your team, that's a value! Especially being a veteran, a catcher and a back-up catcher who understood his role and didn't complain. He was just a great guy to be around."[11] Dyer was traded to Detroit for minor league infielder Jerry Manuel.

As for Palmer, his right elbow began to act up and he had to take cortisone shots in order to alleviate the pain.[12] He felt some pain during the winter league season 1978–79 but never to that level.[13] Another pitcher had to deal with some serious health issues. Bill Gullickson would have to learn to live as a diabetic: "What happened was I got hit with a cold real bad that winter. I went early to spring training to work out and everything. I had all the symptoms, I just didn't know the symptoms, tired after the workouts, thirsty all the time, losing weight because I was working out." After a couple of days of training on the daily chores of how to take care of himself, including injecting insulin, Gullickson was back with the team.[14]

As the camp went along, Williams was somewhat less enthusiastic about the prospect of Rusty Staub being the regular first baseman.[15] The beat writers kept writing that the case was settled anyway.[16] But on March 31, surprise: Staub was dealt to the Texas Rangers for minor leaguers Chris Smith and LaRue Washington. To the astonishment of most observers, Warren Cromartie had won the first-base battle against all odds. Bill Lee voiced his displeasure, saying that the Expos had just let go 100 RBIs.[17] But Larry Parrish's take was a lot more subdued. According to the third baseman, Staub never was comfortable at first base and he also lacked the power that was (and still is) generally associated with the position. Parrish said that Staub couldn't benefit anymore from some ballparks in the American League where fences in right field were closer to home plate.[18] As for Staub, he expected the Expos to settle some contractual issues that had been lingering since the start of the 1979 season, the reason in fact he was traded away from Detroit in the first place. John McHale denied promising anything to Staub.[19] At the end, it was Dick Williams' decision not to give Staub the first base job.[20]

Staub was not the only one to leave the premises. On April 1, the Players Association decided not to play the remainder of the exhibition schedule. The talks for a new Basic Agreement were going nowhere and the union set the deadline of May 22 for a full-scale strike, which would be the first in the middle of a season in pro sports.[21] Free agency was at the core of the negotiations, as the owners wanted some kind of compensation to a team that lost a player to free agency. That left less than two months to reach an agreement.

After the union's announcement, many players decided to leave Daytona Beach, including Rodney Scott, Andre Dawson, Warren Cromartie, David Palmer, Stan Bahnsen and Elias Sosa.[22] But most players from other teams decided to hold their own daily training in Florida, in many cases under some coaches' supervision.[23] In the Expos ranks, it was total confusion, as remembered by David Palmer: "We were told that we wouldn't be able to work out at the complexes and that we just should go home. And so I did. I went to Glens Falls with my wife and we waited and the next thing I knew, they were playing intra-squad games and working out and I wasn't there! It got to the point where I didn't know if it would be worth returning to go back down to spring training, so I wasn't there in Florida like I should have been. So that's why I wasn't ready to start. So I pitched out of the bullpen to start the year. I just took the information I had. I should have just stayed there but I thought that other players would go home but they didn't."[24] Even though Dick Williams severely reprimanded his young pitcher, Palmer was not to blame as a dozen players decided to go their own way as well. And while the Expos were divided and spread out, their main rivals, mainly the Pittsburgh Pirates and the Philadelphia Phillies, kept training together.[25]

Besides Staub's departure, the on-field personnel left very few surprises. Bill Almon replaced Jim Mason, whose career was over. On the mound, only two new faces were added from the beginning of 1979: free agent acquisition Fred Norman and reliever Dale Murray, who was with the team for the final stretch the preceding September.

The season began on April 11 in Philadelphia with the same two starting pitchers who had ended the 1979 campaign: Steve Rogers and Steve Carlton. The Phillies had to wait until their ninth meeting against the Expos to record their first win against their NL East opponent in 1979. Carlton and Greg Luzinski made sure that it wouldn't happen again in 1980 as Luzinski hit a long three-run home run in the bottom of the first inning that paved the way to a 6–3 win. Two of the Expos' runs came in the ninth with Gary Carter's long ball. Carter was not happy with his slot in the batting order as Dick Williams had him hitting sixth, behind Dawson, Valentine and Parrish at the heart of the lineup.[26] On paper, it was hard to argue with the manager's decision with such athletes, but Carter always thrived under the spotlight and hitting sixth is not the same as hitting fourth. For the time being, Valentine would hit fourth.[27]

The Expos began their 12th local season on April 18, after winning two games out of five in Philadelphia and New York. Thanks to a five-run fifth inning, the Expos prevailed, 7–5, against the Phillies. It was Ron LeFlore's

Larry Parrish's value to the Expos was never clearer than after he left the team. John McHale acknowledged that he misread the tall third baseman's contribution, especially his impact in the clubhouse.

first game in his new home and was the catalyser of that first inning, leading off with a single and a stolen base. The game was a solid indication of what was to come for the Expos as five players stole bases, including LeFlore and Rodney Scott. The little second baseman was struggling at the plate with a batting average (.176) that was going down and down until it would reach .103! Scott went directly home from the moment the strike was announced at the end of spring training and was the last player to rejoin the team, not in Florida, but in Philadelphia for the beginning of the season.[28] He would have to wait until June to see his average reach .200 for good. He still remained a favorite of Dick Williams, especially since he had an accomplice with credentials on the basepaths in Ron LeFlore.

Larry Parrish kept going where he left off the year before. The tall third baseman was used to hot and humid weather from his Florida home and was usually slow to start the season under the cold Montreal spring.[29] But in 1980, a more and more confident Parrish showed a .306 average in April with 13 RBIs in 16 games along with an impressive slugging percentage of .597. On April 25 in Atlanta, he hit three home runs and drove in all his team's runs in an 8–7 loss in 11 innings.

From 1976 to 1979, the Expos had to wait until late May before getting the big headlines in the sports media in Montreal as the Canadiens, the most famous National Hockey League franchise, kept piling up Stanley Cup championships. Not in 1980. To everyone's consternation on April 27, the Canadiens lost in the second round of the playoffs against the Minnesota North Stars.[30] It was in fact the first time since 1974 that the Canadiens were ousted that early. It was the beginning of a stretch that saw the hockey team losing four straight playoffs series as they would lose in the first round three years in a row from 1981 to 1983. The Montreal sports landscape was on its way to transform itself as the fans were adopting the Expos more and more.

The Expos concluded the first month with a 6–10 record, tied with the New York Mets for last in the NL East, five games behind the division-leading Pittsburgh Pirates. Pitching and defense were the main culprits of the Expos' early struggles: the team's ERA was 4.38 and the team allowed 18 unearned run in 16 games,[31] a perfect combination to give some more gray hair to any manager. No doubt the time lost with the strike at the end of spring training had something to do with the team's problems in defense, especially a team led by Dick Williams, who always stressed a rigid respect for fundamentals. But the defensive lapses were not his only worry. Ron LeFlore, true to his reputation, showed up late at least three times in the first few weeks.[32] But LeFlore was as charming as one could be and the fans loved him. In May, he launched the French translation of his biography *One in a Million*."[33] He loved the attention and knew how to play with the media. John McHale would even describe him as a very good seller.[34] He came in Montreal to lead the offense as the leadoff batter the team had really been lacking for some years. The Expos knew who they were getting when they acquired him. What was left to know was whether his on-field contribution would offset the headaches he would cause his bosses and, of course, if Dick Williams would let him do as he wished.

The Expos were back in Montreal on May 2 after a short trip to Pittsburgh. After a 4–3 win against the San Francisco Giants on Friday, the Expos lost, 3–2, on Saturday afternoon. More than the game, the Expos also lost Larry Parrish. In the bottom of the fourth inning, Parrish was hit by Ed Whitson's offering and was replaced by Ken Macha. As Parrish later recalled: "In that ballpark in Montreal, the whole time I was there it was open. And the shadows broke up in the day. San Francisco was in town, who Ed Whitson was with. And it was one of those days, a day game, the shadows were out there, and Whitson threw a ball up and in and I lost it. I knew it started up and in but I didn't know if it was a slider, if it would break to the plate or if it was a fastball. I just didn't see it. It was like I saw it just right up front. It wasn't at my head or anything. It wasn't really that bad a pitch. Had it been at my head, it would have hit me because I had lost it and I was still trying to pick it up. When I saw it, all I had the time to do was jerk my hand and it hit me on my right wrist. But it broke a bone. It just wouldn't heal. I just couldn't hold the bat. I could swing but I couldn't hold it, I had to sort of give in as I swung."[35] For the fans, it was hard to pick up the ball at Olympic Stadium on a sunny day as the shadows fell in the middle of the field. One can imagine how hard it was for batters to try to pick it up when these shadows were right between the mound and home plate. Parrish tried to keep playing but in late May, he had to take a break as his average during that month was a paltry .169. He would come back on June 30 but his whole season would be affected by this injury.

The Expos nonetheless began resembling the team of 1979 when they came back to win 6–4 against the Giants, thanks to doubles by Tony Bernazard and Rowland Office and an infield hit by Andre Dawson. That triggered a sequence where the Expos won 13 out of 17 games, allowing the team to reach .500 for the first time in 1980. At the end of these 17 games on May 26, the Expos had reduced the lead from the NL East leaders, the top spot held by both Pittsburgh and Philadelphia, to only a game and a half.

Even with that success, Montreal and the province of Quebec (and the whole country for that matter) had other concerns and worry as the provincial government had scheduled a referendum on May 20 to get the mandate to secede politically from Canada, while maintaining economic ties. In that context, the Expos were far down the list of priorities among the population as the topic was rather passionate from both sides, to say the least. The population finally decided against the government plan with a 59.6 percent proportion.[36]

But political offices in Canada were not the only place where hardball was played. The talks between the owners and the players seemed stalled as the May 22 deadline was looming, the date when the players could go on strike. The stoppage looked inevitable but a last-minute agreement allowed play to keep going. An agreement was reached on benefits, pension and many other topics. One item was left for discussion: the compensation for the loss of a free agent, which the owners were adamant was necessary in the next Basic Agreement. A committee a four persons, two from both sides, was formed to study the matter. Sal Bando and Bob Boone represented the players and Frank Cashen and Harry Dalton came from the management's ranks. In case there would be no settlement on the matter, the owners would then be able to unilaterally impose their own compensation system.[37] As the players were waiting word from the pending talks, they were told by the union leaders to wait for news before flying. Thus, when it was announced that the season would continue, some Expos players had to travel to Cincinnati by their own means, including Ellis Valentine, Bill Lee, Ron LeFlore and Warren Cromartie.[38]

Cincinnati was the first stop on a three-city road trip that included stops in Chicago and St. Louis. The Expos did pretty well with five wins in eight games, remaining in contention two games behind Pittsburgh and Philadelphia. During the trip, shortstop Chris Speier got his regular spot back after a month on the bench. Speier greatly struggled both offensively and defensively as he had to deal again with back problems. Rodney Scott was moved to short while Tony Bernazard was playing second. On May 25, Speier's batting average was a feeble .195. Whatever was hurting Speier seemed to disappear during his time on the bench. It took him only days before he elevated his average to .300 once he got back into the lineup.

Since the beginning of his career and particularly in 1978 and 1979, Ellis Valentine had made headlines with stuff that had nothing to do with his play on the field. In 1980 however, he seemed in the best disposition of his career. In spring training, he insisted that the past should remain in the past and that everybody should be looking ahead.[39] In April, his average was so-so at .234 but he managed to drive in ten runs in 16 games. In May, he elevated his game to where most people thought he should have throughout his career. But on May 30 in St. Louis, his season and also his career took a turn for the worse when he was beaned in the face in the sixth inning by a pitch from Roy Thomas. Valentine suffered multiple facial fractures.[40] Valentine had driven in three runs in that game up to that point. It would take him more than a month before getting back in the lineup. At the end of May, the Expos recalled Bill Gullickson from their AAA affiliate in Denver. Dale Murray was the one sent down.[41] Gullickson seemed to have adapted to his life as a diabetic. In Denver, he had won six of his seven decisions with a 1.91 ERA, which was remarkable in Denver where offense was king due to the altitude.

In early June, a 12-game home stretch was awaiting the Expos against Chicago, St. Louis, San Diego and Los Angeles. The Expos won the first one, 8–7, in 13 innings against the Chicago Cubs. They came back with three runs in the eighth and ninth innings off Bruce Sutter, one of the best number one relievers in baseball. The winning run was scored when rookie Bob Pate drew a bases-loaded walk as a pinch-hitter.[42] It was Pate's first appearance in the majors after a call-up to replace Ellis Valentine. After losing the second game of the series against the Cubs, the Expos went on a ten-game winning streak, quite an accomplishment without two of their best offensive weapons, Larry Parrish and Ellis Valentine. Parrish's name was placed on the disabled list on June 8 as the Expos were facing the St. Louis Cards in a doubleheader.[43] Between games, the Cards fired their manager Ken Boyer! St. Louis was touted as a threat in the NL East but they were dead last with a 18–33 record when Boyer was let go.[44] That winning streak launched the Expos to the top of the NL East. On June 13, they held a two-game edge over the Pirates and four and a half over the Phillies.

Even with the Expos winning, one player was not pleased at all with his situation. Ross Grimsley had pitched only four times before a June 3 start against the Cubs. After the game (which he lost), he expressed his desire to be traded.[45] He would start some more games because of an overloaded schedule but the return of David Palmer and the emergence of rookies Bill Gullickson and Charlie Lea, another call-up, would lead him right to the bench. In his last start, on June 14 at Olympic Stadium, Grimsley was booed heavily as he was being replaced. He responded by saluting derisively to the home crowd.[46] Things had changed drastically for the left-hander since his 20-win season in 1978.

Charlie Lea's call-up from the minors had nothing to do with Grimsley's ineffectiveness. Lea was added to the Expos' pitching corps because of Bill Lee's off-the-field adventures. According to his version, as told in his autobiography *The Wrong Stuff*, Lee got hurt when he fell as he was hanging from a female friend's window.[47] Up to that point, Lee had been very inconsistent, unlike his first year with Montreal. But he had seemed to get untracked just prior to his injury, with two complete games in his last four starts. As for Lea (pronounced Lee), he had won all of his nine starts in AA in Memphis with a minuscule ERA of 0.84 before allowing only two runs in 12 innings after two starts in Denver. His presence was rather surprising as his name was very rarely mentioned during spring training. He was not a first-round draft pick, like more high-profile prospects Bill Gullickson and Bob James. Lea, a Memphis native, was picked in the ninth round in 1978 and reached the majors in less than two years. In fact, he spent most of his time in the minors in his hometown.

As Lea later said: "I was lucky in a lots of respect. It was lucky because I got to stay in the same apartment that I had. My wife had a job that she didn't want to leave at the time, so it was lucky in that regard. We were around some friends. So in a lot of respects it was great. But on the other hand, pitching in front of a home crowd and hometown and your friends is great if you pitch well. But if you don't pitch well or perform well, it can be nerve-wracking as well because everybody who knows you knows what's going on. There are pluses and minuses. But in the end, since I ended up succeeding and doing well, I definitely would say it was a plus."[48] Dick Williams wasted very little time to take a look at his new tall right-hander as he got him to start on June 12 against the San Diego Padres the day after his call-up. "I do remember that game. I had no idea I would be starting a game when I got called up. I went to the ballpark, I got there late in the game, I showed up, had a uniform laid out for me, a locker for me like they would do, and I put it on, and went out on the field and Dick Williams informed me that I would be pitching the next day against the San Diego Padres. I just assumed I would be in the bullpen. I think it was best in hindsight because he just threw me right into the fire and fortunately I did well. I threw eight innings and Freddie Norman came in and finished up the last inning."[49] The crowd gave him a rousing ovation as he completed the eighth inning.[50]

After the ten-game winning streak, the Expos were blanked twice at home by the Los Angeles Dodgers before leaving for the West Coast, where they quickly lost four of their first five games. The standings was getting tighter. The Expos managed to keep the lead up to the All-Star break with a 42–34 record, a half game in front of Philadelphia and a game and a half over Pittsburgh. Contrary to 1979, when the Expos had almost no injuries, reserve players were put to the test, especially Rowland Office, replacing Ellis Valentine, and the third baseman combo of Ken Macha and Brad Mills, replacing Larry Parrish. But what really attracted the fan's attention was the work of the two speedsters, Ron LeFlore and Rodney Scott. Both players struggled for lengthy periods of time at the plate. LeFlore even went through an 0-for-32 slump while Scott took two months to get untracked. But once on the basepaths, these two explosive players were nothing short of spectacular, even though they were quite different. LeFlore was very aggressive, always sliding hard with his feet and spikes ahead. Scott was far more subtle, but could be as annoying to opponents. With the absence of Valentine and Parrish, it was up to Carter and Dawson to carry the team but the show belonged to LeFlore and Scott as the main characters.

On the mound, Steve Rogers and David Palmer were the only ones to show any consistency, with both showing ERAs under three. At the break, Rogers had ten wins. Scott Sanderson and Bill Gullickson had yet to show they could win regularly. In the bullpen, veteran lefty Woodie Fryman was absolutely sublime with an ERA of 1.75. In the first three months of the season, Fryman allowed only 23 hits and seven earned runs in 38 and two-thirds innings. From May 2 to June 7, he threw 23 scoreless innings, allowing only seven hits and seven walks, including three intentionally. It was Fryman's first season as the number one reliever, taking over for struggling Elias Sosa. Stan Bahnsen was the only other reliable member of the bullpen, as Fred Norman, a starting pitcher throughout his career, had a hard time adjusting to being a reliever.

In early July, Dick Williams and Larry Parrish agreed to new contracts. Williams got a one-year extension through 1981; Parrish's deal extended through 1985.[51] In the meantime, Gary Carter, whose deal was set to expire after the 1982 season, wanted to start talks about extending his own contract.[52]

Shortly after the All-Star Game, Ross Grimsley was granted his wish as he was sent to the Cleveland Indians in the American League in a trade for minor leaguer Dave Oliver. Almost three decades later, Grimsley still had a hard time trying to figure out what happened after winning 20 games in 1978: "I was physically OK but I just think it was a combination of just not being able to make pitches and the concentration level not being there. Very possibly, I think after winning 20 games, that's a goal every pitcher wants and once he gets it that's a big thing, I just lost my concentration. It was hard to get it back and I didn't know what to do to get it back. And it just became a battle to do that. I think the stuff was probably the same. Just the concentration level and trying to make pitches, I just couldn't do it for whatever reason. I didn't do it but then I didn't get to pitch very much and they traded me to Cleveland. I didn't want to leave but I had to go in order to pitch."[53] Once in Cleveland, Grimsley unleashed some acerbic comments towards his former manager Dick Williams, saying many players were unhappy in Montreal due to a lack of communication from Williams.[54] As for Grimsley, after a good first impression, he couldn't do better than he did in Montreal, with an ERA of 6.75. His career would end in 1982 in an obscure role as a reliever with Baltimore.

David Palmer's situation was a more serious concern for the Expos. The pain in his right elbow that bothered him in spring training hadn't subsided, even though he still took his regular turn in the rotation. In mid–June, he got a cortisone shot but he finally had to be placed on the disabled list on July 22.[55] The week before, he couldn't go past the fifth inning against the Reds. It was the third time in five starts that he couldn't reach the sixth inning.

The Expos could at last count on their regular lineup after the All-Star break with the return of both Valentine and Parrish. The Expos won three out of five games at home against St. Louis and Chicago. On the following road trip, the Expos played .500 in ten games, which included Bill Gullickson's first career win in the second game of a doubleheader in Houston. He had been quite unlucky as the offense just didn't support him, especially in a three-start span during which he allowed only five runs in 23 and one-third innings. Gullickson was pushing hard for a spot in the rotation, which he would get for good in late July.

Back home, the Expos called up highly-touted prospect Tim Raines.[56] The young second baseman was leading the American Association in batting average and stolen bases. He was the leadoff hitter of one of the best AAA teams in the last 40 years. He had spent two weeks with Montreal earlier in the season but was used only once. This time, he would play on a regular basis. He was expected to boost an offense that wasn't going that badly with 87 runs in its last 15 games since the All-Star Game, an average of almost six runs per game. But Chris Speier's struggles prompted the team to take a closer look at Raines, as Rodney Scott was moved to shortstop.

On July 25, Raines was inserted in the lineup as the number three hitter, which gave the Expos a top of the lineup with speed to spare, with LeFlore, Scott, Raines and Dawson. The Houston Astros were in town for the first of a 15-game stretch at Olympic Stadium for the Expos. Against Nolan Ryan, Raines didn't disappoint with three stolen bases, one hit and two runs scored. The Expos scored their seven runs in the fourth, fifth and sixth innings and seemed to be on their way to an easy win with a 7–2 lead in the top of the ninth. Canadian Terry Puhl led off the ninth with a home run off Steve Rogers. A walk and a double later, Rogers was replaced. Fred Norman and Elias Sosa then allowed four hits and a walk before Woodie Fryman at last put an end to the debacle in what became a 9–8 loss. More than 50,000 fans witnessed what could have been a very devastating defeat for a young team. But the Expos rebounded to end that home stretch with a 10–5 record. Raines would start only three more games before being sent back to Denver after being limited to a mere single in 15 at-bats.

During the Expos' stay in Montreal, the team played the annual Pearson Cup against the Toronto Blue Jays. It was a good occasion to take a look at Hal Dues, who had been so impressive in 1978 before an elbow surgery ended his campaign. He had lost the entire 1979 season but seemed back on track in 1980. He had been named the pitcher of the month in May in the American

Ron LeFlore's only year with the Expos in 1980 was an eventful one, on and off the field. It was established before the end of that season that he wouldn't be back the next year.

Association. In fact, had it not been for fear of a strike in late May, he would have been called up but management wanted to make sure he would pitch, so they left him in AAA. Against the Jays, Dues threw six innings of two-hit ball,[57] a good-enough performance to warrant the team to call him up to Montreal a couple of days later. He would start a game in Chicago but Dick Williams would lose almost all confidence in him. He would pitch three more seasons in the Expos' minor league system without being able to duplicate his 1978 success.

The Expos were not the only team in the NL East winning consistently. On August 10, the Pittsburgh Pirates caught up with the Expos after sweeping a four-game series against Philadelphia. In Chicago on August 9, Dick Williams penciled Jerry White in the lineup, replacing Ron LeFlore who showed up late[58]. White got two hits but the Expos still lost, 3–1. Williams stated that it was not the first time LeFlore wasn't on time.[59] But the Expos needed their leadoff hitter, especially with a race that was very tight with two months to go. Also LeFlore, even with all his shortcomings, wasn't intimidated by anything or anyone. On August 4, in the first game of a doubleheader against the New York Mets, LeFlore pushed his luck to its limit. In the bottom of the eighth, the Expos had already scored twice to cut the Mets lead to one run, 3–2. LeFlore was on third with Andre Dawson at bat and Ellis Valentine on-deck. With a two-strike count on Dawson, LeFlore decided to go for a steal of home, catching Mets pitcher Pat Zachry (and everybody else in Olympic Stadium) by surprise. In his rush to get the ball to home plate, Zachry committed a balk, allowing LeFlore to score the tying run.[60] LeFlore was oblivious about the real possibility to see Dawson swing the bat! Columnist Tim Burke, from *The Gazette*, would say that LeFlore was one of the few who couldn't be intimidated by the Pittsburgh Pirates, the defending World Series champions.[61] LeFlore wasn't done against the Mets as he scored the winning run in the 11th inning after a single, a stolen base and an RBI single by Dawson.

From August 11, the Expos ran into the worst three-week stretch of the season, with only six wins in nineteen games, beginning with the worst defeat of the team's history, 16–0 in St. Louis with Tommy Hutton ending the game on the mound. Scott Sanderson, who had become the team's most reliable starter, couldn't even go past the first inning, allowing seven runs. Sanderson had won nine of his last 11 decisions. The day after, veteran Fred Norman pitched six shutout innings in a 4–0 win. He was going through his best moments with the Expos, as he was used at last as a starter. It was his fourth straight start with at least six innings, including a complete game. After St. Louis, the Expos headed for an important four-game series in Pittsburgh as both teams were tied for first place. The Pirates were as confident as ever, having won 12 of their 15 confrontations, dating back to September 1979. And things didn't get better in that series for the Expos, who lost three out of four and had to wait until the ninth inning of the last game to grab any kind of lead, thanks to a two-run single by Rodney Scott against almost invulnerable (against the Expos, that is!) Kent Tekulve. A loss would have put the Expos four games back of the Pirates. Three losses in Pittsburgh wasn't what Dick Williams hoped for but it could have been worse!

Back home, the Expos lost three straight against the Dodgers, including a cruel 3–2 defeat in the opener, when the bullpen allowed all three runs in the last two innings and Jerry White hit a solid liner off the hand of Dodgers reliever Don Stanhouse to end the game on a double play as runners were on third and first. The Expos managed to salvage the homestand with four straight victories before losing to the Giants as the team was getting set for the second West Coast swing of the season. The Expos could nonetheless gain some ground over the Pirates, who began to struggle with only three wins in nine games. Injuries were taking a toll on Pittsburgh, which was playing without their leader Willie Stargell, who wouldn't be back in 1980.[62]

In Los Angeles, the Dodgers proved again to be too much for the Expos as they won four straight in Los Angeles. But as was the case in the homestand, the Expos redeemed themselves against San Diego and San Francisco with a 5–2 record, including three straight shutouts against the Giants, thanks to solid performances by Bill Gullickson, Steve Rogers and Scott Sanderson. The last game in San Francisco marked the major league debut of Tim Wallach, the team's number one draft choice in 1979 and former collegiate player of the year. In 1979, in only half a season, Wallach had hit 18 home runs for Memphis in the Southern League, a AA circuit. In 1980, Wallach hit 36 home runs and had 124 RBIs. It took him only two plate appearances to record his first major league home run against Phil Nastu, after being walked in his debut. As the team was in San Diego, the Expos traded twice with the Padres. First they acquired Willie Montanez. The veteran first baseman was not very happy going to Montreal, especially since the team had no intention to use him on a regular basis, but mainly as a pinch-hitter.[63] John McHale admitted that he feared that the Pirates would be interested in Montanez, as they were without their leader, Willie Stargell.[64] The player the Expos traded away was a young second baseman, Tony Phillips. The other Padre to become an Expo was hard-throwing pitcher John D'Acquisto. He was sent to Montreal for a player-to-be-named-later, who would be Randy Bass. Bass, a first baseman, had been punishing minor league pitching for many years, including the last two in the Expos' system. He would eventually find his niche in Japan as one of the most feared sluggers in that country. D'Acquisto had a very good arm but could be very erratic as well. He wouldn't be a big factor in September.

In late August, the Expos had to do some damage control after an article in the magazine *Inside Sports* featuring Ron LeFlore made the headlines. LeFlore voiced his real displeasure over being snubbed for the All-Star Game, blaming the fans. Published in a question-and-answer format, LeFlore said that the fans didn't care too much about black players, pointing out how Warren Cromartie or himself weren't voted on for the All-Star team. Some teammates were also the subject of criticism by LeFlore, including Steve Rogers for leaving a game too early (a game the Expos would eventually lose). LeFlore was quoted as saying the team was divided between the rednecks and the militants, and that he was the only one normal there and was able to establish some kind of communication between the factions. As for his then famous tardiness, he said that baseball is a long season and that Dick Williams won World Series with guys who didn't give a crap about the rules.[65] It goes without saying that the local media had a field day with this article. *Le Journal de Montréal* contacted its author, Mark Ribowski, who said that had he written everything LeFlore told him, the speedy outfielder would be in even more trouble than he already was.[66] LeFlore would apologize via a written statement on September 10, showing his appreciation over how he was welcomed by the fans in Montreal.[67] As all this controversy was going on, Larry Parrish expressed some worry about the lack of communication within the team. He believed that Tony Perez was never really replaced as the link among players.[68] Andre Dawson told Michael Farber from *The Gazette* that some rules were erased for some players. Farber made some reference to LeFlore, Rodney Scott and Ellis Valentine.[69] Dick Williams had to do without Valentine for the entire road trip in California in late August and early September. Valentine had driven in 37 runs in 42 games with a .320 batting average and nine home runs when he returned in July. But he had to leave a game at Olympic Stadium on August 20 after hitting a triple, thanks to a sciatic injury.[70]

The Expos were back at home in first place on September 9, a half game ahead of the resurgent Philadelphia Phillies. The Pirates couldn't keep the pace and without Willie Stargell they looked absolutely nothing like the solid team they had been the first half of the season (or the last year and a half for that matter). The Pirates had lost 17 out of their last 22 games. As for the Phillies, they recovered nicely after being swept badly by the Pirates in early August in a four-game series, in spite of increased tension within the team.

The Expos won their return game home, a 3–0 shutout courtesy of Steve Rogers. The day after, Bill Gullickson threw one of the most spectacular games in the history of Olympic Stadium when he struck out 18 batters in a 4–1 win over the Chicago Cubs. Bill Buckner was the only Cubs regular who wasn't a victim of Gullickson. "I knew I threw the ball good but I had thrown the ball good before and had not much success so I never really relied on the bullpen session for the outcome. I knew after the first batter, I struck out the guy with a fastball and threw it where I wanted to with good heat on it. As the game went on, I had a good breaking ball. It seems like I could throw it wherever I wanted with whatever speed I wanted to. Before you knew it, the game was over and I struck out 18 guys," Gullickson would say about that game.[71] Gullickson was on its way to be Dick Williams' most trusted pitcher, even though he was still a rookie, not unlike David Palmer in 1979.

The Expos made it three in a row with a 6–5 win over the Cubs on September 11, but Ron LeFlore got hurt when he went after a foul ball along the left-field line. Said LeFlore: "It was a line drive. Dave Kingman hit the ball and I didn't know how close the wall was to the line there. I don't know what was on my mind but you know I was so anxious about going to the World Series. I was running at the ball, and I should have known when Dave Kingman hits a ball down the left-field line, it should have been foul. I just ran and when I looked up and saw the ball going foul, the wall was right there. My first defense was to put my hands up and I broke a bone in my left wrist area."[72] He tried everything be get back in the lineup, including shaving his cast. "But John McHale wouldn't allow me to do this. I thought it was healed enough for me to try to play. And they were saying, we're not going to risk your career. But when you have an opportunity like that, when you see guys play in the Super Bowl, a guy like Jack Youngblood play with a broken leg, when you get an opportunity like that, it wasn't coming around every year, and I thought that was the year for the Expos."[73] He would be used exclusively as a pinch-runner from that point on.

Even though LeFlore had a subpar year, his loss came at a very inopportune moment as the next visitors were the Pittsburgh Pirates, who had just shown some life, with two straight wins against St. Louis. The Bucs were three and a half games out of first place and even though there was still some weeks to go, they sensed that they had to win that three-game series to remain in the heart of the NL East race. On September 12, the first game saw Scott Sanderson oppose Rick Rhoden. As was the case with some Pirates players, especially pitchers Kent Tekulve and Don Robinson, Rhoden seemed at his best against Montreal, with five career wins in six decisions. That game would be no exception as he allowed only one run through seven innings. But that was one run too many; Scott Sanderson limited the Pirates to five hits in a complete game effort in a 1–0 victory, his 15th of the season. Larry Parrish drove in the only run in the second with a single.

In the meantime, the Phillies were swept in a doubleheader against the lowly Cardinals. With 21 games to go, the Expos had increased their lead to two games over the Phillies. The Expos split the other two games with the Pirates, winning the Sunday game, 4–0, on another spectacular performance from Bill Gullickson. Not surprisingly, "Gully" was named the NL player of the week. Ellis Valentine was back in the lineup for that last game, which was settled when the first four batters reached base via hits against John Candelaria. More than 56,000 fans attended that game, even though rain delayed it for an hour and a half. The Phillies again were on the Expos' tail after winning the last two against St. Louis. The gap was only one game in favor of Montreal.

The Expos were then headed for a two-week road trip that included stops in every NL East opponent city, in order: New York, St. Louis, Pittsburgh, Chicago and the pièce de résistance, Philadelphia. The Expos would then spend the last week of the season at home. Given that the Expos had been far better at home than away, that one-game lead looked very thin. The Expos split the first six games, winning two in New York and one in St. Louis. The September 19 loss in St. Louis was particularly hard to swallow as the Expos blew a 7–2 lead in the seventh inning. The Expos took the lead in the ninth, thanks to a sacrifice fly by Ellis Valentine as a pinch-hitter, but Elias Sosa couldn't retire a single batter in the ninth, allowing a two-run double to George Hendrick. Valentine would be used in the last two games in St. Louis but hurt a hand while checking his swing.[74] His season was over.

Two weeks to go and everybody was thinking about the upcoming Philadelphia three-game series. But the Expos had to deal first with Pittsburgh and Chicago in short two-game series. The Pirates were four games back and they couldn't afford to lose any more ground. In fact, these were desperate times for that team. Jim Bibby provided them with some relief with his 18th victory in a 4–2 win. The Phillies took care of business with a 3–2 triumph in St. Louis to climb back to first place, a half game ahead of the Expos.

On September 23, Steve Rogers was scheduled to face the Pirates. Rogers had only one win in five decisions up to that point against the Pirates, who badly needed that game. A loss would however be a huge big blow against their slim chances to overcome Montreal and Philadelphia. Rogers delivered in a decisive, 7–1, win. The Expos got to Bert Blyleven with six runs, three unearned, in the sixth inning. Blyleven was completing his worst season in his eleventh major league season. There was a good chance he wouldn't be back with Pittsburgh, as he was very unhappy with the way manager Chuck Tanner used him, complaining of being relieved too soon from games.[75] The righty even left the team in May to voice his protest. The "We Are Family" atmosphere of 1979 was then just a distant memory in Pittsburgh!

The Expos had regained the lead with the Phillies' loss in St. Louis but two games had to be played in Chicago before heading to Philadelphia. The Expos and Cubs split that short two-games series. The Phillies could score only three runs in two games against the Mets, but that was enough for two, wins 1–0 and 2–1.

Ten days to go, only a half-game separated both teams as they were scheduled to meet six times in the last week and a half, beginning with three games at Philadelphia's Veterans Stadium. Both teams had split the first 12 games. In 1979, the Expos had to battle a team (the Pirates) that showed an image of harmony and togetherness under their theme song "We Are Family." Well, the Phillies looked nothing like that and it was a secret to no one that it was a rather explosive unit that the writers had to deal with. Their manager,

Dallas Green, had taken over the Phillies towards the end of 1979 and his style was completely different from the man he succeeded, Danny Ozark. The latter had won three straight NL East championships but still Ozark could never get any credit. Even under heavy pressure, Ozark had always protected his players and would never ever criticize one of his own, to the point where some players were getting too comfortable, at least to the eyes of Dallas Green, who didn't refrain one bit from voicing his displeasure to the media about players. Green complained about the general atmosphere of the team, which didn't sit too well with some veterans who were used to Ozark's way of doing things, players like Larry Bowa, Greg Luzinski, Garry Maddox and Bob Boone.[76] In early August, the temperature reached its boiling point in Pittsburgh between games of a doubleheader after a third straight loss to the Pirates (the Phillies would lose the second one as well). In a speech that could be heard by the writers even with doors closed in the clubhouse, Green blasted his players. During the second game, Green and Ron Reed, two huge men, almost went at it and had to be separated by other members of the team.[77] In early September, after a second straight loss in San Diego, a 10–3 shellacking at the hands of a team that was going absolutely nowhere, it was general manager Paul Owens' turn to admonish his players. Garry Maddox was one of the main targets of Owens' diatribe, as the usually reliable outfielder had lost two balls in the sun the day before and had yet to wear his sun glasses the following day.[78]

Earlier in the season, in early July, the *Trenton Times*, a New Jersey daily, reported that some Phillies players had received amphetamines illegally, thanks to a Reading, Pennsylvania, physician. Pete Rose, Steve Carlton and Greg Luzinski's names were mentioned in the article.[79] The tension was thus palpable throughout the season. Jayson Stark, who would later work for ESPN, was then a beat writer covering the Phillies. He acknowledged that the atmosphere was quite tense around the team: "There was a tension that hung over the 1980 Phillies that was different from the atmosphere surrounding just about any other great team I've ever encountered. But there were reasons for that tension. This was a team built to win it all that had never been able to find a way to win The Big Game and fulfill its mission. Won 101 games in 1976 but got swept by the Big Red Machine. Won 101 games in 1977 but was done in by Black Friday. Won the East again in 1978 and got bounced by the Dodgers. Signed Pete Rose in 1979 and had too many pitchers get hurt. Those failures created a pervading sense of the whole world is against us. And they also caused their easy-going manager, Danny Ozark, to get fired. The man who replaced him, Dallas Green, publicly challenged their whole even-keel approach. Benched veteran players like Greg Luzinski and Bob Boone, and ripped them in the media. So all that did was heighten a tension that was already there, had already built to unusual heights and pervaded that team every day it took the field."[80]

The stage was set in Philadelphia for that Friday, September 26, encounter. David Palmer was assigned as the Expos' starting pitcher against Dick Ruthven. Palmer came back in late August but had started only three games since. Ruthven was a tough right-hander, the kind who gave the predominantly Expos righty lineup all kinds of trouble. The atmosphere at Veterans Stadium was electric as more than 50,000 filled the venue, which was quite different for the Expos from the 6,000 who attended both games at Wrigley Field the preceding two days!

The Phillies scored first in the second inning on Garry Maddox's 11th home run of the season after two outs. Palmer had retired the first five batters in order before Maddox's shot on the first pitch. When Palmer got back in the dugout, Dick Williams shouted to Palmer: "We told you he was a first ball hitter!" Palmer, being as big a competitor as one could be, was already pretty upset over himself, so he didn't really need Williams to remind him of his gopher ball.[81] Ruthven easily disposed of the first 11 batters before Rowland Office hit a single, but was left stranded. In the sixth inning, Ruthven seemed in perfect control when after two outs, Jerry White, who had assumed Ron LeFlore's leadoff spot, hit a double and went on to score on Rodney Scott's single. Ruthven was replaced after seven innings and Tug McGraw took over. He retired all six batters he faced. It was still tied at one when Bake McBride came to the plate in the bottom of the ninth. The Phillies had only one hit against Palmer since the fourth inning, a single by McBride. In spite of feet and knee injuries, McBride was in 1980 one of the most steady players on his team. On that Friday, on a team full of superstars like Pete Rose, Mike Schmidt and Steve Carlton, McBride was the king of the city as he ended the game with his ninth home run of the season, giving the Phillies a 2–1 win and more important, a one and a half game lead over the Expos. David Palmer remembers vividly his solid performance, even though he ended up in the losing end of the game: "I threw Bake McBride a curveball about a foot off the ground and he just golfed it. Cro (Warren Cromartie) went back to the wall and I thought he was going to catch it and it barely went over but it went over. He was circling the bases and the place went absolutely berserk. I just stopped, I waited for him to cross, to pass me before I went off the field, I didn't want to cut in front of him. And I just looked up in the stands and said, man, what an awesome game! I mean, I was extremely disappointed we didn't win the game but it was just an awesome game and an awesome atmosphere."[82]

The task at hand on Saturday seemed huge with Steve Carlton on the mound for Philadelphia. Carlton was a true physical phenomenon with a very specific training regimen. At 35, Carlton pitched at least seven innings in 32 of his first 36 starts in 1980, accumulating more than 300 innings, the last pitcher to do so. In his other four starts, he threw at least six innings, never allowing more than two earned runs! His 23 wins led the league and his ERA was 2.34. He was facing Scott Sanderson who was going through a rough time, allowing eight earned runs in 13 innings in his last two starts. Both teams traded home runs from Mike Schmidt and Gary Carter early on. The score was tied at two when the Expos took the lead for the first time in the series, thanks to Jerry White's RBI double. The Expos got an insurance run in the eighth against Warren Brusstar. That run was to be of some importance as the Phillies scored once in the ninth. Elias Sosa was on the mound to start the ninth for what was his third inning of work. Greg Luzinski and Manny Trillo began the inning with singles but Sosa induced two force-outs before rookie Keith Moreland drove in one to get the Phillies within one run. Then, Dallas Green and Dick Williams decided to play a little game of chess. Former Expo Del Unser was announced as a pinch-hitter, to which Williams countered with lefty Woodie Fryman. Then, Green made his last move by bringing a solid young hitter, another rookie, Lonnie Smith. Both Moreland and Smith were instrumental in the team's success. Dallas Green, who used to be in charge of player development, knew both very well. Smith's batting average was a robust .337 when he came in to face Fryman. After taking the lead in the count, Fryman threw Smith a backdoor slider that umpire Harry Wendelstedt called a strike to confirm the Expos' victory. Fryman remembered that at-bat very well but was very humble about the outcome: "It was a hard slider that froze him at the plate. But it was just one of those things that happened. What happened in a situation like that, if you're going good, the hitter is looking for a pitch and you just cross him up. The hitter wasn't ready for that, he got frozen up. But if he's looking right, he might have hit a home run. It goes both ways."[83] That time, Expos fans were just happy it went Fryman's way!

After two pressure-packed games, it was back to square one. A loss would have meant a risk of being swept and leaving Philadelphia three and a half games behind. That Saturday win removed a lot of pressure off the players. Still, there was that third game to take care of. Steve Rogers and rookie Bob Walk were on the mound. The Expos were leading, 2–1, in the sixth when they added three runs, including two on a triple by Chris Speier, a liner that Garry Maddox lost in the sun, not unlike what happened in San Diego, which again frustrated Dallas Green.[84] Gary Carter added to the lead with his second home run of the game, a two-run shot, for a 7–1 lead. The Phillies scored twice in the eighth but as Rogers threw a complete-game five-hitter in an 8–3 win. The Expos were back in first place, a half-game over the Phillies.

Even though he had a hard time being accepted by his own teammates, catcher Gary Carter was the face of the Montreal Expos for several years. His departure, due to owner Charles Bronfman's dissatisfaction over his contract, marked the end of an era.

For the first time since his arrival in Montreal, Gary Carter was at last the Expos' go-to guy. His performance through the weekend (4-for-10, 3 HRs, 5 RBIs) was a reflection of his contribution in September. Through August, Carter's batting average was a mere .246, his slugging percentage was only .449 and his on-base average was a lowly .308. After the series against the Phillies, all his numbers had significantly increased to .267, .491 and .330, respectively. Even though the catcher's position is without a doubt the most demanding in baseball, Carter had been in the starting lineup every game since August 31. His next day off would have to wait! But considering the context, Carter had no complaint. He was showing he could thrive under pressure and he loved the attention.

Monday, September 29, the Expos were back at home to host the St. Louis Cardinals for a three-game series. The Phillies were facing the Chicago Cubs four times in Philadelphia before the final showdown in Montreal for the last three games. Against the Cards, Dick Williams picked Bill Lee, even though he had not started a game since August 4. Nine days earlier, Lee had been perfect in four innings in relief against the Cards in a 5–4 win. The Cards had the reputation of being more vulnerable against lefties. The decision to pitch Lee was made easier by Charlie Lea's struggles, as he couldn't go past the sixth innings in each of his last four assignments.

The Expos were facing Pete Vuckovich, a 15-game winner in 1979, who had yet to show the great potential most observers saw in him. But Vuckovich was pretty efficient that night, limiting the Expos to only five hits in eight innings, including Andre Dawson's solo home run. Vuckovich even drove in one of his team's two runs (Vuckovich's batting prowess would be more in the limelight as the Clu Haywood character in the movie *Major League*). Bill Lee was every bit as good, also with two runs in eight innings.

In the top of the ninth, the Expos got a major league scare. With two outs and two runners on, Dane Iorg came to bat as a pinch-hitter. If there was such a player that should have been named an Expo killer, Iorg would certainly have been a very worthy candidate. In 1980, up to that point, Iorg was hitting a whopping .478 (11-for-23) against Expos pitching. Stan Bahnsen was on the mound from the start of the inning but there was no way Dick Williams was going to let the righty pitch to Iorg. Woodie Fryman induced Iorg to hit an infield pop-up. The Expos ended the game in the bottom of the ninth, thanks to a three-run home run by pinch-hitter John Tamargo. It would be the last hit of his career.

In Philadelphia, the tension was again building up within the Phillies, as if it was possible. In the first game against the Cubs, Dallas Green put Del Unser and Lonnie Smith in the lineup, replacing veterans Garry Maddox and Greg Luzinski. Maddox had told a coach that he was bothered by an injury but was ready to go.[85] The game went into the 15th inning when the Cubs took a 5–3 lead with two unearned runs against rookies Dickie Noles and Kevin Saucier. The fans in Philadelphia, well-known for voicing their displeasure in no uncertain ways, gave it to the players, booing them unmercifully. But Cubs pitcher Doug Capilla opened the door by walking the first two batters in the bottom of the 15th. A wild pitch advanced the runners to scoring position and after two outs, Garry Maddox, who entered the game in the 12th inning, tied the game with a single before Manny Trillo completed the comeback with a game-winning single of his own. Larry Bowa, who was all worked up by that improbable win and also by the treatment the team was subjected to, clearly signalled his frustration in the direction of the fans with an obscene gesture, which didn't go unnoticed.[86] In this pre-Internet era, the hard-core Expos fans didn't have to wait to get the results as the airwaves from the flagship Phillies station, KYW 1060, could be heard in the Montreal area during the night.[87]

The Expos and Phillies had no problem winning their games on Tuesday and Wednesday. In the latter game, David Palmer threw a very impressive six-hit shutout, with ten strikeouts and no walks. Palmer's last two starts were among the gutsiest one could get from a pitcher whose elbow was killing him, to the point where he would have to miss significant time after surgery.[88] Another youngster was helping the Phillies tremendously: pitcher Marty Bystrom. A September call-up, Bystrom won his fifth straight start in the 5–0 win over the Cubs. He was a huge help for the pitching staff, as Steve Carlton and Dick Ruthven had been the only reliable starters up to that point.

The Expos were idle on Thursday but the Phillies had to complete their four-game series against the Cubs. With the score tied at one at the top of the seventh inning, Jim Tracy led off with a triple. But Bob Walk got out of that jam by retiring Jesus Figueroa, Mike O'Berry and Scot Thompson. The Phillies went on to win, 4–2, leading to the final confrontation with the Expos with both teams tied for the top spot.

Like in 1979, the Expos were going to end the season at home on the last weekend of the season with the season NL East title on the line. The Expos and the Phillies had identical records at 89–70 but the Expos seemed to have an edge as they were the toughest team at home for the last two seasons, winning almost two-thirds of their games at the Big O. The Expos were riding a five-game winning streak while the Phillies had just swept their four games against the Cubs. Sixteen-game winners Scott Sanderson and Dick Ruthven were going to start the first game. Ruthven's choice was quite interesting in that he hadn't pitched for a week. He wasn't injured at all and the only reason he didn't pitch was to keep him rested for the Expos. Dallas Green wanted him to face the Expos once again to offset the right-handed power of the Expos' lineup.[89]

The Phillies struck first in the initial frame with one run. Sanderson escaped what could have been a bigger inning as the first two batters, Pete Rose and Bake McBride, hit a single and a double, respectively, to get into scoring position with no outs. Mike Schmidt drove in a run with a sacrifice fly and Sanderson got the other men out. That run held until the sixth inning when the red-hot Schmidt hit his 47th home run of the season, a solo shot.

The Expos got that run back in the sixth on a sacrifice fly by Andre Dawson but that was all the Expos could muster against Phillies pitching. Tug McGraw, the Phillies' number one reliever, was brought in the eighth inning and was nothing short of spectacular. Since a short stint on the disabled list, McGraw had been almost unhittable. In 47 and one-third innings, he had allowed only three earned runs for a 0.57 ERA. Since July 17, he had 12 saves with four wins against only one loss. That night in Montreal, he pitched his 15th game in September. As was the case for the second part of the season, he was perfect, striking out five of the six batters he faced. The first round belonged to the Phillies and they needed only one win to advance to the NL Championship Series.

The weather for the second game was horrible for a baseball game, with rain pouring in Montreal so the start had to be delayed. Tall righty Larry Christenson faced the Expos, another one who made life difficult for Expos batters. In fact, his lifetime record against Montreal was 11–5. The Expos took the lead in the third on Jerry White's two-run home run. The Phillies came back and took the lead in the seventh against Steve Rogers before the Expos scored two on Jerry White's sacrifice fly and a double from Rodney Scott for a 4–3 lead. During that inning, pinch-runners Ron LeFlore and Tim Raines stole three bases. Rogers left with three runs allowed in seven innings but was either very lucky or clutch in the fifth inning when he allowed only one run after allowing the first four batters to reach base. But Rogers struck out Mike Schmidt and Greg Luzinski followed by lining out into a double play. The score was still 4–3 in the top of the ninth with Woodie Fryman on the mound. He had struck out pinch-hitter Garry Maddox to end the eighth with two men on, but allowed leadoff hitter Pete Rose to reach first via a walk. After two groundouts, Bake McBride, who had forced out Rose, was at second and the Expos were only one out away from forcing a winner-take-all Sunday match-up. Bob Boone was the last batter to stand between the Expos and that much-needed win. Boone hadn't even started the game — he had started only twice in the last six games—and had only two hits in his last 24 at-bats. He had no RBIs in his 17 starts in September. Against all odds, Boone got a good piece of a pitch that caught too much of the plate, to Woodie Fryman's own admission,[90] that went through the infield to Andre Dawson who was powerless as McBride crossed the plate with the tying run. Again Tug McGraw was summoned from the bullpen in the ninth. He struck out the first two batters when the pitcher's turn at bat was due. Dick Williams sent young Tim Wallach to the plate, but McGraw got him on a pop-up. In the tenth, leadoff hitter Jerry White reached on a single and went to second on a sacrifice by Rodney Scott. But Rowland Office and Andre Dawson couldn't advance the runner further.

In the eleventh Stan Bahnsen was pitching his second inning as Pete Rose led off with a single. After an out, Bahnsen had to deal with Mike Schmidt, who became in 1980 the number one player in the National League. Nobody had hit more homers since 1974 than Schmidt (263). He led the league in home runs from 1974 to 1976, but many pointed out his high strikeout numbers and a low batting average, even though he got more than his share of walks. In 1979, he hit 45 homers and on Saturday, October 4, 1980, he had 47 when the day began. Nobody else in the National League had more than 40. Schmidt was destroying opposing pitchers as of late, with seven hits in his last 14 at-bats, including three home runs.

On the other hand, Bahnsen was also having success, as he hadn't allowed a single run in his last ten innings, allowing only four hits by the opponents. Bahnsen had every reason to feel confident against Schmidt, as the Phillies' slugger had been limited to five singles in twenty at-bats, with three walks, against the veteran reliever.[91] The situation bore some resemblance to when Ross Grimsley was called upon specifically to retire Willie Stargell, in what appeared to be a mismatch. Dick Williams was dealt the right hand with Grimsley in 1979, but not this time. With a 2–0 count, Schmidt got his pitch to hit his 48th home run of the season that left no doubt as soon as the ball left the bat. In his autobiography, Gary Carter stated that he wanted a breaking ball but was shook off by Bahnsen.[92] After the game, Bahnsen acknowledged that he thought Schmidt would be expecting a breaking ball.[93] Some people wondered why Schmidt was allowed to hit with back-up catcher Don McCormack on deck. But a walk to Schmidt would have pushed Rose to second base, a situation Dick Williams wanted to avoid. Tug McGraw had no problem sealing the win, finishing the game by striking out Larry Parrish. McGraw would admit that he never threw as well as he did during that weekend.[94] In five innings, he allowed one runner and struck out nine with a save and a win. The Expos won a meaningless game on Sunday, which left them one game behind the Phillies in the final standings.

As was the case in 1979, the Expos were again beaten by the team that would win the World Series. But the similarities about both seasons end there. In 1979, the team went through the season almost without injury. In 1980, several players missed significant time, most notably Parrish, Valentine, LeFlore and Palmer. To this day, Parrish thought his injury cost the team the title: "I was always notorious to start slow and to finish up strong. And I don't know what it was, maybe the weather. I didn't like cold weather, I was born in Florida and I still don't like cold weather. 1980 was the only year I got a strong start. I think that was the best start I ever got. I think on May 2, that year, I had seven home runs and 28 RBIs or something like that. I think I wound up with 11 home runs and finished with 50 RBIs. In my mind, that year, if I'm able to play anything like the year before, we win going away. We don't need the last weekend because we win by 10 games."[95]

John McHale believed the most crushing blows were the injuries to LeFlore and Palmer.[96] Some players thus had the opportunity to play a little more. Jerry White did a very nice job filling in first for Ellis Valentine and then for Ron LeFlore. In fact, White's on-base percentage, at .351, was better than LeFlore's at .337. Gary Carter and Andre Dawson were the main threats offensively, Carter leading the way with a September rush that put him in the 100-RBI club, the second Montreal player to reach that number after Ken Singleton in 1973. Dawson, considered then among the best overall player in the majors, ended up with a .308 batting average, 17 home runs, 41 doubles, 34 stolen bases and 87 RBIs. Ron LeFlore and Rodney Scott stole a combined 160 bases, a record for teammates since broken. LeFlore led the league with 97. In fact he "stole" the thief title away from Omar Moreno when he stole second and third as a pinch-runner in the last game of the season. Notwithstanding his horrible start, Rodney Scott remained one of Dick Williams' favorites. The manager was often heard praising his second baseman and went as far as say he was the most valuable player on his team.[97] Warren Cromartie's transition from outfield to first base went smoothly. He was more than adequate defensively, far better than what Rusty Staub showed at spring training, and he showed more power at the plate with 14 home runs, which helped hike his RBI total to 70.

On the mound, Steve Rogers and Scott Sanderson led the team with 16 wins each. Two rookies made significant contributions, Bill Gullickson and Charlie Lea. David Palmer was hampered by an elbow problem and had to go through surgery, which left in doubt his availability for 1981. Bill Lee's season was full of ups and downs, both on and off the field. In the bullpen, 41-year-old Woodie Fryman was the team's most reliable man, as Elias Sosa went through tougher times than in 1979. Stan Bahnsen did a creditable job in long relief, notwithstanding the gopher ball to Mike Schmidt that did in the Expos in the next-to-last game of the season. Fred Norman could never justified himself in a relief role, with an ERA of 4.88 from the bullpen. As a starter, the veteran lefty could still hold his own (3.42), even though he was used only sporadically in that capacity.

That second-place finish was rather hard to swallow, harder in fact than 1979, as they were then looked at as a potential force in the National League. But the team was still young and, furthermore, they had some bona fide prospects coming along. In 1980, the Expos' main affiliate in Denver literally dominated the American Association, both offensively and on the mound. They finished with a record of 94–44, 17 games over the Springfield Redbirds, a St. Louis farm team. Seven members of the Denver Bears made the postseason all-star team.[98] That team was chosen among the top 100 all-time minor-league teams by researchers Bill Weiss and Marshall Wright as part of the celebration of the 100th anniversary of minor league baseball in 2001. In AAA ball, only the Albuquerque Dukes of 1981 were rated better than the 1980 Bears among teams in the previous 50 years.[99]

The main prospects with the Bears were Tim Raines and Tim Wallach. Raines was named Minor League Player of the Year.[100] He led the American Association with a .354 batting average and 77 stolen bases. Wallach and Randy Bass, the latter traded to the Padres late in the season, provided power with 36 and 37 home runs, respectively. On the mound, the team finished second with a 4.23 ERA, quite impressive given that Denver, as everybody came to know when the Rockies joined the majors in 1993, was a launching pad for hitters. Steve Ratzer led the team with 15 wins but his name rarely made headlines when future moundsmen were discussed. The Expos even allowed him to find another team during the season.[101] The two pitchers who were deemed as real future Expos were Bob James and Kevin Mendon.[102] James was just back from elbow surgery after the 1979 season. The fastball pitcher seemed to be back in form with 79 strikeouts in 87 innings and a very respectable 3.83 ERA. But his control was still an issue as his number of walks was too high at 74. Mendon was a curveball artist who wasn't afraid to throw strikes. He won 14 games in a season spent in both Memphis (AA) and Denver. He allowed only 58 walks in 169 innings. By the way, the Memphis Chicks had their share of success as well with an 83–61 record.

At the gates, the Expos were as popular as ever, with 2.2 millions fans who showed up at Olympic Stadium, 100,000 more than in 1979. The team's popularity was on the rise, to the point where the O'Keefe Brewery coughed up $35 million over the next five years in a sponsorship agreement with the Expos, the most lucrative deal of that kind in the majors.[103] The organization seemed on solid ground, both on and off the field.

Among the regulars, Ron LeFlore was the only one who had the opportunity to become a free agent. He was very popular with the fans but it became clear as the last days of the season unwound that he wouldn't be back. Shortly after the season ended, super-scout Charlie Fox said when asked if the team would try to sign LeFlore: "No, and I hope he doesn't let the door hit him in the butt!"[104] Dick Williams didn't want him with the club either.[105] John McHale was rather evasive when asked why the Expos didn't want to retain LeFlore, but it was understood that there was more to it than his play on the field: "I don't want to go into details but you wouldn't believe all the problems we had.[106] He was a talent, but he brought with him baggage that was not good."[107] LeFlore spent only one year in Montreal, a year where he didn't go unnoticed. In an interview, LeFlore insisted he wanted to stay with the Expos:

"I wanted to stay in Montreal. They only wanted to give me a 1-year contract. I would have liked to have a 3- or 4-year contract."[108]

With LeFlore out, the next important case to take care of was that of Ellis Valentine. Valentine had his best campaign, with 67 RBIs in only 86 games, with a .315 batting average and 13 home runs. But the organization had enough of his overall attitude. In late September, most media outlets questioned the seriousness of his hand injury.[109] Valentine was also unhappy over certain behavioral clauses in his contract that he had to fulfill in order to get a $2,000 monthly bonus. According to that uncommon agreement, Valentine had to (a) perform on the field offensively and defensively; (b) work hard in games and practices; (c) cooperate with the organization and show leadership on the field; (d) be in good physical condition; and (e) be a model citizen. According to his agent, Tom Selakovich, Valentine didn't get his bonuses in June and September, two months when he barely played. Selakovich also said that the Expos threatened to suspend Valentine in late September if he didn't go back to Montreal to have his wrist examined. The real reason for that threat, according to Selakovich, was that Dick Williams didn't want him around anymore, after seeing him laugh on the bench as his team was battling for a playoff spot.[110] John McHale admitted that these special clauses didn't have the expected effect.[111] Valentine was visibly upset by this criticism. He told columnist Tim Burke: "Sometimes I think I've become a prisoner of my own talent."[112] Valentine had doubts about his future in Montreal, a city where he felt comfortable, but he obviously had problems coping with the huge expectations put on him since his debut in the organization. John McHale was beginning to gauge that Valentine was not at ease with this superstar tag: "Maybe he doesn't want to be the king of the town. He still is very popular with the fans."[113]

McHale's two priorities were a solid left-handed batter and a starting pitcher.[114] David Palmer was operated on in November but nobody knew when he would be back.[115] Rogers, Sanderson and Gullickson were the only sure things in the rotation, while Bill Lee, Charlie Lea and Fred Norman were also options. As for that lefty bat, Al Oliver was again on top of John McHale's list.[116]

In the free agent market, the Expos targeted veteran pitcher Don Sutton. He had spent the first 15 years of his career with the Los Angeles Dodgers and looked as if he could still pitch, as he led the league in ERA in 1980 at 2.20. The Expos' brass, including owner Charles Bronfman and financial controller Harry Renaud, invited Sutton for a visit to Montreal in late November. The Expos' offer was for three years but as was the case with Reggie Jackson three years earlier, Sutton declined a very compelling package and opted to go to Houston. The Expos were never close to landing Sutton. When Charles Bronfman asked him up front what the Expos' chances were to sign him, Sutton didn't try to hide his true feelings, saying that they were not very good.[117] When the Astros introduced Sutton in a press conference, he listed the New York Yankees and the Milwaukee Brewers as the other teams competing for his services, without uttering a single word about the Expos.[118]

At the winter meetings, the Expos were almost idle, with only one transaction that at the time looked like a minor move, when they sent utilityman Tony Bernazard to the Chicago White Sox for lefty Rich Wortham. Bernazard was deemed expendable as Rodney Scott was Dick Williams' favorite at second baseman. Wortham had won 14 games in 1979. He faltered badly in 1980 with control issues, along with his unhappiness about being demoted to the bullpen to begin the season,[119] but the quality of his arm still drew rave reviews. Peter Gammons wrote in The Sporting News that Wortham could win 15 games with a good team.[120] Stan Bahnsen could have left as a free agent but the veteran pitcher got a deal to his liking, a $1 million three-year contract that made him one of the best-paid long relievers in the game.[121] Bahnsen did a very creditable job in long relief, producing ERAs of 3.15 and 3.05 in 1979 and 1980, respectively. Moreover, Bahnsen saved the Expos more runs than he let in with runners on base.[122] He was also a calming influence among the young pitchers on the team.[123]

In January 1981, the Expos announced that Andre Dawson had agreed to a long-term deal. The contract extension ran through 1986 for a total of $4 million.[124] At the press conference, Dawson said to be very happy with his new deal and that he would never ask for it to be renegotiated,[125] words that he would very soon regret. Jerry White, who was "the best fourth outfielder in the league"[126] according to Dick Williams, also accepted a three-year deal.[127] Infielder Ken Macha's contract was sold to the Toronto Blue Jays, a move that displeased Bill Lee, who thought that the Expos misunderstood Macha's real value to the team, not only on the field but also in the clubhouse.[128]

In February, Valentine, who was still with the Expos to the surprise of many observers, agreed to a one-year contract. Writer Serge Touchette reacted in a rather ironic way: "Valentine is lucky to not have been offered a half-year agreement!"[129] A couple of days before the start of spring training, Gary Carter told an Ottawa writer that Valentine wouldn't be back with the team in 1981.[130] Lastly, after striking out with Don Sutton, the Expos had to be content with what appeared to be a consolation prize in veteran Ray Burris. The veteran righty was still without a job but was highly recommended by Woodie Fryman, who was a teammate of his with the Cubs in 1978.[131] Burris had always been tough on the Expos with 12 wins, his highest total against any team, and a respectable 3.25 ERA.

In 1979, the Expos showed for the first time on the field how good they could be. In 1980, they showed lots of character through a season of adversity (and distractions as well), a year where they were again picked as the Team of the Year in the annual poll of the *Canadian Press*.[132] In mountain climbing, the last part is always the hardest to reach. The Expos were at that point. It was to be seen whether they were up to the challenge.

6

1981: They Made the Playoffs!

The start of spring training was not without some contractual rumblings, not only within the Expos but also throughout the majors. A new threshold had been set with Dave Winfield's monster contract with the Yankees that called for an average of $2 million per year for ten years.[1] It was almost the double what the best players were then currently getting. Most players wanted to get their share, trying to use the Winfield comparable to their advantage. John McHale insisted that most of these players had yet to reach their free agent status and, consequently, no comparison should be made.[2]

Without much fanfare, McHale was able to get everybody to sign, including Rodney Scott who had gone through arbitration in each of his first two years with the team. Scott always had a high opinion of his value to the team, which was of course reinforced by Dick Williams time and again. Scott said that the stats really didn't tell the truth as to his real contribution: "I knew my value to the team. I knew I was good enough for that. I just figured that I would be compensated. That's all there was to it. Without me, I don't think they would have finished in those positions we had finished."[3] Scott agreed to a one-year contract which called for a $235,000 salary, not including bonuses.[4]

Surprisingly, Willie Montanez decided to return even though he was a free agent. But Montanez planned to play regularly in 1981 and expected to do so, especially in light of a bonus that would be earned should he reach 400 at-bats. The Expos had been looking almost desperately for some power from the left side. Montanez looked like an interesting option, given his track record. He was also above-average defensively. On top of that, he had played well in the winter leagues.[5] But his signing was more an insurance policy in case Tim Raines couldn't prove he could hit major league pitching.[6]

Spring training was moved for 1981 from Daytona Beach to West Palm

Beach, where they would have to share space though with the Atlanta Braves.[7] It was the second time the Expos would be at West Palm Beach, where they held their annual southern preparation from 1969 to 1972. The Expos were getting closer to most of the training sites in Florida. Since Daytona was the northern most city in the Grapefruit League, the Expos had to travel long hours to get to their road games. But the move left behind many Quebecers who had come in greater numbers to Daytona than to West Palm Beach.[8] From an organization standpoint, the move made good sense, especially when one considers that West Palm Beach was also the Florida State League affiliate of the Expos.

As seemed to be the case every single year since he became the Expos' manager, Dick Williams began spring camp by warning that he would be more rigorous regarding his players' discipline.[9] Williams had been the subject of some criticism, even from his own players, including Andre Dawson, who rarely raised his voice.[10] One could imagine that Ron LeFlore's departure, whose tardiness was then legendary, would make the manager's job a little easier.

The big topic in March concerned Tim Raines. He had played second base throughout his minor league career but was now being asked to play left field. He was scheduled to play winter ball in the Dominican Republic to get familiar with left field, but these plans were thwarted, thanks to a local regulation that stated that the players be used in their natural position.[11] Williams had no intention to dislodge Rodney Scott from second baseman, as he considered him as the best defensive player at this position.[12] In fact, Raines was told as early as September 1980 by Williams that he would be the team's left fielder in 1981 (which confirms that Ron LeFlore's fate had already been sealed before the season ended).[13] Even with his lack of experience in the outfield, the Expos' brass was still confident that Raines would succeed. To give an idea of Raines' value not only within the organization but also throughout the big leagues, Jim Fanning revealed that the Expos could have acquired almost anybody had they decided to put Raines on the market.[14] Writer Pierre Ladouceur, from *La Presse*, predicted that Raines would easily make people forget Ron LeFlore.[15]

The only other uncertainty with position players again involved Warren Cromartie. He first had to wait on whether Raines would make the transition to left field and if Dick Williams intended to play Montanez at first base. The Expos wanted also to take a close look at another prize prospect, Tim Wallach. He had hit more than 50 home runs in the previous year and a half in the minors and had nothing to learn by returning there.

On the mound, starting pitchers Steve Rogers, Bill Gullickson and Scott Sanderson were a lock to form a more than adequate trio. It became more and more obvious that David Palmer wouldn't be available until May, at the very least.[16] Charlie Lea and Ray Burris were expected to get every opportunity to battle for the other spots, along with Rich Wortham. Four veterans were assured a spot in the bullpen, Woodie Fryman, Elias Sosa, Stan Bahnsen and Bill Lee. Since Dick Williams had already stated that Wortham would be on his staff, that left at most only one opening.[17] Fred Norman's perspectives looked rather grim, especially with rookies Kevin Mendon and Steve Ratzer knocking at the door.[18] Ratzer had earned some points during the winter. With Escogido, in the Dominican Republic, Ratzer, pitching under manager Felipe Alou, was used exclusively in relief and showed impressive stats: an ERA of 1.21, with 11 saves and five wins in six decisions.[19]

As pitchers and catchers were making their way to the training sites, the Players Association and the ballclub owners weren't going anywhere in their attempt to sign a new collective bargaining agreement. In fact, the two factions remained where they were a year before. The gap was as large with the same contentious topic: the owners' demand for compensation after the loss of a free agent. The union suggested a pool of unprotected players from the teams taking part in that process; 25 players on each team would be protected. The owners wanted a more direct compensation. When it looked as if the two parties wouldn't budge from their positions, the owner's main negotiator, Ray Grebey, announced on February 19 that the owners would unilaterally implement their own system.[20] The players counter-attacked six days later by taking a strike vote. The following day, it was announced that there would be a work stoppage on May 29 if no agreement was in place.[21] There were still three months to try to reach a settlement.

March wasn't there yet, but Ellis Valentine managed to attract a lot of attention. He showed up early in West Palm Beach and, as was the case in 1980, he promised to behave.[22] But in an article in *The Gazette*, Valentine criticized his manager Dick Williams, complaining about a lack of communication. He said that it was the players, not Williams, who ruled the clubhouse, adding that managers were responsible for no more than seven or eight wins per season.[23] As the hitters were getting set for the exhibition games, Valentine refused to take part in a batting practice session, complaining about the background. He explained that he couldn't see the ball and after being almost killed and blinded the season before, he didn't want to hit in such conditions. The right fielder was also quite unhappy about the way some teammates were making fun of him and his past injuries. He asked to be traded and threatened to physically challenge those who would keep teasing him.[24] In the next few days, the three Montreal daily papers, *Le Journal de Montréal*, *La Presse* and *The Gazette*, published columns where the authors, Serge Touchette, Jean Aucoin and Michael Farber, respectively, wrote unequivocally that Valentine had to go. Touchette and Aucoin were particularly harsh in their critics. Farber was a little more subdued but nonetheless wrote that for everybody involved, it would be best that Valentine was sent elsewhere.[25]

As the Expos were going through their Grapefruit League schedule, the organization was preparing for a decision from the commissioner's office that would have important long-term repercussions on the team's visibility and finances. After a complaint from the Toronto Blue Jays, the commissioner's office was asked to take a look at the territorial broadcast rights of both Canadian teams. The Blue Jays wanted to limit the number of games that were broadcast into Ontario, especially to the greater Toronto area, the most important market in Canada. The fact that two breweries were heavily involved with both organizations surely triggered that move by the Jays, who were owned by Labatt.[26] The Expos' main sponsor, O'Keefe, had just agreed to pay $35 million for five years, a very lucrative deal.[27]

In mid–March, John McHale was very concerned about the outcome. In *The Gazette*, columnist Tim Burke wrote that the Expos' games were as popular as the traditional "Hockey Night in Canada" throughout the country. In the article, John McHale told Burke that the Expos had to buy their own TV time in their first two years in the National League and that the organization had worked very hard to become the team of the country. The agreement with O'Keefe included 32 games nationally, and three more during the final weekend, if these games became meaningful, as was the case in both 1979 and 1980. What really bothered McHale was the lack of knowledge of the Canadian market in the commissioner's office. "I don't think there's five people in the U.S. who know the TV and radio broadcast situation in Canada," he said.[28] His fears were more than justified when the decision was announced on March 11: the Expos would be limited to only 14 games nationally, which included the greater Toronto area, comprised of Toronto, Hamilton, London, Peterborough and Barrie, which represented more than 40 percent of the country's TV market. The number of games would fall to 12 in 1982. Ironically, the day of the announcement, the Expos won, 4–3, in the Grapefruit League over the Toronto Blue Jays.[29]

In an interview some 25 years later, John McHale maintained that this decision really hurt the Expos' organization: "We had the best television contract in baseball. And then we were kept from having our games going to Ontario by the Blue Jays. Really, it was a Labatt Brewery decision more than a baseball decision: they took the protest to the commissioner who turned it over to the radio-television guy who didn't understand the Canadian television market at all. In the meantime Turner and Atlanta and the Cubs were doing exactly what we had done, except they were doing it in a different tech-

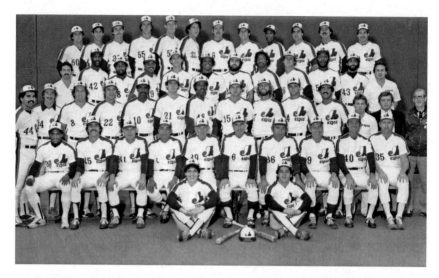

The Expos reached the playoffs for the first and only time in 1981. The team defeated Philadelphia in the NLDS that year, but fell to the Los Angeles Dodgers in the NLCS and did not reach the World Series. Seated: Tino Di Pietro, Frank Albertson; first row (left to right): Tim Raines, Steve Rogers, Steve Boros, Ozzie Virgil, Pat Mullin, Jim Fanning, Galen Cisco, Vern Rapp, Norm Sherry, Woodie Fryman; second row (left to right): Bobby Ramos, Chris Speier, Gary Carter, Stan Bahnsen, Andre Dawson, Scott Sanderson, Ray Burris, Larry Parrish, Bill Lee, Bill Gullickson, Elias Sosa, Mike Kozak, Peter Durso, Harvey Stone; third row (left to right): John Silverman, Anthony Johnson, Jerry White, Grant Jackson, Mike Phillips, Warren Cromartie, Larry Parrish, Rowland Office, David Palmer, John Milner, Jerry Manuel, Ron McClain; fourth row (left to right): Tom Wieghaus, Terry Francona, Tim Wallach, Dave Hostetler, Charlie Lea, Tom Gorman, Bryn Smith, Pat Rooney, Wallace Johnson, Brad Mills, Dan Briggs, Rick Engle.

nical way. They were doing it with satellite. We had to do it directly because we didn't have the capability to do it that way. So when Montreal became a Quebec-only team and no longer had the right to compete in Canada, that was a very telling blow to the financial picture of the Montreal Expos."[30]

René Guimond succeeded Roger D. Landry in 1981 as the marketing director and he acknowledged that the curbing of the TV market was a big blow. "It was very hard financially because we had an agreement with CBC and Radio-Canada to cover the whole country. The Jays succeeded in getting a blackout for Toronto, to protect their market. The CBC then had less interest, since they couldn't cover the Toronto area. And they had to deal with their image, as lots of baseball fans were upset over not having the Expos anymore, who had many fans in Toronto. Later, TSN (The Sports Network, the first all-sports TV station in Canada) began broadcasting some Expos games, but they really were more inclined to broadcast the Jays' games, and they just ceased to show any Montreal games. Because of the nature of the Canadian market, the Expos became the team of a single province, with almost no way to technically cover the whole country."[31]

The long-term consequences of that decision were yet to be felt however in March 1981 and the attention was directed more towards what was going on in spring training. Dick Williams was then again the subject of some harsh words, this time from one of his former players, Ron LeFlore. In a *Chicago Tribune* article, LeFlore, who had signed a three-year contract with the White Sox, said that Williams was the only one responsible for his bad reputation in baseball, stating that he never had any problems with his mangers before. According to LeFlore, nobody liked Williams, including Carl Yastrzemski, who was considered one of the true gentlemen in the game. LeFlore had however some problems of his own with his new manager, Tony LaRussa, as he had already shown up late ... before the season had even begun![32]

On the field, Rich Wortham had problems throwing strikes, a condition that highly displeased Dick Williams. Wortham, who seemed to be a sure-thing with the pitching corps, was sent to the minors. He would never pitch for the Expos. Ray Burris, thanks to a very impressive training camp, won the fourth spot in the rotation. His ERA was 1.33 with three wins in four decisions.[33] Charlie Lea and Steve Ratzer would complete the staff, Ratzer almost by default, as Kevin Mendon couldn't justify himself because of arm problems.[34] His professional career was practically over. Fred Norman was released and would not pitch again.

With no clear-cut number one reliever, the Expos were willing to give a tryout to Mike Marshall, the same Mike Marshall who had chosen the Minnesota Twins over the Expos at the eve of the 1979 season. With Wortham's control problems combined with Ratzer's unspectacular showing in West Palm Beach, the Expos were willing to take a look at Marshall. The veteran was jobless and available but few teams were willing to take a chance at an outspoken and unpredictable 38-year-old pitcher.[35] He was thrown in an exhibition game against the Tigers. His second pitch was hit far over the right-field fence by a highly-touted young outfielder, Kirk Gibson.[36] The rest of the outing went better but the experiment didn't go farther. Marshall said that he had nothing to prove, except that his arm was sound. The Expos didn't want to decide anything after only one preseason appearance, to the detriment of other pitchers who had been battling for spots on the staff.[37] Marshall would end up with the New York Mets.

Among position players, Tim Raines won the left-field job. Even though Tim Wallach had no set position for the time being, he was still kept on the roster, along with newcomers Bobby Ramos and Jerry Manuel. Larry Parrish looked as if he was back to his 1979 form and swinging the bat well.[38] Jerry

White, Rowland Office and Tommy Hutton were anchoring the bench, while John Tamargo was let go.

For the first time, the Expos were established as the favorites to win the NL East in many publications, including the three Montreal dailies as well as UPI.[39] Before 1979, they hadn't showed yet that they could contend with the best. In 1980, lots of specialists doubted that the Expos could repeat their success of the year before, as they had lost two solid 10-game winners in Dan Schatzeder and Rudy May and the fact that they had almost no injuries in 1979, which was quite unlikely to happen again. They still overcame injuries, controversies and came within one win of winning the NL East title. But in 1981, the Expos had matured enough, according to most observers. Even John McHale, as conservative as one could be baseball-wise, went as far as to say that the 1981 edition of the Expos was the most powerful of the team's existence.[40] The only weakness seemed to be the bullpen. In 1980, 40-year-old lefty Woodie Fryman was summoned to take over the number one spot, after Elias Sosa lost some of his effectiveness.

The way the season began gave a very good indication of what Expos fans would see in the next decade or so from rookie Tim Raines. The Expos started the season in Pittsburgh against 18-game winner Jim Bibby. Raines was the very first batter for Montreal and got on first on a walk. He stole second and continued to third as catcher Steve Nicosia's throw went all the way to the center fielder. He scored on a double by Andre Dawson. The lead was short-lived as the Pirates tagged Steve Rogers for four runs in their first turn at bat. But the Expos came back with single runs in the eighth and ninth innings to win, 6–5, thanks to four hitless relief innings by Stan Bahnsen and Woodie Fryman. Andre Dawson finished with three hits in as many at-bats, an omen of things to come.

After a 3–2 loss in Pittsburgh, the Expos were back at home for the local opening against the Chicago Cubs on April 15, one day later than scheduled, thanks to bad weather. The Expos won twice against the Cubs and kept it going, winning ten out of eleven games, giving them an 11–2 record on April 26, in first place in the NL East, one game over the St. Louis Cardinals and two over the Philadelphia Phillies, who were swept in a three-game series in Montreal during that sequence. In the second game against Philadelphia, a 10–3 win, the Expos stole seven bases. Tim Raines added four hits to raise his average at .444. Even though it was a few months too late for some, and a very small consolation at that, Tug McGraw was the losing pitcher in two of those three games.

At the end of the month, Ellis Valentine was at least hitting a little better, after a horrendous start, with only two singles in his first 27 at-bats. Heavily criticized since the end of 1980, Valentine was visibly perturbed by all the attention, something he surely wanted to avoid. He said that if his presence became a burden on the team, then he wanted to be traded.[41]

After the quick visit to Philadelphia, the Dodgers came to Montreal. The Dodgers had always been a good draw in Montreal. They were good, they had some characters and it had been only twenty years since the International League Montreal Royals left town. The Royals had been a Dodgers affiliate for many years and many baseball fans still felt some allegiance towards the Dodgers. But the real attraction was a Mexican left-handed pitcher who was the toast of the whole baseball world, Fernando Valenzuela. The rotund south-paw had won and completed his first five starts, four of them being shutouts. He struck out at least ten batters three times and his ERA was a minuscule 0.20. Adding his September 1980 stint with the Dodgers, when he went score-less in 20 innings, and his career ERA was 0.14! Being Mexican and playing in Los Angeles, Valenzuela had all the publicity one could hope for and more. But the Expos had a very solid rookie of their own in Tim Raines. In the first month of the season, Raines' batting average was .355 with 16 stolen bases without being caught even once. Valenzuela was scheduled to pitch on Sunday, May 3, the third game of that four-game series. As if to make a statement, Raines won the first game for the Expos by hitting a walk-off home run in the 13th inning in a 9–8 victory. It was his first major league home run. He added three stolen bases for good measure. The Dodgers got even on Saturday as Jerry Reuss, a notorious Expos killer,[42] shut them out, 4–0. For the first time in the season, Raines was caught stealing by Mike Scioscia.

On May 3, more than 46,000 fans showed up at Olympic Stadium to see Valenzuela against Bill Gullickson. The Dodgers scored first in the opening frame and it was the only run until the Expos tied it in the eighth in what was an epic pitching duel. Valenzuela and Gullickson were both dominating. Chris Speier was the first batter to hit the ball to the outfield in the sixth inning against Valenzuela. The only hit so far was a first-inning infield single by leadoff batter Tim Raines. Gullickson in the meantime allowed only one runner to reach first base after the first-inning until the tenth. He was still on the mound in the tenth when at last the Dodgers scored five runs against him and Woodie Fryman for a 6–1 triumph. The game was of course a dis-appointment for the hard-core Expos fans but they had just witnessed great pitching from two of the best young pitchers in the majors. The Expos would win the next game against Los Angeles to get even. The team played that series without Ellis Valentine, as some fluid had to be remove from an aching knee.[43]

The Expos still had seven games to play at home before going on their first West Coast swing of the season. They won two out of three against San Diego, but lost their first three against San Francisco, including the first game of a doubleheader, a game when they were limited to four hits by journeyman Tom Griffin, who threw a complete game. The Expos were trying to salvage the series by sending Charlie Lea, who had pitched only 11 innings since the beginning of the season, allowing 16 hits and four walks. In his two starts, he wasn't able to go past the fifth inning. In spring training, Dick Williams was pushing him hard, saying that he wouldn't do so if he didn't believe in his potential.[44] So far, the Expos hadn't really needed a fifth starter, thanks to days off and cancelled games due to inclement weather. But Williams would have to make a decision soon between Bill Lee and Charlie Lea.

Lee had pitched the first game against the Giants, allowing four runs in eight innings, an honest outing. But Lea did the unexpected to say the least: he threw a no-hitter, the third in the team's history. Bill Stoneman had pitched the first two in 1969 and 1972. Lea couldn't relax much during the game as it was still scoreless in the seventh inning. Tim Wallach provided Lea some relief when he hit his second home run of the season off Ed Whitson. Rodney Scott and Andre Dawson would add RBI doubles in the same inning for a 4–0 lead. After the game, Lea was surprisingly very calm: "When I was warming up, I never felt like I had great stuff. I always felt I had to scratch and claw and that's what I think made me successful. I had thrown no-hitters before in college or university, I had thrown shutouts and any pitcher knows when the game is going on how many hits they've given up. I mean they may not voice it but I knew I had a good game going on. At some point, I saw the no-hitter was within reach. But as far as thinking I have no-hitter stuff today, no I never pitched a game with that on my mind."[45]

After Lea's gem, it was off to Los Angeles, where the Expos always seemed to have problems. That trend was confirmed as the Expos were swept in a self-destructive way. In the first game, they were shut out, even though they finished the game with ten hits and four walks. In the second game, the Dodgers scored four unearned runs in the bottom of the ninth for an 8–6 victory, Ron Cey hitting the game-winning home run. In the last game, Andre Dawson tied the game, 2–2, with a home run in the top of the ninth with two outs against Fernando Valenzuela. But the respite was short-lived as Pedro Guerrero, the first batter in the bottom of the ninth, deposited one of Steve Ratzer's pitches over the left-field fence. Ratzer would pitch only one more game with the Expos (and in the majors). The Expos ended that series in third place in the East, two and a half games behind St. Louis. Philadelphia was one game back from the lead.

In San Francisco, the Expos lost for the fourth time in a row before Charlie Lea got the team in the win column with another superb outing against the Giants, a four-hit shutout. On May 20 in San Diego, Steve Rogers became the first Expos starting pitcher other than Charlie Lea to win a game since

May 7. As the team was in San Diego, Andre Dawson voiced some criticism toward his manager Dick Williams, reproaching him to play the same players over and over again, contrary to Chuck Tanner with the Pittsburgh Pirates.[46] Dawson was known as a man of few words, which added some weight to his comments. Furthermore, Dawson, along with Tim Raines, were the only players who contributed offensively. After the West Coast swing, Dawson's batting average was .311 and his slugging average was an impressive .593. On the other end of the spectrum, Larry Parrish was again bothered by his right wrist, the one that was injured in May 1980. His average was under .200 and he had only one home run. According to the physicians he consulted, he would have to learn to play with pain for the rest of his career, a possibility that wasn't very alluring, to say the least.[47]

The Expos had one more series in Chicago before getting back to Montreal. The Cubs were absolutely horrible with only six wins in thirty-three games, by far the worst record in the majors. They still managed to win two out of three against the Expos, the only win after another solid performance from Charlie Lea, who pitched seven more scoreless innings. May was supposed to mark the return of David Palmer but he had to go back to Montreal after a setback in his rehabilitation program.[48]

On May 25, the Expos were back at home but the task at hand would not be easy, with the reinvigorated St. Louis Cardinals, led by their manager Whitey Herzog, who was also the team's general manager. In less than a year, Herzog had completely transformed the Cards, adding catcher Darrell Porter and reliever Bruce Sutter, one of the best in the business. Youngsters Tommy Herr and Ken Oberkfell were also added to the team as regulars in the infield. Herzog wanted a team built with speed, tailored for the vast Busch Stadium. But the next series would be played in Montreal, where the Expos were most at ease. True to their reputation, the Expos swept the Cards in that three-game series, thanks to solid performances from Bill Gullickson, Steve Rogers and Charlie Lea, who combined for 22 innings, allowing seven runs. It was Lea's fourth straight win. The three victories over the Cards took the Expos closer to first place, only a half-game behind Philadelphia and St. Louis.

The Expos got a day off on May 28 but the baseball world was not without news, quite the contrary. The strike date was fast approaching and talks didn't seem to progress. But as was the case in 1980, the fans did get a reprieve of some sort. The National Labor Relations Board filed an injunction request on behalf of the Players Association, asking the U.S. District Court to delay the owners' decision to impose their own system of compensation for the loss of a free agent. The Board had ruled favorably after a complaint from the Players Association, who alleged that the owners had negotiated in bad faith. Both owners and players agreed to wait until the Board's injunction request before making the next move, thus delaying the strike indefinitely.[49] But the decision was expected to occur very soon.

After the Cards, the Expos hosted the Pittsburgh Pirates. The first game on Friday, May 29, went the Expos' way, 3–2. But the biggest news of the day was announced right after the game: Ellis Valentine became a New York Met, the Expos getting in return reliever Jeff Reardon and minor league outfielder Dan Norman. Valentine hadn't played since May 19 in San Diego and missed time in three different instances since the beginning of the season because of leg injuries. Serge Touchette didn't waste time to applaud the move: "Good riddance!"[50] That transaction put an end to the Valentine-Expos marriage, a tumultuous one that should have and could have had a better dénouement.

What happened to the player who was the jewel of an organization that was full of bona fide prospects? Ellis Valentine's talent was never an issue and everybody who saw him play, teammates, coaches, executives, writers, would attest to that.[51] His arm was compared to the best there was. Mel Didier, who was in charge of player development when Valentine was drafted, was unequivocal regarding Valentine: "He had the greatest arm and the most accurate arm that I've ever seen. And that goes back to Rocky Colavito, Clemente, all those guys. He had the better arm and the thing was, he was deadly accurate. I mean, he wasn't all over the place and he would throw runners out. I've seen him go back to the wall, pick up the ball off the wall and throw the ball on a line drive, no more than 10 feet high all the way to third base. And he could do that. He was an unusual player. He had good power, a quick bat."[52]

Jim Fanning would go along: "Ellis Valentine had really outstanding ability. He could do all those five tools: run, throw, hit, field, power. I think he had better all-around tools than Andre Dawson. He would take a ball to home plate and throw it over the left-field fence. In fact he did it one time, I saw it from the press box, I went down and scolded him like a little child, don't ever do that again."[53] Larry Parrish was his roommate in the minors: "He still has the most talent of any player I've seen to this day. There was nothing he couldn't do. He had a pristine arm, he could run, he had power, could hit for average, and could find a way to hit a tough pitch and go to right field for a double and the next time up hit it out to left center. There was nothing he couldn't do other than handle himself away from the ballpark!"[54]

Wayne Twitchell went as far as to compare Valentine to one of the best ever: "Ellis Valentine had as much talent as Mike Schmidt. He could do it all! I think maybe the first game I pitched for Montreal was against Cincinnati. It was real early there and I remember distinctly Pete Rose being on third base. A fly ball being hit to right-field, and I knew it was normal right field depth. I just assumed I was going to give up a run, Pete would tag up and score. I ran back behind Gary Carter and I was looking for the ball coming and of course Pete Rose coming. The ball was coming but Pete Rose was nowhere to be seen, I looked to left and he was standing on third base, arms folded. Ellis Valentine threw a one-hop strike. I guess Pete Rose was aware of Ellis Valentine's arm. I had just seen enough to make the observation that it was phenomenal, it was refreshing."[55] Of course, Twitchell was used to the Phillies' outfield with Greg Luzinski and Garry Maddox. Luzinski's best defensive position was probably linebacker on a football field! As for Maddox, he covered lots of field but was not known for the power of his arm.

The supreme compliment to Valentine came from one of the most respected scouts in the majors, Jim Russo. He was mostly known for his scouting report on the 1966 Dodgers as he was working for the Baltimore Orioles in preparation for the World Series. The Dodgers, who were the favorites, not only were swept by the Orioles but they were also shut out in the last three games. Russo was nicknamed "Superscout" thereafter, which was also the title of his autobiography. In the book, Valentine's was first on his list among the greatest underachievers he saw. He had seen a lot of Expos games in spring training from 1976 to 1979 and he was seldom as impressed by a player as he was by Valentine, pointing out that he also thought he was superior to Andre Dawson.[56]

Not only was Valentine very talented, he also had a unique charisma that made him a fan favorite. John McHale said he was the most popular player everywhere he played through the Expos' farm system.[57] Hall of Fame broadcaster Dave Van Horne, who was the Expos' voice from 1969 to 2000, also chipped in when asked about Valentine's popularity: "He loved playing the game and he showed his happiness on the field with that great big smile and when he would come across home plate after a home run or after the team had won a game out on the field or after a great terrific catch or a great throw, he would show that smile to the fans and that won them over. Of course he had a huge smile and you could see it in the highest rows of the stadium. I think he had that magnetism on the field, he had star quality. Ellis Valentine had star quality, he had a presence, the way he carried himself, that size of course. But it was that big smile that won the hearts of the fans and Ellis played the game hard."[58]

A good example of the aura of Valentine could be best exemplified by a public appearance he made in Montreal. The last weekend of May 2002, many former players were invited for a special promotion. Before the Saturday, May 25, game, media members were on the field as the Expos' alumni were getting ready to play a short exhibition game. Among the ex-players were Mack Jones, Balor Moore, Dale Murray, Al Oliver, Floyd Youmans, Andy McGaffigan and Tim Burke. As soon as Ellis Valentine set foot on the Olympic Stadium carpet, it was as if everybody stopped doing what they were doing to converge towards that big man with the black suit and infectious smile.[59]

Among all the impressive young players the Expos groomed in the mid–70s, Ellis Valentine was considered the jewel of them all. His infectious smile made him a fan favorite everywhere he played. A beanball and substance abuse curtailed what, to many, could have been a Hall of Fame career.

All this, talent, charisma, charm, led the Expos and especially John McHale to be extremely patient with their gifted right fielder, even though rumors about him being available began surfacing as soon as 1977 when California scout Bob Zuk said that Valentine had been on the market the year before.[60]

According to the overwhelming majority of those who were in contact with him, Valentine's career was curtailed by drugs. Jim Bay, a Montreal broadcaster who was among the closest to Valentine among the media, said that his problems began very soon after his arrival in Montreal.[61] Jean-Paul Sarault told an anecdote that happened right after the All-Star Game in 1979 as the Expos were in Los Angeles. Valentine was scratched from the starting lineup and according to the team's official statement, he was suffering from some stomach ailments, which was farthest from the truth as any statement could be. When pushed by the writers, Expos trainer Yvon Belanger, after some hesitation, told them: "The real reason is that he is loaded! But keep it to yourselves!"[62] Warren Cromartie wrote in his autobiography *Slugging It Out in Japan* that Valentine smoked even on the team's bus (and it was not cigarettes).[63]

Dave Van Horne and Larry Parrish insisted that Ellis Valentine should have never gotten into drugs. Parrish remembered meeting Valentine's mother as they were both playing in Florida in the minors: "Actually, his mother came down, we were in the Florida State League and she stayed like a month down there and she would cook for us. At that time, you just could not see Ellis getting into the problems that he went through."[64] Said Dave Van Horne:

"Ellis would be the first one to tell you, he wasn't brought up that way, even though he was brought up in a very tough area. His mother was a very strong influence in his life, and kept him on the straight and narrow until he got away from home and got involved in baseball and unfortunately picked the wrong people to surround himself as far as friends are concerned."[65]

Ellis Valentine became very honest with what happened, with time. He would admit taking drugs, but still he was very proud of his accomplishments in baseball. Questioned about whether drugs was the main reason he failed to reach the level expected out of him, he pointed out the ball he got in his face that night in St. Louis on May 30, 1980. To him, that pitch from Roy Thomas was a more devastating blow than the drugs he took during his time in the majors, adding that he didn't think it was an accident.[66] Lots of people associated with the team at that period suspected that Valentine was under the effect of drugs when he was hit that night and thus couldn't react accordingly.[67] Confronted by these allegations, Valentine didn't deny it but was still upset over being singled out: "What difference does that make? Even if I would have been straight, do you think my body would have been drug-free? Other players like Dickie Thon and Art Howe were hit like I was and nobody questioned them. I would have appreciated if the Expos had taken care of me like the Orioles did with Gary Roenicke."[68] At the start of the 1979 season, Roenicke was hit in the face by an offering from Lerrin LaGrow, of the Chicago White Sox. Roenicke admitted that it took him a full year to get really comfortable again at the plate.[69] Valentine said he really felt alone after his face was shattered by the pitch in St. Louis. John McHale was at his side when he woke up at the hospital. Larry Parrish was one of the very few other members of the organization to pay him a visit, a gesture that Valentine never forgot.[70]

The Expos tried as they could to change Valentine's ways, to no avail. According to Serge Touchette, only two people could have some influence on him: his mother and John McHale.[71] Jim Bay would go as far as to say that McHale considered Valentine as almost his own son.[72] "I'd like to have a quarter for every day I talked to his mother about Ellis," said McHale.[73] Even with all his problems, Dick Williams persisted in penciling him fourth in the lineup, knowing full well that his team wasn't the same without him. Valentine knew that he was a player who could deliver when it really counted. "There were players who could get RBIs in blow-ups. I didn't care much in those games. But I was there when they really needed me," said Valentine, proudly.[74] He liked the attention of both the media and fans when things were going well, but he despised all the responsibilities that went with being a superstar, a fact confirmed by Larry Parrish: "I heard him say at different times, 'I don't want to be great, I just want to be good and be left alone!' When you think sometimes about the Tiger Woods of the world, the Michael Jordans and guys like that, they have not only the physical ability but also the mental ability to be much better than the others. To me, Valentine, that was the part he didn't have."[75]

Michel Lajeunesse, who covered the Expos for the French service of *Canadian Press*, would point out that despite his shortcomings Valentine was a very sound baseball player: "He was very accurate with his relays from the outfield and there was a reason for that. He had learned to play the right way in the minors. That's why that generation of players was so good. I met him many years later after his career was over and we were taking a look at Vladimir Guerrero. He told me, 'Look at him, he could be so much better. He has yet to learn and doesn't want to. I'd like to work just 30 minutes with him: he would learn some stuff.'" Lajeunesse added that Guerrero will probably end up in Cooperstown but will never know how to play the game correctly.[76]

Pierre Ladouceur, from *La Presse*, defended Valentine for years and was one of his fans. He thought the Expos should have understood and accepted that Valentine was going to give them 130 games per season. As for his nonchalant attitude, Ladouceur wasn't concerned one bit: "When I was playing juniors, we had a third baseman who took a lot of crap from opponents because of the way he carried himself, in a cocky way. He was the subject of taunts from opponents and fans. We were laughing at it, but once on the field, he performed."[77] The player was Ron Fournier, who would eventually become a National Hockey League referee before embarking on a successful broadcasting career in Montreal. Former major league pitcher Claude Raymond, who became a color analyst for the Expos for radio and TV in French, was also not overly concerned about Valentine's tardiness. "Who cares, as long as the player performs on the field?"[78] That statement was quite surprising, coming from someone whose respect for the game was infinite. In fact, Raymond had voiced that opinion as early as 1980 when he wrote his analysis for the coming season. He let it be known then that Valentine should be left alone and that the Expos would benefit from his contribution.[79]

Ellis Valentine never wanted to leave the Expos and Montreal.[80] Even if he had asked time and again to be sent elsewhere, they were words more akin to a teenager in search of more freedom who threatens to leave the house. Valentine treated life, and baseball, like a big playfield where one could and should enjoy every single moment. "He was a big kid," said Serge Touchette. "In that world of adults, he always had problems. He just liked to play, all the time. He liked to have fun and always had that big smile."[81] Maybe it is not surprising that Valentine was at his best with kids. He would go unannounced to visit kids in a hospital. In fact, in 1979, he bought $200 worth of Expos caps to distribute them to sick children, without the presence of any media.[82]

The fallout between Valentine and the Expos was hard for both parties. When John McHale announced the transaction, Serge Touchette said he never saw McHale that nervous: "We had the impression he had just traded a member of his family. He had always taken Valentine under his wing. He was very hard to control with a little rebellious side. I'll never forget the scene. McHale had a little cupboard glass with coffee and cognac. He was so nervous he pierced it. I still can see the cognac dripping on his nice black leather shoes. I'm sure it was a difficult moment for him."[83] As hard as it was, McHale admitted that it was inevitable, as he would say that the players didn't want him around anymore.[84] Valentine was obviously shaken. Twenty years later, he still thought he could have stayed in Montreal: "We could have found a way. It was not a matter of money."[85] When the transaction was announced, Valentine, even with his paltry .211 average and his horrible start, managed to get 15 RBIs in his last 16 games.

Valentine would never again be a major factor in baseball. He would leave the Mets after the 1982 season. About his time in New York, he would first say: "I hated every minute of it." He would point out thereafter that no matter where he would have been sent, his reaction would have been the same and that it had nothing to do with New York.[86] He then signed with the Angels before a brief stay with Texas in 1985, his last hurrah in the majors. In 1986, he decided to go to a rehabilitation center. Since then, he's been helping kids and families who were having problems of their own. In 2002, he was honored for his work at the annual gala of BAD (Baseballers Against Drugs).[87]

Life without Ellis Valentine began for the Expos with a 3–2 loss to the Pirates on May 30. Jeff Reardon pitched his first game with his new team and escaped the only inning he pitched unscathed, even with a runner on third with no outs. Reardon was in his second complete season in the majors. With the Mets, he was the second man in the bullpen, behind Neil Allen. He was a fastball pitcher and had considered himself at least the equal of Allen but couldn't prove his worth as a true closer.[88] This was something he was expected to do with the Expos, as the leader in saves at that point was Bill Lee, a pitcher whose profile didn't fit that of a number one relief man. But the Expos would have to wait a little to see more of Reardon, as he left the team to be with his ailing father. He would be back four days later, to the exasperation of Dick Williams.[89]

The Expos won the last game against the Pirates before an important four-game series in St. Louis. The standings in the NL East were close, with Philadelphia a half game up over the Expos, who were a half game in front of the Cards. Things looked rather well with Charlie Lea on the mound for the first game. Lea had just been named the pitcher of the month in May[90] but the Cards got the best of him. St. Louis won three out of four games, which left the Expos two games behind first place. Veteran Ray Burris was the only winner for the Expos. From St. Louis to Cincinnati, the Expos seemed unable to get the offense going, being limited to 11 hits in three games as they lost all three games. The only one to shake things up a little was Rodney Scott, when he was involved in an altercation with a waiter who refused to serve him a drink late at the hotel.[91] The Expos dropped further back to fourth place, as the Pirates went past them.

Ray Burris was doing a creditable job as the team's fourth starter. He was a keen observer of what was going on and couldn't help but express some concerns about the lack of preparation of some teammates when the team was on the road, an opinion shared by Woodie Fryman.[92] It was not very surprising to see these two agreeing about how the players should act off and on the field. They were always together on the road and their professionalism was exemplary. David Palmer recalled joining the duo in 1982: "Woodie Fryman took me under his wing my first day in the big leagues when I was 20 years old. He told me the dos and the don'ts; if you're 15 minutes early, you're late, that sort of things. And then the next year when I made the team, I lockered next to him. He just wouldn't let me complain about any of the little things. Like when I was walking in and said, 'How they can put that kind of socks in my locker.' He said, 'Just be happy to have a locker. Don't worry about the little things.' Woodie would go over the hitters with me, saying pitch to your strengths, not as much as to their weaknesses. Woodie taught me a lot about being a major league player, how to act on the field, off the field. Show up early and watch the other team take extra batting practice. And when Ray came over, he just kind of fit right in with me and Woodie and did the same things!"[93]

Another veteran, Stan Bahnsen, had another interesting observation about the way the Expos' batters were being handled. He thought they were too undisciplined and that was common knowledge throughout the league. He went farther, saying he would never throw a fastball if he had to pitch against the Expos.[94] Bahnsen had a valid point as very few Expos hitters were good at drawing walks, with the exception of Tim Raines.

Off the field, the Expos were going through some important changes. Harry Renaud, who had been the team financial adviser since the very first day of the franchise, was leaving to take charge of BC Place, a new indoor facility in Vancouver. Renaud had witnessed many changes since the first year in the business: "In 1969, Maury Wills became the first black player to get $100,000 a year and we had it publicized. The business has changed completely as we talk about millions of dollars." His departure had nothing to do with the on-going talks between owners and players. Renaud let it be known in December 1980 that he would leave. Expos owner Charles Bronfman told him that he would have been his first candidate to succeed John McHale as the team's general manager. "I didn't know baseball. I really enjoyed the environment but there was a lot that I didn't quite catch."[95] Just before leaving, the Expos had hired René Guimond to replace Roger D. Landry as the marketing director. Within days, he got more responsibilities and was elevated to the rank of vice president.[96]

More comfortable in Montreal, the Expos got back to business with convincing 12–1 and 11–2 wins over the Atlanta Braves. But those wins were second in the baseball news as Justice Henry Werker rejected the injunction request of the NLRB and ended his decision with a resounding "PLAY BALL!"[97] The owners applauded the outcome, but the players were quick to react: they would go on strike in two days, on June 12. As both parties had retained their respective positions for more than a year, it was quite unlikely that 48 hours would not be enough to curb a work stoppage. After an unspirited 7–0 win over the Braves, the players went on strike, the first time it happened in pro sports during a playing season.

Considering the importance the Expos had at the time in the sports landscape, not only in Montreal but throughout Canada, the void was huge locally and the media tried their best to fill the space, whether in the newspapers or on the airwaves. In *The Gazette*, Michael Farber and Red Fisher defended the players' and owners' positions, respectively[98] while Tim Burke published an open letter from an Expos part-owner, Sidney Maislin, to the attention of Steve Rogers,[99] who was heavily involved with the Players Association. The Expos' English flagship radio station carried for some time the games of the Denver Bears on its airwaves.[100]

Even if there was no breach among the players' ranks, many of them were affected. With the Expos, Bill Lee had to leave in the middle of the radio show hosted by Jeff Rimer.[101] Lee had always been passionate about the game and the strike couldn't happen at a worst time for him, as he was going through some rough times personally with his wife.[102] *La Presse* decided to publish old stories, like the first game of the Expos' history in 1969[103] or when Jean-Pierre Roy, a Quebecer who had a cup of coffee with Brooklyn in the 1940s, won his 25th game with the Montreal Royals in 1945[104] or Jackie Robinson's very first game with the Montreal Royals in Jersey City in 1946.[105] The newspapers tried their best to satisfy their readers' thirst for baseball, something the Expos had been cultivating for some years.

In the first week of July, Pierre Ladouceur wrote that the strike would end a month later, as soon as the last strike insurance payment from Lloyds of London would be make (it was due on August 8).[106] Ladouceur was right on the target as an agreement was announced on July 31 with a return date set for August 10. A total of 712 games were cancelled.[107] Both parties claimed victory, even though there would be no direct compensation for the loss of a free agent, but rather a pool of players like the one suggested by the players in the first place. That system would last only a couple of years when some teams lost players without being active in the free agent market, one of the most famous cases being that of Tom Seaver, selected by the Chicago White Sox from the Mets after losing Dennis Lamp to the Toronto Blue Jays!

After the settlement, teams had less than two weeks to get ready to resume the season. The Expos decided to gather their players not in Montreal but rather in West Palm Beach.[108] Right before the return to action, the All-Star Game was held in Cleveland. Three Expos players were there, Tim Raines, Andre Dawson and Gary Carter. The latter was named the player of the game when his two home runs led the National League to a 5–4 victory. It was a rather sloppy exhibition for an All-Star Game. Even American League manager Jim Frey looked rusty as he was left at the end of the game with no option but to let pitcher Dave Stieb bat in the ninth because nobody else was left on the bench.

There was still some debate as to how to handle the shortened season. At first, John McHale, a staunch defender of traditional baseball, was against a split-season format,[109] where the winner of the first half of the season (games played before the strike) would meet the winner of the second half (games played after the strike) in a Division Series to determine the teams to advance to the Championship Series. But most ballclubs bought into that idea, which had been used for years throughout the minors. The two most ferocious opponents were the St. Louis Cards and Cincinnati Reds, as both teams were close to the lead in their divisions at the time the strike interrupted the season.[110] Both would have to start from scratch. The American League voted overwhelmingly for the split-season format, but it was a lot closer in the National League, which needed nine votes out of twelve to get approval. With the Cards and Reds opposed, the opponents needed only two more votes to get this proposal overturned. The Phillies joined in but they couldn't get a fourth team to back them. John McHale had already voiced his opinion on the matter, but finally changed his mind when came time to vote, which proved to be crucial.[111]

The baseball conflict was over but another national labor strike was making headlines in the U.S. The 13,000 air controllers decided to go on strike on August 3. Two days later, President Ronald Reagan fired 11,350 of them (those who had refused an order to go back to work).[112] To show their solidarity, the Canadian air controllers decided to boycott some flights from the U.S. The four Pittsburgh Pirates who took part in the All-Star Game, Dave Parker, Bill Madlock, Phil Garner and Mike Easler, had to fly from Cleveland to Burlington, Vermont, before renting a car and driving an hour and a half to get to

Montreal.[113] The umpires would also be late and missed the first two games of the series.[114]

Those who thought that baseball fever would subside in Montreal after the strike were in for a big surprise: more than 70,000 people attended the first two games against the Pirates. Pitchers were limited to a set number of pitches as they were not deemed quite ready to go full steam after only a 10-day training camp. The Expos split both games, losing the second one after the bullpen blew a superb performance from Bill Gullickson, who had allowed only one hit in seven innings. The next two games opposed the same two teams, this time in Pittsburgh as the Expos prevailed both times.

The Expos were back in Montreal to face the Cards. Both teams were established favorites for the second half, with the Phillies already assured of a playoff spot by having won the first half of the season. But thanks to bad weather, they could manage to play only one game, a Cards 3–1 win with pitcher Joaquin Andujar, a notorious Expos killer, the winner. He was acquired right before the strike from the Houston Astros. The quality of his arm was acknowledged by most people, as was his famous temper. He was used as a swingman in Houston but with the Cards he was added in the rotation to stay.

After the Cards, the Expos entered a sequence where they faced Houston, Atlanta and Cincinnati for a combined 20 times in the next 21 days. First in Houston, the Expos won one out of three games before splitting the four games in Atlanta. Against the Braves, Jeff Reardon got his very first save with the Expos, which was the team's 22nd game since he became the closer. It was clear Dick Williams didn't have the utmost confidence in Reardon as his number one man in the bullpen.[115]

During that trip in the South, the Expos made two changes. First, they brought up Terry Francona from Denver.[116] He had been the team's number one draft choice in June 1980. Since then, he hadn't stopped hitting. In 1980 with Memphis, he hit .300. In 1981, he was even better, hitting .348 at Memphis and .352 in Denver. Francona was chosen the collegiate player of the year in 1980, an award Tim Wallach had won the year before. He was also named MVP of the College World Series, leading University of Arizona to the national title. The Expos had tried to modify his style, which was to make contact and use the whole field. The team's brass wanted him to swing more for power.[117] But given Francona's numbers, it was very hard to argue with his success. Second, after Francona's call-up, the Expos traded disgruntled Willie Montanez to the Pittsburgh for another first baseman, John Milner.[118] Montanez expected to play more but was used mostly as a pinch-hitter.

In Montreal against Cincinnati and Atlanta, the Expos had five straight wins when their pitchers allowed only four runs. The Expos were only one game back from the Cards. The Braves ended the Expos' streak on August 30 with a 5–4, 12-inning win. But the loss became irrelevant when Steve Rogers got hurt in the eleventh inning. Summoned from the bench as a pinch-runner for Gary Carter, Rogers injured himself in the ribs when he slid awkwardly into second base, trying to break up a double play after a grounder by Warren Cromartie.[119] The timing of the injury couldn't be worse as Charlie Lea was really struggling. In fact, he was nursing an inflammation in the right elbow and his season would be over in mid–September.[120] David Palmer, who had been with the team at the mini-camp following the strike, was sent home when it became obvious he wouldn't be able to help the team down the stretch.[121] It was not the first time Williams had used Rogers to run the bases. But the pressure began to mount around the Expos and the manager was criticized more and more. Rogers, who had his share of differences with his manager, defended the strategy, saying it was not the first time he was used on the basepaths.[122] What further fueled the speculation about Williams was the fact that he was in the last year of his contract. Seven games were to be played against Cincinnati and Houston before entering the final stretch against the Eastern Division foes. But they could do no better than winning two of them, being blanked twice. The tension was palpable. Against the Reds, Williams and Rodney Scott had a very heated exchange after the second baseman was removed for a pinch-hitter.[123]

With rosters expanded on September 1, the Expos acquired veteran lefty Grant Jackson from Pittsburgh. The Expos had their eyes on John Curtis but he refused to go to Montreal.[124] Two young pitchers were called up from the minors, Rick Engle and Tom Gorman. In Houston, the Expos released the founder of the BUS Squad, Tommy Hutton. He immediately retired and moved up to the broadcast booth.[125] More players were called up that day, including Wallace Johnson, Dave Hostetler and pitcher Bryn Smith.

Even with all their problems, the Expos were only two and a half games back from the Cards. And they could take care of business as the rest of the schedule was against NL East opponents, beginning with a three-game series in Philadelphia. The Expos split the first two games, but a story from respected UPI writer Milt Richman was making the rounds. According to Richman, Dick Williams had agreed to manage the Yankees in 1982.[126] Bob Elliott, who was covering the Expos for the *Ottawa Citizen*, was able to reach John McHale, who refused to comment.[127] The following morning, September 9, McHale announced the firing of Dick Williams and the appointment of Jim Fanning as the new manager.

After a little less than five seasons, Dick Williams was let go. In his autobiography *No More Mr. Nice Guy*, the often irascible manager said that McHale told him the rumors with the Yankees were the source of his firing.

Williams always denied having an agreement with the Yankees and, in fact, would never manage the Bronx Bombers.[128] To the media, McHale said that Williams took the news like someone who already had a contract with somebody else. He also pointed out the lack of communication between the manager and the players.[129] The real reason of course came down to the same old stuff: the Expos were simply not winning enough to the management's liking. Williams' firing was not that surprising. The real surprise was that Williams lasted that long at the helm of the team.

Williams and John McHale couldn't be more different, both professionally and personally. McHale was extremely conservative while Williams only cared about winning, no matter the means or how his players behaved or looked, as long as they were ready to play. It wouldn't be that far-fetched to compare the Williams-McHale tandem to Felix Unger and Oscar Madison from *The Odd Couple* sitcom fame! McHale confided in an interview that towards the end of Williams' tenure in Montreal, it became increasingly difficult to work with him: "Dick's style was different than mine and he was very difficult to get into a meeting to sit down and having a meaningful conversation about your ballclub. I always admired though what Dick had done. We had the kind of club that I thought needed more tender loving care than it needed more of a whip." He added that many players became malcontent. "Dick, by that time, had seemed to have come to the point where the players were so upset with him and the agents kept calling me about him. I guess we came to the conclusion that we were not going to win this thing if this continues. The central figure in of all of this scene, to be withholding a chance to win, was Dick. Dick was a very good baseball man, a very sound ability and background for winning but at this point, he just couldn't seem to take it over the top."[130] Owner Charles Bronfman agreed that Williams and McHale just didn't share the same values, baseball-wise.[131] Williams was convinced that he contributed to the growing of this group of players and that they could win on their own, no matter who the manager would be.[132]

It didn't take long for players to react and most who talked weren't very kind, to say the least. Stan Bahnsen, who had backed Williams in 1979, remarked that he never played for a manager who was that negative towards his pitchers.[133] Steve Rogers said that during spring training Williams would write on the board in the clubhouse the number of walks his team had just allowed after a game.[134] "He had no sympathy for pitchers," said Rogers.[135] Tim Wallach was in his first season and was not playing regularly and had few contacts with Williams, "except to blast me."[136] In New York, Rudy May expressed some worries when told about the rumors leading Williams to the Yankees: "If he comes here, I'm out of here!"[137] May obviously hadn't forgotten how he was used (or not used) in Montreal in his last season in 1979.

But some players were ready to give Williams credit for the team's success in the preceding two years. David Palmer considered him the best manager he played for: "When the game was going on, it just seemed like he always made the right move. It seems he always put the team in the best situation to win. Whitey Herzog was about the same way. And Dick was just great in putting us in a position to win."[138] Steve Rogers agreed: "Dick Williams, as far as the managing of the game, during the game, knowing and anticipating and positioning the team, whether with relievers, he was sometimes two, three, four, five hitters ahead of what was happening and I thought he was probably a good, if not the best, game manager that I've been around."[139]

Galen Cisco was his pitching coach in Montreal and would be so in San Diego. He was another one who praised Williams' savvy: "I learned a lot from him and all he wanted to do was win. That was his personality, there's all different kind of managers but that was Dick's personality and that was a part of the reason why I think he was such a successful manager. The players didn't like him, but I think after they played for him for a while, they appreciated him a little more afterwards. My take on Dick Williams was a guy that really wanted to win."[140]

If Williams' firing was not such a surprise, the name of his successor was: Jim Fanning. *Sports Illustrated* even sent a writer (Steve Wulf) to Philadelphia to see what was going on.[141] The move was not however without precedent. Towards the end of the 1979 season, the Phillies installed Dallas Green as manager. He was basically the Jim Fanning of the Phillies at that point, overseeing the player development department. Fanning hadn't managed for almost 15 years, never in the majors. But Fanning had been John McHale's right-hand man since the birth of the Expos' franchise. Fanning never refused anything for McHale but contrary to Dallas Green in 1979, Fanning and the Expos still had a legitimate chance to make the playoffs. But Fanning had less than four weeks to do so and catch up to the Cards. His debut was non-spectacular as he lost his first two games, 11–8 in Philadelphia and 6–5 in Chicago, where he used 18 and 21 players, respectively, unlike Dick Williams who trusted his veteran players a lot more. Rodney Scott and Warren Cromartie were quick to complain about the new manager's way, especially where they were directly involved. "He can go to hell," said Scott.[142] "I have no respect for him," added Cromartie.[143]

Fanning earned his first managerial win as Steve Rogers, in his first game since his rib injury, threw a three-hit shutout at Wrigley Field. Larry Parrish hit a home run in the sixth inning, his fifth in the second half — he had only two before the strike — and was showing some kind of return to form. The day after, he drove in three more runs with two hits, including a double in a 10–6 win. But in that victory, Tim Raines broke his right hand when he slid at home plate in the fifth inning.[144] His absence was indefinite but it was certain that he wouldn't be able to face the Cards in the all-important five-game series at Olympic Stadium. The Cards were still ahead in the NL East standings, with a two and a half games lead. Two double-headers were scheduled on September 15 and 16 and both were split, with the Expos winning the second game each time. Bill Lee was called to pitch the second game of the series and managed to get his third win of the campaign after a one-run seven-inning effort.

The Expos were on the brink of being swept in the second twin bill. After losing the first game, 7–1, Charlie

Jim Fanning was never able to garner the respect of his players during his time as Expos manager. Yet he's the only man to skip Montreal to a post-season berth.

Lea was removed in the first inning after allowing three runs. It was still 3–0 in the seventh when the Expos got to Lary Sorensen for one run and then Bruce Sutter for two more to tie the Cards at three. The Expos won it in the 11th on an RBI single by Larry Parrish. After the first four games, it was the status quo and the fifth one looked as if it would be a very important one. But the Cards, thanks to a five-run third inning, ran away with the game for a 7–4 triumph and more importantly, a three and a half game lead with only two and a half weeks to go. Jean Aucoin wrote in *La Presse* that the season was over, as far as the Expos and post season were concerned.[145]

But the Expos refused to let it go. After splitting the next two games against the Cubs, they embarked on a seven-game winning streak, that was launched by a spectacular 17-inning, 1–0 triumph, against the Phillies. Steve Carlton and Ray Burris both threw scoreless ball for ten innings, allowing three hits. Both teams had plenty of chances to score in extra innings. Stan Bahnsen threw two and two-thirds innings and allowed a hit and four walks but miraculously escaped unscathed, thanks to three runners caught stealing in the 15th and 16th innings. Andre Dawson ended that marathon with a walk-off RBI single against rookie Jerry Reed. Bryn Smith got his first major league victory, but he was no ordinary rookie. At 26, he was older than most rookies and had been in the minors since 1975. In 1981, he had just completed his first complete season in AAA, leading Denver with 15 wins and more important, a 3.05 ERA, which was very impressive in Colorado.

As the Expos were getting back to business, the Cards inexplicably went into a tailspin, losing seven of their next eight games, mostly against teams they should have handled, mainly the Mets and the Cubs. They finally won twice in a row against Pittsburgh to set up a final two-game showdown against the Expos at Busch Stadium the last week of the season, beginning Monday September 28, with the Expos in the driver's seat, with a one and a half game lead. But again, the Expos faltered miserably in a crucial time, losing both times, 6–2 and 8–4. Scott Sanderson and Bill Lee, the two starters, allowed a combined ten earned runs in six innings.

Both teams still had five games before the end of the season, all on the road. The Expos would play twice in Pittsburgh and three times in New York. The Cards would go to Philadelphia and Pittsburgh, respectively. The Expos won both games in Pittsburgh while the Cards could only split with the Phillies, allowing the Expos to take the lead. Cards manager Whitey Herzog could only scratch his head as his team couldn't take advantage of the young-sters on the mound for the Phillies throwing against his team. In September, Dickie Noles, Mark Davis, Dan Larsen and Mike Proly started games against St. Louis, with the Cards being able to win only one of those. In fact, Herzog was wondering whether the Phillies wanted to face the Cards more than the Expos in the playoffs.[146]

The stage was set for the final weekend of the season. Steve Rogers was scheduled to start the first game against the Mets against Pat Zachry. Warren Cromartie gave the Expos a 1–0 lead with a home run in the third inning. That was enough for Rogers, who threw a real gem with a two-hit shutout in a 3–0 win. Cromartie had missed the last two games with an ankle injury but he was a big reason for the team's surge. Since taking over the leadoff spot from Tim Raines on September 18, Cromartie, who had the reputation of swinging at everything within the area code, had literally transformed himself. In 12 games, he accumulated 21 hits and 11 walks for a .467 batting average and an astronomical .571 on-base percentage.[147] The Cards lost that night, 8–7, in Pittsburgh as the Pirates scored the winning run in the bottom of the ninth off Bruce Sutter. The Expos would need one more win to assure themselves a place in the playoffs.

On Saturday, October 3, Scott Sanderson was facing the Mets but couldn't go past the third inning. In the opening frame, he held the Mets scoreless, even though he allowed a single and a walk. In the second, the Mets took a

1–0 lead and added two more runs in the third before Bryn Smith took over. The Expos got on board in the fifth after an RBI grounder by Brad Mills. The Expos got another run back in the sixth with Gary Carter's home run. In the seventh, manager Joe Torre decided to go with his closer, Neil Allen. Terry Francona led off, reaching first base on shortstop Frank Taveras's error. With one out, John Milner was walked and was replaced by pinch-runner Rodney Scott, who was sidelined due to an injury.

Bill Lee was due next to bat. Everybody expected a pinch-hitter but to the surprise of most, rookie switch-hitter Wallace Johnson was summoned to the plate. Johnson had been a sixth round draft choice in 1979 and thus never got the publicity of those who were picked earlier in the annual amateur draft. But since then, he did nothing but hit, everywhere he was sent in the Expos' minor league system. In 1980, he won the Florida State League batting championship with a .334 batting average. He could also draw walks with 61. In 1981, he was destroying AA pitching with a .363 average when he was moved up to Denver, where he hit .298 before his call-up to the Expos. Allen was used to high-pressure situations as the Mets' number one reliever. Johnson could see that Allen was trying to intimidate him with his fastballs.[148] But with two strikes, Johnson got good wood on a pitch and hit the ball solidly to right-center field. Neither center fielder Lee Mazzilli, who was playing Johnson a little to the left, nor right fielder Ellis Valentine, was close to the ball as it made its way to the fence, allowing Jerry Manuel (who had reached on a fielder's choice) and Scott to score and Johnson to reach third with a two-run triple that gave the Expos the lead for the first time that afternoon. Johnson was clapping his hands as he got up to third base.[149]

Johnson's September call-up was probably the most unexpected with the Expos. As Johnson recalled: "Because I didn't get to Denver in AAA until probably past the half way point, there were guys who had been there all season, like Danny Briggs, and guys like that. At that point of time in my career, we're trying to win, we were trying to win a championship that year, under Felipe Alou in Denver. Just playing on a championship team was really awesome. And the icing on the cake was a bunch of the guys being called up in September." Manager Jim Fanning knew all the players in the Expos' system, which helped, according to Johnson. "I think it was definitely an advantage because Mr. Fanning had basically saw me come up through the ranks. We never really had long conversations but, having been the farm director, he knew the players in the minor leagues and what they could do, probably more than the reports that major league managers probably got and those kinds of things. I think that didn't hurt."[150]

In the eighth, the Expos added a much-needed insurance run on Jerry Manuel's double against Allen. The Mets scored once in the eighth with Mike

Cubbage's home run off Jeff Reardon. The Expos went scoreless in the ninth and they were only three outs from reaching the postseason. Reardon got the first two batters easily, Mike Jorgensen on a pop-up and Hubie Brooks on an infield grounder. Dave Kingman was the last man standing between the Expos and the postseason. Kingman, even though his batting average was traditionally among the lowest among everyday players, was the last hitter a team would like to see at the plate in such a situation, as he was also one of the most dangerous home run threats in baseball. But Reardon prevailed, inducing Kingman to hit a soft fly ball to left that Terry Francona caught running. The Expos lost a meaningless game to the Mets on Sunday with Dave Hostetler being the only point of interest, as he hit his first career home run, a shot that landed over the bullpen behind left field.[151]

The Expos benefited of course from some particular circumstances to reach the playoffs, especially with the split-season format. As the winner of the second half in the NL East, the Expos were slated to play Philadelphia (the first half winner) in a Division Series to determine the NL East champion. In fact, both the St. Louis Cardinals and the Cincinnati Reds were crying out foul, as they were out of the postseason even with the best record in their own division for the whole season, with the Reds showing the best overall record in all of baseball. Even Red Fisher in the *Montreal Gazette* voiced his displeasure about the outcome.[152] But the rules were known right from the moment play resumed in August and honestly, the Cards had only themselves to blame, as they failed miserably against teams they had no business losing against, even though they handled the Expos almost at will in September.

With the Expos, some veterans upped their game a notch after the strike. Larry Parrish was the team's Player of the Month, with a .295 average, a .500 slugging percentage and 25 RBIs in 31 games, including some very important ones down the stretch. It was not by chance that Parrish was able to deliver at that particular time; the wrist wasn't bothering him anymore: "I came back in 1981 and it was still bothering. I went to see a doctor up in San Francisco. He looked at it and said, 'I won't touch you, I won't operate on you. If you were an accountant I would.' And I go on, 'If I was accountant I wouldn't need an operation. The only time it hurts is when I try to swing a bat.' He said, 'I can't guarantee that if I operate on it, I can fix it.' I said, 'What am I going to do?' He said, 'You have to learn to play with it or think about retiring.' And right about then, the strike came. It didn't help anybody else but maybe me! I went home at that time and didn't know if my career was over. Because I just couldn't perform anymore. During that time we had off, I swung a hammer every day and had calluses at that time and I had to rebuild some stuff at home. And when I came back after the strike was over, it never bothered me again the rest of my career. And when I came back, I swung the bat! I was back! Back to where I was."[153]

Warren Cromartie also was a big contributor to the team's success: "I always wanted to lead off because Pete Rose was one of my idols and always leading off, and the leadoff hitters always get things going, set the tempo for the rest of the team. The guy who makes the pitcher work a little bit more, the guy who comes back to the dugout and relays the message to the other guys, what he's throwing, how hard he is throwing. You get the chance to be the first one to score, the first one to get a hit. Just like playing first base, the last one to make an out, always in the middle of things, always catching the ball. Leadoff was a dream of mine, leading off in the majors."[154]

As was the case in 1980, catcher Gary Carter didn't benefit from any break in the last five weeks of the season. Offensively, he drove in 38 runs in 50 games in the second half, while being outstanding defensively. Andre Dawson became what was considered then the most complete player in the majors. He slowed down some in September but still managed to drive in 17 runs. Pitchers began to fear him a little more, as he got 13 walks in September, a very high number for Dawson. He finished the season among the leaders in many offensive categories, including batting average, total bases, home runs, RBIs, and runs. His defensive excellence was also acknowledged by everybody and he was immensely respected by his peers, both for the quality of his game as for his professionalism.[155]

On the mound, the Expos were able to count on a very consistent quartet of Steve Rogers, Bill Gullickson, Ray Burris and Scott Sanderson. Among them, only Sanderson had problems towards the end of the season. Rogers led the group with 12 wins, but the other three could have had more than their 25 combined wins with better luck and better offensive support, as they all had ERA around 3.00.

In the bullpen, Jeff Reardon was the main beneficiary of Dick Williams' firing. Reardon never had Williams' confidence and the bearded reliever wouldn't hide his disdain for his former manager.[156] But in September and October, Reardon allowed only 14 hits in 28 and one-third innings with a 1.27 ERA. Fanning used him 14 times in September, while Williams had called on Reardon only seven times in the three weeks of August.

John McHale, against all odds, had gambled and won when he picked Jim Fanning to replace Dick Williams, even though many people had scratched their heads when the change was announced. Fanning didn't refrain from making unpopular decisions, even though some of them might have looked irrational. But since winning was the ultimate goal, both men could boast, "Mission accomplished!" It was however far from over, as there was still some real baseball to be played in 1981: Expos, welcome to the postseason!

7

1981: Post-Season

When the Expos made their way back to Montreal from New York after concluding the regular season, there were more than 10,000 fans waiting for them at the Dorval Airport, more people than had ever greeted the famous Montreal Canadiens of the National Hockey League.[1] In fact, the Canadiens were beginning their season in almost total obscurity, which was enhanced by Team Canada being humiliated, 8–1, by the Soviet Union in the final of the Canada Cup in mid–September at the Montreal Forum. The attention sports-wise was thus turned almost exclusively towards the Montreal Expos in their first-ever postseason appearance.

The Expos faced the Philadelphia Phillies in a best-of-five Divisional Series, with the first two games played in Montreal. The Phillies had basically the same team that had won the World Series in 1980, with the exception of left fielder Gary Matthews, replacing Greg Luzinski. Pete Rose had a season of revival in 1981, leading the National League with 140 hits with a .325 batting average. He had overtaken the Stan Musial atop the all-time National League hit list in August. But the most dangerous threat remained Mike Schmidt. He led the National League with 31 home runs, 78 runs, 91 RBIs, 73 walks, in slugging percentage and on-base percentage. While Andre Dawson was deemed by many as the most complete player,[2] Schmidt was by far the best hitter in baseball. On the mound, Steve Carlton and Dick Ruthven remained the workhorses among the starting pitchers with 13 and 12 wins, respectively, although Ruthven's ERA was somewhat high at 5.15. No other starting pitcher won more than four games during the season. Tug McGraw was again the main reliever from the bullpen.

Weather was rather cold in Montreal in early October 1981, even by Canadian and Quebec standards.[3] The Phillies weren't very happy with these conditions, especially Mike Schmidt.[4] The first game featured the pitching aces from both teams, Steve Rogers and Steve Carlton. They had faced each other 13 times in their career at that point and both pitchers showed identical records, five wins and five losses. They first met on July 26, 1973, in Rogers' second career start. The Expos' rookie then pitched a complete-game one-hit shutout.[5] He had no complex whatsoever against the tall lefty. Carlton was considered among the elite pitchers in baseball. But he seemed to have his share of problems against the Expos, who were loaded with right-handed batters. Since 1977, Carlton had won only five of his 12 decisions, even though his ERA wasn't that bad at 3.13. It was still off what he compiled overall in that same period, with a 94–47 record and 2.77 ERA.

The Expos had to make changes on the roster, thanks to injuries to Tim Raines and Rodney Scott. Wallace Johnson and Tom Gorman were kept, while Jerry Manuel would play at second base. The first postseason major-league baseball game ever outside the U.S. was played Wednesday, October 7, at Olympic Stadium. Some 34,000 showed up in spite of the frigid weather. A local female teenager, who was garnering some attention locally, sang the national anthem. Her name: Céline Dion.[6]

The very first batter was Lonnie Smith and he got on board with a single, but was erased when Pete Rose hit into a double play. Gary Matthews and Mike Schmidt followed with a triple and a walk, but Rogers struck out Bake McBride to end the threat. The Expos scored first when Warren Cromartie, an on-base machine since mid–September, hit an opposite-field single; after a fielder's choice, Jerry White stole second and scored on Gary Carter's double after two outs. Keith Moreland tied the game when he led off the top of the second with a home run. Up to that point, Rogers had only been able to retire two of the first six batters. The Expos took the lead again in the second on consecutive doubles by Tim Wallach and Chris Speier. The shortstop had been horrible in the second half of the season with a .185 average and only seven RBIs. Speier scored the team's third run in the third after a walk, a sacrifice and another hit by Cromartie. In the fifth and seventh innings, Andre Dawson reached third base with nobody out but was left stranded there each time. But these runs were not necessary as Rogers was holding the Phillies to a single run. In the ninth, he had retired the previous 12 batters when he allowed two-out singles to Moreland and George Vukovich. Jeff Reardon got the third out, not without trouble as Manny Trillo lined out to left fielder Terry Francona to end the game.

The second game was played at night and featured Bill Gullickson and Dick Ruthven on the mound. Gullickson had been the most consistent starter in 1981. He allowed more than three earned runs only twice in the season, both times in May. His ERA since the strike was only 2.09. His seven wins were not indicative by any means of his real effectiveness. Ruthven, quite the contrary, had taken advantage of some solid offensive support to notch 12 victories. Ruthven's ERA in the second half ballooned to 6.75! True, the

Phillies had nothing to gain in the last two months of the season, as they had clinched a playoff spot by winning the first half of the season, but there was still reason for concern.

The Expos broke first with an RBI single by Speier. The Expos could do no more damage when both Jerry Manuel and Bill Gullickson were retired with runners on the corners. In the third, the Expos added two runs. Cromartie led off with a double and after two outs, Gary Carter hit the first Expos home run in postseason history. Gullickson held the Phillies scoreless until the eighth when Lonnie Smith tagged him for a two-out double, followed by an RBI single by Pete Rose and another double by Bake McBride. Rose stopped at third base as Mike Schmidt was the next batter. Jeff Reardon was summoned from the bullpen and he gave Schmidt a free pass, loading the bases, a risky move as he represented the go-ahead run. But Reardon prevailed by retiring Gary Matthews on an infield pop-up. Reardon got the Phillies in order in the ninth for a second consecutive Expos 3–1 triumph. All that was left to do was win one in Philadelphia, on the road where the Expos were a lot more vulnerable than at home, and the Expos would be NL East champs.

There was no off-day between Game 2 and Game 3 and, not only that, Game 3 was played in the afternoon after a night game in a different city. Larry Christenson was the starting pitcher for the Phillies, a surprise since he hadn't started once since August 24. But in relief, since September 19, he had allowed only one run in 12 innings. He could be a tough customer on the mound, especially against a predominantly right-handed lineup like that of the Expos.

In the second inning, the Expos took a 1–0 lead after another clutch hit by Chris Speier. But that would be the only moment of celebration for the Expos as they played one of their sloppiest games in recent weeks, with four errors in a 6–2 loss, Ray Burris being the loser. The Expos had a second chance to clinch the NL East title on Saturday afternoon in Game 4 with Scott Sanderson. But in his last two starts, both on the road, he pitched a combined six and one-third innings, which was cause for concern. Sanderson's performances at home and on the road mirrored that of his own team. At the Big O, the tall righty won eight times with a 1.74 ERA, but he could do no better than a 5.85 ERA on the road, with only one win. 1981 was not an exception as his home career ERA was 1.97 at that point, and 4.45 on the road.[7] Dickie Noles, his opponent, joined the rotation at the end of August and did a creditable job with a 3.15 ERA in eight starts. Sanderson did nothing to reassure Expos fans, allowing two runs in the first inning on Mike Schmidt's home run. In the third, Fanning decided to remove Sanderson after two outs and runners in scoring position. Stan Bahnsen allowed these runners to cross the plate on Keith Moreland's single, doubling the Phillies' lead to 4–0.

The Expos celebrate a victory on the turf at Olympic Stadium on their way to winning the NL East Division Series during the strike-shortened 1981 season (Archives Nationales du Québec).

The Expos scored their first run in the fourth on Gary Carter's home run. They scored another run in the fifth but could have inflicted a lot more damage as they had the bases loaded with nobody out. In the sixth, Fanning played the right cards as pinch-hitters John Milner and Wallace Johnson each drove in runs with singles to tie the game at four. Gary Matthews got the lead back for the Phillies with a home run against Woodie Fryman in the sixth, but again the resilient Expos evened things up on a Gary Carter double that scored Jerry White. In the bottom of the seventh, Garry Maddox reached third base with one out, but Jeff Reardon retired Mike Schmidt and Gary Matthews to keep the score tied. Nobody reached base on either side in the 8th and 9th innings. In the 10th against Tug McGraw, Gary Carter led off with a single, but Larry Parrish, who was trying to bunt his teammate to second, hit into a double play. Fanning kept Reardon, the third batter of the inning, in the game and he struck out. In the 10th, George Vukovich, who had three hits in four at-bats in the series, put an end to the hostilities with a solid liner that barely made it over the right-field fence for a walk-off home run for a 7–6 win. Up to that point, Reardon had only allowed one baserunner to reach base among the 13 batters he faced, and that was an intentional walk to Mike Schmidt in the second game.

The stage was set for a second showdown between the two Steves, Rogers and Carlton in Game 5. The Phillies looked as if they had the edge, as they were playing at home and as Carlton was used to playoff pressure, having won the World Series with St. Louis in 1967 and Philadelphia in 1980. As for Rogers, it was his first experience in postseason. After the first game, he didn't change anything about his routine, as if he was going to pitch on Sunday.[8] It was not the first time he would show that control over himself in moments like these. Bill Stoneman was his roommate when Rogers made his debut in the majors in 1973. Stoneman said that Rogers had no problems dealing with the demands of the media in his rookie season, even on days he pitched, and there were lots of them as he went on to win ten games with a minuscule 1.54 ERA. Stoneman had to be fully concentrated when he was starting. "But Rogers was able to manage all the media attention," remembered Stoneman.[9] Rogers explained that his time as a pitcher with the University of Tulsa prepared him to face the pressure: "In my college career, I was very fortunate to have played on the baseball teams at the University of Tulsa, as two of those years we went to the College World Series. We played for the national championship, we were eliminated in the championship game, came in second in the nation, and then we were eliminated in a semi-final game two years later to come in third. Nonetheless, I had been afforded the opportunity to pitch in some very big games and to be part of a media setting that I dealt with in college."[10] Rogers was named the tournament's best pitcher in 1971. If Rogers took the means to get prepared for the biggest game of his life, he still had to shake that reputation of somebody who couldn't win the big one, a reputation that was no doubt fueled many times by Dick Williams. In his last four starts, Rogers' ERA was 1.09 and was partly able to get rid of that label. But a bad performance in Game 5 would surely trigger the same comments.

The Phillies had to cope with some unwelcomed rumors: Dallas Green was said to be ready to leave the Phillies after the season to join the Chicago Cubs.[11] In two seasons as the team's manager, he had led the Phillies to a World Series title and another postseason berth. Green had always felt comfortable with the Phillies and was considered as their heir apparent to GM Paul Owens. But after the 1980 World Series conquest, the team owners, the Carpenter family, decided to sell the team as the game's landscape was changing fast, most notably with player free agency.[12]

For the moment, Green was the Phillies' manager and he inserted George Vukovich in the lineup, hitting him third, replacing Bake McBride in right field. In the first inning, Carlton struck out the side. Rogers allowed two singles but the Phillies couldn't capitalize. In the fourth inning, Gary Matthews tried to score from first after a single by Manny Trillo but was easily thrown out at the plate.

In the fifth, Carlton got into some trouble as Larry Parrish led off with a single and Tim Wallach followed with a walk. Chris Speier hit into a force-out before Jerry Manuel loaded the bases with another walk. There was only one out but the next two batters were pitcher Steve Rogers and Warren Cromartie, a lefty hitter. Even though Rogers was a pretty good athlete (he did some running in track and field),[13] hitting in the majors was not something in which he had proven anything. His batting average was .138, even below that of an average pitcher. But Carlton threw a slider that was too much to the liking of Rogers, whose solid grounder went between second baseman Manny Trillo and shortstop Larry Bowa.[14] Two runners came in to score and the Expos were leading for the first time since the third inning of Game 3.

In the sixth, the Expos added a third run when Andre Dawson scored on a double by Larry Parrish, who was thrown out at third trying to stretch the hit to a triple. In the bottom of the sixth, the Phillies at last threatened. Lonnie Smith and Pete Rose reached base via a single and a walk leading off and Rogers would have to face red-hot George Vukovich and Mike Schmidt. Vukovich was handcuffed and Rogers had a perfect double-play ball but Speier's relay to first was not on target and Schmidt came up as the tying run. In Game 2, the Expos gave Schmidt a free pass when he came to the plate as the tying run late in the game, but this time Fanning let Rogers pitch to Schmidt, who had put an end to the Expos' hopes in 1980 with a home run in extra-innings against Stan Bahnsen. But this time, Rogers and the Expos won big, as Schmidt hit into an inning-ending double play that, this time, was executed perfectly.

The Phillies put one runner on base in both the 7th and 8th innings to no avail. In the 9th, Rogers was set to face Mike Schmidt, Gary Matthews and Manny Trillo. The first two batters were retired on fly balls to the outfield. Manny Trillo ended the Division Series with a liner that was caught by first baseman Warren Cromartie. In their 12th season, the Expos were now the NL East champions and headed to the NL Championship Series.

That performance from Steve Rogers shut many people up, those who still doubted his guts in important games and under pressure. Rogers had heard enough about these critics and when the first question at the press conference following his shutout of the Phillies was about his bad reputation in big games, Rogers snapped back: "Next question!"[15] Some people believed that Rogers' direct involvement in the conflict between the players and owners made him mature, a theory he wasn't ready to accept. "I guess it did give me the education of being stonewalled, being forced into a corner that you really have no way to get out of, and through no fault of your own," he would say. But as was the case with Larry Parrish, Rogers was a major beneficiary of the time off the strike provided the players. "My last start before the strike, my shoulder was bothering me. I had some shoulder problems. Then, I had 50 days off. Entering the second half, as everybody was getting in shape, the shoulder felt fine. Instead of going into August 1 with 175–200 innings pitched, I went into August 1 with 100 innings pitched. I just had so many fewer innings pitched to that point that I never hit that wall in August and in September. I was as strong as an ox. That being said, I was strong in August and September. I wasn't fighting the fatigue factor of having pitched 250 innings going into September. All those things said, I did pitch the best baseball of my career in that second half but it was as much about being strong as about anything. And it just had to be that was September and October at that time because we had a split season. I guess, people can put whatever spin they want on it but I know from a physical standpoint, I was just ten times stronger in the months August in September than I had been in any other year because of the number of innings pitched."[16]

As for the Phillies, in the next few days, Dallas Green would indeed leave the Phillies to become the Cubs' new GM.[17]

The best-of-five NL Championship Series saw the Expos face the Los Angeles Dodgers, who had just defeated the Houston Astros for the NL West title after losing the first two games. That series featured high-caliber pitching, especially from the Dodgers who limited Houston to a meager six runs in five games. The Dodgers had lots in common with the 1980 Phillies. They had had powerful teams for some years but had yet to win the World Series, falling short all three times they represented the National League in the 1970s (1974, 1977 and 1978). In 1980, they finished tied with the Astros for first place but lost a one-game playoff. Like the Phillies, it looked as if the window of opportunity was passing by without a title to show for it. Since the team moved to Dodger Stadium in the early 1960s, the Dodgers had featured several high-quality pitchers and with good reason: their scouting had always been good and the ballpark was really kind to pitchers.[18] In 1981, Fernando Valenzuela was the main attraction among the Dodgers' pitching staff, but Jerry Reuss, Burt Hooton and Bob Welch were a very solid backup crew. In the playoffs, manager Tommy Lasorda decided to go with three starters, leaving Welch in the bullpen. For almost a decade, the Dodgers had featured the same four regulars in the infield: Steve Garvey, Davey Lopes, Bill Russell and Ron Cey. Cey, injured in early September after being hit by a pitch, was due to be back against the Expos after missing the Divisional Series against the Astros. The Expos could count on the return of both their speedsters, Tim Raines and Rodney Scott. Wallace Johnson and Tom Gorman were left off the roster.

The first two games were played in Los Angeles, where the Expos seemed to always find ways to lose. In their last 19 games at Dodger Stadium, the Expos had won only once, dating back to July 1979. Since then, they had lost nine in a row there. Bill Gullickson had the first game assignment on the mound for Montreal against solid but unheralded Burt Hooton. Hooton, whose outpitch was a knuckle curve, had always played in the shadow of fellow Dodgers Don Sutton, Tommy John and, in 1981, Fernando Valenzuela. In 1981, his ERA was 2.28, even better than his Mexican teammate. His eleven wins were second on the staff.

The Expos got runners on base in each of the first two innings but were erased both times on double plays. In the bottom of the second, the Dodgers scored first on a double by Ron Cey in his very first at-bat in more than a month and a successful squeeze bunt by Bill Russell. That's the only inning in which Gullickson would give in to the Dodgers in his seven innings of work. The Expos in the meantime just couldn't pull it off against Hooton, even though they had runners on base in every inning. Of course, hitting into three double plays didn't help! Jeff Reardon came in the eighth but was tagged for three runs after two outs on successive home runs by Pedro Guerrero and Mike Scioscia. The Expos scored once in the ninth on a double by Larry Parrish but after another hit, a single, Chris Speier ended the game by hitting into the team's fourth double play of the afternoon.

The situation looked grim for the Expos, as they were facing the real possibility of going back home two games behind. They would have to cope with Fernando Valenzuela in Game 2. In twelve home starts, his ERA was 1.57 with seven wins, including five shutouts. In two games against the Expos, in 18 innings, he had allowed only eight hits, one walk and three runs. His opponent was veteran Ray Burris. He had been a solid and consistent performer in 1981, with nine wins and a 3.05 ERA, which was remarkable given that he started 13 of his 21 games on the road. Down the stretch, he won six out of eight decisions, which didn't include his masterful 10-inning performance on September 21 against Steve Carlton.[19] Even with Burris' solid 1981 pedigree, nobody thought he had a chance against Valenzuela and everything seemed to lean towards the Dodgers.

Tim Raines hit a leadoff single but was picked off by the Valenzuela. In the second inning, after one out, Larry Parrish and Jerry White hit successive singles before Warren Cromartie doubled in one run. White had to stay on third. Chris Speier was walked, loading the bases. After Burris struck out, Raines drove in a second run with a single but Cromartie was thrown out at home. The Expos were leading, 2–0. As Burris was taking care of his business on the mound, the Expos scored once more in the sixth when Andre Dawson scored from first on a single by Gary Carter, combined with a Dusty Baker fielding error. In the seventh, the Expos had two runners in scoring position with one out, but just weren't able to push them across. In the bottom of the ninth, Burris ran into some trouble after one out when Steve Garvey hit a single and Ron Cey reached on an error by Chris Speier. Pedro Guerrero, a dangerous batter, was coming to the plate as the tying run. But his liner was caught by Speier whose relay to second doubled up Garvey, ending a 10-game losing streak at Dodger Stadium and allowing the Expos to return home with the NLCS tied at one game apiece.

In one start, Burris became an instant hero in Montreal. When he signed for one year days prior to spring training, he was viewed as an insurance policy and nothing more, given the uncertainty surrounding David Palmer's elbow.[20] Burris had a solid camp and won himself a spot in the rotation. He couldn't choose a better moment to pitch the game of his life. When asked if that performance was the highlight of his career, his answer might surprise lots of people: "I wouldn't consider it the highest point of my career. I would consider it a point in my career. It was a chance for me to show people I could perform in that arena at the highest level of what a lot of people consider pressure. Because pressure is everything in the Championship Series. Going to the World Series, that's the highest you can go, there is no other level to be. I knew what I could do. I accepted and enjoyed that opportunity and that was an opportunity that every player loves to have, and that's to get to the playoffs. There are even some great players who never got to the playoffs, or World Series, like Ernie Banks, with all the great years he had with the Cubs." Very early in his career, Burris was confronted with lots of pressure. After being picked in the 17th round in the 1972 draft, he was sent directly to AA, which was quite unusual for someone chosen that low. But the Cubs liked that he threw strikes. In 1973, he made his major league debut. As a tall African American, the comparisons with future Hall of Famer Ferguson Jenkins were almost immediate. Burris insisted that he wasn't hurt by the comparison. In 1975, he joined the Cubs' starting rotation and would win 44 games in the following three seasons. In 1981, the pitcher who was considered more of a journeyman could at last enjoy some recognition from the baseball world.[21]

After a day off when teams traveled from California to Montreal, the players prepared for a radical weather change. The *Los Angeles Herald Examiner* wrote on the front page "From Burris to B-R-R-R!"[22] Steve Rogers and Jerry Reuss were the pitchers scheduled for Game 3. Rogers was in the best form of his career but Reuss was also hot. The blond lefty had allowed only one run in his last 27 innings and in the series against the Astros he blanked them in 18 innings. Against the Expos, Reuss had had some success with 14 wins against five losses. It wasn't the first time Rogers and Reuss were opponents in a championship game. Fourteen years earlier, in 1967, Rogers, from Glendale High School, started the semi-finals of Missouri state championship against Reuss, from Ritenour. Reuss led his team to the final.[23]

With these two red-hot hurlers, no one expected any offensive fireworks.

In the first three innings, both teams were limited to three hits combined. The Dodgers led off the fourth with singles by Steve Garvey and Dusty Baker. Rogers retired the next three batters but nonetheless the Dodgers scored on a groundout by Ron Cey. Reuss looked to be in a zone, allowing only three singles in the first five innings, extending his scoreless streak to 23 innings. He began the bottom of the sixth by retiring Tim Raines and Rodney Scott before Andre Dawson tagged him for a single. Gary Carter followed with a walk, the first free pass in the game by either pitcher. Dawson came in to score and tie the game on Larry Parrish's single. Then came Jerry White, a switch-hitter. In that series so far, he had hit the ball with authority, with three hits, including a double, in nine at-bats with a walk, after a season-ending slump that saw him getting only five hits in his last 36 at-bats for a paltry .139 average. Physically, White didn't instill the same fear at the plate as the three hitters who preceded him, namely Dawson, Carter and Parrish. But White, like Burris two days earlier, became an instant hero when he belted an inside pitch over the left-field fence for a spectacular three-run home run that triggered one of the loudest reactions ever at Olympic Stadium from the 54,000 fans. Recalls White: "The first time up (against Reuss), he kept pitching me inside and hard with a cutter and he was really buckling me in and I was a pretty good hitter on the inside part of the plate. So, I think he jammed me one time and then the next time I ended up hitting the ball well to left field. Actually I had hit the ball to the wall and the outfielder caught it. And then I felt I'd make an adjustment from there and make an adjustment to the inside part of my hand and he's gonna come in again because he had success there. And he tried it again and it didn't work that time. I knew it was gone when I hit it."[24]

The Dodgers were retired in order in the 7th and 8th innings. The Dodgers put the first two runners on base in the ninth, with singles by Garvey and Cey. But Rogers induced Pedro Guerrero to hit into a double play. Rogers struck out Mike Scioscia to end Game 3. The Expos were only one victory away from reaching the World Series! It was another solid performance in a crucial time by Rogers. Even though that outing was not as spectacular as his two-hitter in New York or his Game 5 shutout in the NLDS against Philadelphia, the Dodgers were never able to hit the ball solidly against him. All seven hits were singles and only one out was an outfield fly.[25] In short, it was another colossal effort by Rogers.

For Game 4, Jim Fanning decided to skip Scott Sanderson and pitch Bill Gullickson with three days rest. In 1981, Gullickson made three starts on short rest. He had a 2.93 ERA, which at first glance didn't look bad. But that was a little misleading, as he allowed 20 hits and three walks in 15 innings, a ratio that was far too high. Sanderson on the other hand had thrown only nine innings in his last three starts, all on the road. But even though Sanderson was more at ease at Olympic Stadium, the manager went with Gullickson. The Dodgers countered with Hooton for a repeat of the Game 1 match-up.

The Dodgers scored first in the third on a double by Dusty Baker but the Expos evened the game in the fourth on Warren Cromartie's single. Gullickson was almost on a survival mode on the mound as he allowed the first batter to reach base in five of the first six innings. In the seventh, he retired the side in order for the first time. In the eighth, Dusty Baker led off with a single and Steve Garvey was due next. Garvey had hit safely in every playoff game so far, including Game 4 against the Expos. He had yet however to drive in a run. But Garvey, like a predator, was sensing that Gullickson was getting tired.[26] Garvey didn't miss and hit a two-run home run for a 3–1 Dodger lead. After a walk to Ron Cey, Gullickson was replaced by Woodie Fryman. The Expos put two runners on base with one out in the eighth but reliever Bob Welch squelched the rally by retiring both Larry Parrish and Jerry White. The Dodgers scored four more times in the ninth for a 7–1 win. After the game, Gullickson admitted that the game was a real struggle and that he had to fight every single pitch to keep his team in the game.[27] Larry Parrish believed that the lack of poise and experience cost the Expos in that particular game: "We all wanted to be the hero that day. We all wanted to hit the home run. We must have made something like 15 outs that day when we had great swings but we hit high fly balls in right center and left center. To me, had we been there before, if we had already gotten over the hump, we would have scored 10 runs that day. But I think it was a strain to get over the hump that day and everybody wanted to be the hero and nobody turned out to be the hero."[28]

Game 5 was scheduled for Sunday, October 18, but was postponed to Monday thanks to bad weather. Ray Burris and Fernando Valenzuela were due up and many wondered how the Mexican was going to react under such frigid conditions, with the air temperature around the freezing point. After an out in the top of the first inning, Bill Russell hit a triple but neither Dusty Baker nor Steven Garvey could get him home. In the bottom of the first, Tim Raines reached second on a double. Then, the Dodgers botched a sacrifice bunt attempt by Rodney Scott and everybody was safe, which meant two runners on the corners with no outs. Andre Dawson, who was mired in a deep lethargy since the beginning of the playoffs, was next. He had no extra-base hits since the beginning of the playoffs and no RBIs. In nine games, he drew just one walk. He was very anxious and less and less patient at the plate, at a time when the chips are high and the pitching is above-average. Dawson was very tense, more so than he should have been,[29] and Valenzuela coaxed him to hit into a double play. Raines went on to score but a potentially big inning that could have put Valenzuela under pressure was quashed.

The score remained 1–0 Expos until the fifth inning. Rick Monday and Pedro Guerrero hit leadoff singles, Monday reaching third. Mike Scioscia hit a liner into the hands of second baseman Rodney Scott for the first out. Valenzuela was next but he was no ordinary hitter for a pitcher. In fact, in 1981, he managed to get 16 hits for a .250 batting average and seven RBIs. As Valenzuela was at the plate, a pitch eluded catcher Gary Carter, not far enough for Monday to score but enough so that Guerrero could advance to second. Valenzuela then pulled a Ray Burris pitch to second that scored Monday with the tying run. Had Guerrero stayed on first, the Expos would have had a good chance at a double play.

It was still 1–1 in the eighth when Ray Burris was replaced by pinchhitter Tim Wallach, who grounded out. A new pitcher would then face the Dodgers in the ninth. Two pitchers were warming up, Jeff Reardon and Steve Rogers.[30] Jeff Reardon thought he was the one being asked for, as Jim Fanning was making signs for a bearded one.[31] But it was Rogers, who had began to grow a beard of his own, who was Fanning's choice. Rogers was no doubt the hottest pitcher on the staff, with a ridiculously low 0.50 ERA in his four playoff starts, covering 35 and two-thirds innings. But it was only the third time in his career that he was used as a reliever.

Steve Garvey, Ron Cey and Rick Monday were due up for the Dodgers in the ninth. Rogers retired the first two batters. Garvey hit an infield popup for the first out. Cey hit a high fly ball to left field that Tim Raines caught at the base of the left-field wall near the foul line. When he crossed Rick Monday on his way back to the dugout, Cey told Monday that it would be almost impossible to hit one out that day.[32] Monday was the only left-handed power hitter in the Dodgers' lineup. It was only his second start of the NL Championship Series. Rogers threw two balls. On the third pitch, Monday had a good swing but only tipped the ball to the screen behind home plate.[33] When a ball is fouled that way, it means that the hitter was dangerously timed with the pitch. Monday knew it and was almost already blaming himself for missing such an inviting offering. Rogers threw another ball, a third one against one strike, to create a hitter's count. Monday always had a good eye and could choose his pitch. He found one to his liking and propelled it high into rightcenter field. Dawson ran to the wall and many thought he would catch the ball, as the alleys in Olympic Stadium were quite vast. But the ball disappeared over the wall, silencing the crowd as the homer put the Dodgers ahead, 2–1. Rogers then retired Pedro Guerreo on strikes.

The Expos had one last chance in the ninth. Valenzuela dispatched Rodney Scott and Andre Dawson for two outs. Gary Carter was up next but Valenzuela refused to throw him anything close to the plate and was walked. Jerry Manuel was called upon to run for Carter with Larry Parrish the next batter. Parrish was looking for a pitch to drive in the alleys[34] but never got what he was looking for and ended up drawing another walk, pushing Manuel to second base with the tying run. Jerry White, the hero of Game 3, had another chance to make a name for himself. Tommy Lasorda had seen enough of Valenzuela and decided to use right-hander Bob Welch instead of his number one reliever, Steve Howe. White was a switch-hitter and there was no way Lasorda would let him bat from the right side in that situation after witnessing his three-run homer against Jerry Reuss in Game 3. As Welch was warming up, Gary Carter told White to be ready for a first-pitch fastball.[35] But Welch threw him a sinker on his very first pitch, that he pulled for a grounder to second. Davey Lopes caught it before relaying the ball to first for the last out of Game 5 and the NCLS. White regretted thereafter to having listened to Carter: "I was not going to get a fastball because the Dodgers knew I was a good inside hitter. I had success against Howe in the past. And Welch, I don't really remember much about him, but he threw me a pitch, a sinker or a splitter that looked like a fastball and I wanted to swing but I was caught in-between swinging. I should have tried not to pull the ball, but to hit it to left field."[36]

After the game, most questions concerning the Expos were about Steve Rogers being on the mound in the ninth inning. Many years later, Rogers would repeat that he was good to go, maybe a little too much: "I was throwing hard in the bullpen, as hard as I had ever thrown. The only thing was, I wasn't throwing the way I needed to be throwing. I was overthrowing. And that basically undid me."[37] Before the game, it had been established that if he was asked to pitch, it would be to begin an inning. After the game, Rogers told the media that he felt good but that he had not been technically right. But why Rogers and not Jeff Reardon? According to Rogers: "The discussion prior to the game had been that if Ray Burris fell through, like in the third to sixth innings, it would be me. If it went extra innings, I needed to be ready. If it was the seventh inning, it would be one of the relievers. Jeff Reardon was throwing next to me. And they asked him how he was, and he said he was fine. And he was throwing the ball well. I could tell that he was in pain but what he was throwing was good. I just think at that moment Jim (Fanning) felt that he would go with me to start an inning because there was nobody on base and that was the way to go. I went into that inning, like I said, I was overthrowing the fastball, so my sinker wasn't sinking. It would stay flat. Nobody remembers, but the guy who almost ended up the hero was Ron Cey. He hit a ball to the base of the left-field wall on a 2–2 pitch, a hanging sinker. It was the exact same pitch that Monday hit out, 3 and 1. It was just because I was overthrowing the ball. I wasn't handling the adrenaline of the moment

Andre Dawson was considered the most complete player in the major leagues in the early 1980s by his peers. His eagerness to make the difference prevented him from performing up to his standards in important moments, like the playoffs.

like a reliever has to learn how to handle. Physically, I was absolutely fine."[38] As for Reardon, not being called in the game in that situation was among the biggest disappointments of his career. Charles Bronfman would tell him that he didn't want him to risk his career.[39] Some thought Reardon was still shaken by his last two outings in Los Angeles and Philadelphia, allowing three home runs to the last seven batters he faced. According to Pierre Ladouceur, Reardon, by making it known his back was bothering him, was not mentally ready to pitch in that fateful Game 5.[40]

Manager Jim Fanning would defend his decision many years later: "We were rained out on Sunday. Monday was the day Steve Rogers was scheduled to pitch on the sidelines. He came to us on Sunday after the rainout, to Galen Cisco and I, and said he would be ready to pitch on Monday. I remember telling him that if we do get that far or whatever, I will not ask you to come in during an inning but if you come in, it will be only to start an inning. So, it was for that reason that we brought him in late in the game. He was the best pitcher in the National League in that last month of the season, had outstanding stuff and that was my gamble, that was my choice, and I have not lost sleep over it. If I had brought in somebody else and we lose, I probably would have not gone to bed yet. But I knew that this was the best guy at hand."[41] Fanning's decision was not unique. In 1977, Kansas City manager Whitey Herzog had called in Dennis Leonard, a starter, to protect a ninth-inning lead in Game 5 of the American League Championship Series against the New York Yankees, a game and a series the Yankees eventually won. Twenty years after Steve Rogers, Arizona's Randy Johnson would pitch in relief in Game 7 of the World Series against the Yankees.

Ray Burris thought his buddy Woodie Fryman should have been asked to pitch on Monday: "In that situation, you got Jeff Reardon, the right-hander, and Woodie Fryman, the left-hander down there. And it was their expertise (in relief). And I thought, in that situation, Woodie Fryman and Jeff Reardon would be the people you go to. Now we got Steve Rogers for extra innings. I think everybody was available for doing some duty in that game. You can look back now and second-guess a lot of people. That's not where I'm coming from. I am not trying to second-guess anybody. What I'm saying is that you have a left-hander hitter in Rick Monday, I thought Woodie Fryman should have been in that game in that situation."[42]

When talking to the main actors in that game and Series, another factor was brought up by Larry Parrish and coach Norm Sherry: the lack of a roof over Olympic Stadium. They both said that had there been a roof, the Sunday game would have been played and that it would have been easier to get to Valenzuela on short rest.[43] "If we have a roof at the time, first I'm not getting hit in 1980 and in 1981, Valenzuela wouldn't have been able to pitch the fifth game on Sunday. We got rained or snowed out or whatever and on Monday he was able to pitch and at that time, he was on top of his game," said Parrish.[44]

Andre Dawson took the loss very hard. He told the media after the last game that even though he couldn't do it all alone, he felt responsible for the teams's elimination. He added that it was not a matter of pressure, but in his estimation he should have contributed more.[45]

Scott Sanderson had a hard time accepting being demoted. Worse, he wasn't even asked once to warm-up against the Dodgers: "I think that we all realized that what he (Steve Rogers) was being asked to perform was a Herculean feat! Having just started two days before (it was three days actually). It certainly was out of the ordinary. It certainly was a gamble, one that didn't pay off. I think the rest of the guys on the pitching staff were scratching their heads, asking themselves what are we here for? We all helped the team get to this place, and then try to get through the playoffs really on a four-men pitching staff. I think their attempt there was to try to have Steve, Ray Burris, Bill Gullickson and Jeff Reardon. They pretty much were the only guys that they try to get by on, that's a hard thing to do; you win as a team, you lose as a team. I remember just thinking that what Jim was asking Steve to do was a pretty tough task."[46]

Even if the loss was hard to take for the whole organization, Jim Fanning was applauded heartily when he left the podium following his post-game press conference.[47] And for the third consecutive year, the Expos were eliminated by the eventual World Series champions.

After the season, Andre Dawson was chosen the Player of the Year by both Associated Press and *The Sporting News*. He finished second in the MVP voting to Mike Schmidt. Chris Speier had played with the great Willie Mays and thought that Dawson was very close to reaching his status.[48] Gary Carter's defensive excellence, along with Dawson's, was recognized with a Gold Glove. Both players also received the Silver Slugger award. Tim Raines finished second to Fernando Valenzuale for the Rookie of the Year award. John McHale was named the Executive of the Year by *The Sporting News*.

The 1981 season was over, but McHale didn't have much time to savor this award as he had some business at hand, beginning by whether to bring back Jim Fanning as manager or not. Andre Dawson and some teammates had voiced their preference for coach Steve Boros soon after Fanning's hiring.[49] Dawson thought Boros would have the backing and respect from most of the players. But McHale couldn't turn his back on Fanning, who had been as loyal to him as one could be since the inception of the franchise. It was McHale's turn to show Fanning his loyalty. In mid–November, it was announced that Jim Fanning would return as the Expos' manager, a decision that was praised by most, except by columnist Michael Farber from *The Gazette*. Farber thought Fanning to be too good a man to be a manager.[50] But after leading the Expos to the postseason, Fanning deserved a chance to prove his worth as manager for a full season, according to McHale.[51]

The Expos made a big splash in the coaching ranks with the hiring of respected hitting instructor Billy DeMars, who had been with the Philadelphia Phillies.[52] Dallas Green had just left the organization, which was being sold.

DeMars was thus available and would be replacing Pat Mullin. Mullin would not be the only one to leave the Expos as Norm Sherry and Ozzie Virgil would join the San Diego Padres to work with their new manager, Dick Williams, late of the Expos.

McHale's offseason was far from over as he had to try to reach a contract agreement with his all-star catcher Gary Carter. Talks had been going on and off since the start of 1981 and management showed some signs at times that they were quite annoyed at the length of this negotiation, especially since they thought they had an agreement on a couple of occasions.[53] During the playoffs, it was reported that Carter had refused an offer of $10 million for eight years.[54] Carter's current pact was due to expire at the end of the 1982 season.

While both parties kept talking, McHale and the team's brass concluded that they had to improve the team's offense, namely at second base and short-stop that were patrolled by Rodney Scott and Chris Speier, respectively. McHale said that the team couldn't afford to carry two .230 hitters.[55] The Expos were thinking about moving Tim Raines back to second, where he had played all his minor league career, but Raines was rather cold to that possibility.[56] Speier was a free agent but it looked as if he would be back, given the lack of free agent candidates at that position and nobody ready yet in the minors to take his place. Ray Burris didn't lose time and agreed to a new three-year contract with the Expos.[57]

In early December, as the Expos were getting ready for the annual winter meetings, *Sportmania*, a French sports magazine, published a story in which Bill Lee blasted manager Jim Fanning. The article was written as Lee in the first person. He said that to consider Fanning a savior was a fallacy. To him, the Expos' presence in the playoffs was due to the fact that they played one more game than St. Louis (hence the one-half game difference in the second-half standings). He admitted that the team was going through difficult times when Dick Williams was fired, but that the Expos would have come out of it, no matter whether the manager was Williams, Fanning or Donald Duck! According to the eccentric lefty, Gullickson should have never pitched Game 4, saying that Fanning told Lee he would pitch that game before changing his mind at the last moment. Fanning was unable to manage, contrary to Williams who just didn't want to manage anymore at the end. Lee thought that Fanning was far too nervous, in that he made every single situation a life-and-death issue. He insisted that most players agreed with him, but didn't want to ruffle feathers.[58] There was no immediate consequence to the article as it was the offseason. The Expos made only one move, sending Steve Ratzer to the New York Mets for shortstop Frank Taveras, an interesting move in light of McHale's wanting to add some punch to his offense. His defense was somewhat suspect but his speed was not, as attested by his 296 career stolen bases in eight complete seasons, including a league-leading 70 steals in 1977 with the Pittsburgh Pirates.

The Expos were also targeting pitcher Dave Stieb, from the Toronto Blue Jays, and (again) Al Oliver, with the Texas Rangers.[59] The Rangers wanted a regular position player and a prospect for Oliver, according to McHale.[60] Stieb, who had some contractual problems with the Jays, established himself as one of the finest young pitchers in baseball in the previous two years. According to rumors, the Expos were ready to part with Larry Parrish to get him.[61] Lefty Gary Lucas, of San Diego, was also mentioned but with Dick Williams with the Padres, there was no way he was going to Montreal, even for Rodney Scott, one of his favorites with the Expos.[62] The New York Mets wanted to know if the Expos were interested to have Ellis Valentine back. The right fielder would surely have jumped to the occasion but the Expos had definitely turned the page.[63]

For the third consecutive year, the Expos were chosen the Team of the Year in the national poll held by *Canadian Press* of its subscribers, namely most media outlets in the country.[64] Just to show how the Expos had become the supreme sports attraction in Montreal, columnist Yvon Pedneault from *Le Journal de Montréal* wrote in December that the team was number one in the heart of sports fans.[65] That testimony was revealing, especially from someone whose expertise was linked a lot more to ice hockey than baseball.

8

1982: A Missed Opportunity

After the 1981 season, Expos fans really thought there was only one way to go, and that it would be up. Everybody had reason to be optimistic: the core of the team was still young and most thought the Expos were on the brink of coming to maturity. Among that group of young players was All-Star catcher Gary Carter. At the start of 1982, he had yet to sign a contract. He always had a good idea of his value and, of course, wanted to be paid accordingly. But talks seemed to go nowhere. Andre Dawson said that the Expos should think about trading Carter if they couldn't sign him and even threw in the name of Mike Scioscia, of the Los Angeles Dodgers, as an alternative. Dawson warned that if the Expos were to agree to Carter's salary demands, it could lead to a negative reaction throughout the team.[1] Dawson had signed a multi-year deal after the 1980 season, which covered both parties through 1986, but he already had second thoughts about that contract that earned him about $800,000 annually.[2]

In mid–January, it looked at last as if there was some hope as agent Jerry Petrie assessed the chances to reach an agreement at more than 50 percent.[3] There was still lots of work to do, especially to iron out the fiscal ramifications of the contract as Carter had to deal with four jurisdictions: the province of Quebec, Canada, the United States and the state of Florida. Furthermore, Canadian Minister of Finances Allan MacEachern had presented a controversial budget that would impact professional athletes playing in Canada.[4] To sort out that mess, two Charles Bronfman fiscalists were assigned to work on that case along with two people from Gary Carter's side.[5]

As these tax specialists were doing their best to come to some kind of agreement, the Expos, not surprisingly, signed Chris Speier to a three-year contract.[6] The Expos also hired substitute catcher Tim Blackwell, to give Carter a break.[7] Carter had played more than 90 percent of the team's games since 1977, a pace, if maintained, that was certain to take its toll at some point in the not so distant future. The Expos also traded veteran left-handed reliever

Grant Jackson, a September acquisition, to Kansas City for minor-league first baseman Ken Phelps. In the meantime, Larry Parrish's name was mentioned left and right in rumors.[8] The Expos wanted Tim Wallach to play regularly and there was no way he would be left on the bench again, as was the case in 1981. But the Expos had options, because Wallach could also play first base and right field. In fact, in that latter position, Dawson suggested to the Expos the name of Ellis Valentine.[9] Again, the Expos showed absolutely no interest, even though it would have cost them next to nothing to acquire him.

Less than a week before pitchers and catchers were to report to spring training in West Palm Beach, the Expos announced that Gary Carter had agreed to an eight-year $15 million contract.[10] John McHale insisted that the Expos just couldn't win without him. McHale tried to smooth out the deal, by telling people that the pact should be counted as ten years because Carter had been underpaid the last two years. But it was clear that McHale was pretty upset after having been forced to cough up that kind of money and he even refused to be included with Carter in pictures at the press conference.[11] Carter became one of the best-paid players in the majors, following Dave Winfield's contract that was signed prior to 1981.

The Expos were the NL East Division defending champion for the first time ever, but ironically, the lineup was far from set at spring training. Before the first day, manager Jim Fanning said that Tim Raines had the potential to be another Joe Morgan,[12] the best second baseman in the 1970s. Fanning also had kind words for Wallace Johnson, whose main position was second base, and he had every intention of giving him the opportunity to win that infield job.[13] That didn't look good for incumbent Rodney Scott, who was told to work with batting coach Harry Walker. Walker appeared to be a good fit for Scott, as he specialized in teaching how to slap the ball on the ground. But Scott was very reluctant to go along with the Expos' request.[14] There were also doubts about who would patrol right field. Wallach was the main candidate but Terry Francona and Jerry White, who did a creditable job in 1981 in the outfield, were also in the mix.

On the mound, very few changes were expected as starters Steve Rogers, Bill Gullickson, Ray Burris and Scott Sanderson were all back. Charlie Lea looked as if he had the edge for the number five spot. Jeff Reardon was touted as the closer, with Woodie Fryman his main accomplice. But it was evident that some veterans were in danger, including Bill Lee, Stan Bahnsen and Elias Sosa. Bahnsen saw the writing on the wall, but insisted it would be unfair to judge him on his performances in 1981, a season unlike any other, since he had suffered some pain in the right shoulder after the strike.[15] In training camp, Bahnsen, a veteran, knew how to pace himself to get ready for the long season. But when the strike ended, he had only ten days to prepare for the second half, which led to his lack of preparation and some ineffectiveness. Bob James, who had so impressed Dick Williams in 1979, was out of options and the Expos had no intention of giving him away. The Expos were interested in veteran Doyle Alexander, but his contract had a limited no-trade clause that included Montreal.[16]

The second-base situation and by the same token Wallace Johnson's performance were the focus of the first part of the camp. In mid–March, many observers doubted that Johnson was ready, especially defensively. Shortstop Chris Speier thought the position was still a big question mark.[17] Pierre Ladouceur wrote that Johnson just couldn't turn a double play[18] and that Rodney Scott was still the best option.[19] Scott thought that a personality conflict with Jim Fanning was depriving him of a chance to have his job back[20] and that the decision had been made already.[21]

In the meantime, the Texas Rangers had a player who was quite unhappy with his contract situation, designated hitter Al Oliver. He had listed five teams where he would like to be traded: New York Yankees, California Angels, Atlanta Braves, Baltimore Orioles and Kansas City Royals.[22] All these teams were contenders, except for the Braves who had an impressive group of young players, especially Bob Horner and Dale Murphy, and a new manager who was very respected, Joe Torre. Even though the Expos weren't named, rumors continued to swirl over the team, but Steve Rogers warned that the Expos should think twice before overhauling the group already in place.[23] Oliver had been the subject of talks around the Expos for years and Montreal scouts had been following him in Pompano Beach,[24] which was only a 45-minute drive from the Expos' camp in West Palm Beach. After only a few days of talks, on March 31, the Expos announced they had acquired Oliver for Larry Parrish and Dave Hostetler. The trade was made a few hours before the deadline for interleague transactions. Parrish was extremely disappointed after going through three very emotional seasons. He was really looking forward to 1982 and working with new batting coach Billy DeMars.[25] Hostetler had no future with the Expos, even though he had hit with authority in winter-league baseball and in training camp. Rangers GM Eddie Robinson would have made the deal straight up, Oliver for Parrish,[26] but McHale, in his haste to get his coveted batter, offered to include Hostetler right from the beginning to make it known he was serious.

In Oliver, the Expos got that elusive left-handed bat, an established hitter with a solid track record who could drive in runs. The Expos' brass had come to the conclusion that this was the missing ingredient that could lead the team to the ultimate goal, a berth in the World Series. To McHale, the Expos' offense had just improved by 25 percent with Oliver.[27] Even at age 35, Oliver was in exceptional shape. He had hit at least .300 in his previous six seasons and in 1980 he drove in 117 runs with 17 home runs and 43 doubles to go along with his .319 batting average.

The media people covering the team were very enthusiastic about the trade,[28] and some would go as far as to predict a pennant in the NL East, an opinion that was shared elsewhere in the majors. With a lineup featuring Oliver, Dawson, Carter and Tim Raines, the Expos just couldn't miss, it was said. However, Chris Speier had some concerns because Oliver's arrival meant that four players would be displaced defensively.[29] Oliver would play first base, moving Warren Cromartie to right field. Tim Wallach became de facto the regular at the hot corner. The other change had nothing to do with Oliver as Wallace Johnson was expected to play second. Even though the defense seemed suspect at first glance, the Expos believed the offense would compensate. Without surprise, some veteran pitchers were sent elsewhere. Stan Bahnsen was released while Elias Sosa's contract was sold to Detroit. Sosa had asked to be traded following some financial problems he had, according to John McHale.[30] Sosa was never able to duplicate his 1979 season, his first in Montreal. Sosa would admit that he had problems that were not related to baseball that contributed to his not performing up to his capabilities.[31] With Charlie Lea and Bob James, the Expos started the season with nine pitchers.

The first series of the season in Pittsburgh was entirely wiped out due to bad weather. Steve Rogers had nonetheless some good news, when it was announced he had agreed to a contract extension through 1985, that would pay him $700,000 annually.[32] Rogers celebrated his new pact with a complete-game three-hit shutout to start the Expos' season with a 2–0 win in Philadelphia on April 9. Andre Dawson gave the Expos the lead in the top of the first with a home run, which was enough for Rogers. The Expos' offense exploded for 11 runs the day after. Oliver got three hits, including his first home run with the Expos, against Dick Ruthven. In the third game, Ray Burris gave up only one unearned run but lost, 1–0, against Mike Krukow.

The Expos were due to begin their local season on April 13 against Pittsburgh but thanks to Mother Nature they had to wait one more day. Scott Sanderson then won his first start, allowing only three hits in six innings. But the defense was responsible for two more unearned runs after errors by Oliver and Chris Speier. Sanderson was not very happy when he was removed for a pinch-hitter in the sixth with two men on board and the Expos trailing, 2–1. But Jerry White made him a winner by hitting a pinch-hit three-run home run, leading the way to a 5–4 win. The Expos were on their way to win for the fourth time in five games but back-to-back home runs by Dave Parker and Jason Thompson tied the game at three. In the ninth, an Al Oliver miscue led to the winning run as the Pirated won, 4–3.

The season was only a couple of weeks old but already some voices were heard disputing the Expos' status as the favorites to win their division. Mike Schmidt pointed out that the Expos had no established closer and that Jeff Reardon had proven nothing.[33] Bill Madlock, the Pirates' third baseman, said that the Expos would miss Larry Parrish.[34] Schmidt and Madlock may have had valid points but one thing was certain: the other teams were concerned about the Expos and there was no doubt that these comments were intended to shake things up, at least in part.

After that short two-game stint in Montreal, it was down to New York against the Mets where they won two out of three games. Al Oliver was the first-game hero with a ninth-inning home run in a 4–3 victory. Ray Burris lost a second heart-breaker, 2–1, in the second game before Charlie Lea earned his first win in his first start. The Expos were back at home for five games against the Phillies and the Mets, winning three of them. They were blanked in the two losses, even though Scott Sanderson and Burris allowed only three earned runs in a combined 16 innings. Burris had allowed only three earned runs, was leading the league in ERA but had an 0–3 record to show for it! Burris didn't complain publicly about his lack of support, but some of his teammates were quite unhappy about the playing conditions in Olympic Stadium.[35] The artificial turf there was deemed one of the worst in the majors, thanks to the seams that were uneven and made the ball bounce in funny ways at times. The surface was also very hard and players were very reluctant to dive on it. Some repairs were scheduled during the forthcoming trip to the West Coast starting April 27, but the turf in Montreal would be a concern all through the Expos' stay in Montreal.

The Expos first flew to San Francisco, but without Rowland Office, who was let go. John Milner, who had been on the disabled list, replaced him on the roster. The Expos, at 8–5, were two and a half games back of the Cardinals with a record that was quite acceptable, which could have been better with a little more support from the offense and the defense. The first three leaders in ERA in the National League were all Expos: Ray Burris (1.17), Scott Sanderson (1.23) and Steve Rogers (1.54).[36]

Off went the Expos to the West Coast in San Francisco, Los Angeles and San Diego, respectively, and given their poor record historically in California, they didn't fare that badly with four wins in eight games. In Los Angeles, they managed to win the series, winning two out of three, which was quite a feat after losing 18 of the last 19 regular-season games at Dodger Stadium. Just before that series, the Expos announced that Wallace Johnson was sent to the minors, recalling Bryn Smith. His offensive contribution couldn't overcome his defensive shortcomings. He was hitting .353 after five games but it had been downhill since then, down to .184. He had only one hit in his last 21 at-bats and only one walk and no extra-base hits.

Johnson's demotion was the first sign of what was awaiting the Expos in 1982, especially at second base. It was clear to most people who attended spring training that he was not ready. Not only that, the Expos intended to use him as an outfielder in the minors from then on.[37] Johnson would remember how the pressure was very high and that's why the direction couldn't wait. "I think it was extremely disappointing. I think I was a work in progress. What basically happened was because of my hitting, I hit so well, but my defense hadn't caught up to my hitting. But I continued to work hard on my defense, knowing that I could play second base. But the funny thing is, the background of it is, that we were in a situation in 1982 where we almost won it in 1981 and we're going to win it in 1982. So I think the organization was going for the brass ring, I guess. We started 6 and 4 out of the gate. It wasn't a real bad start the first 10 games. But I think the pressure on the organization, now, was we can't take a chance with this rookie guy. We can't take a chance. That had a lot to do with them demoting me and then, basically, my whole career after that became one of going up and down, up and down, up and down. I'll never forget Jeff Reardon said, 'The way it happened that guy's probably never going to get back to the big leagues again.' That's probably true except that the faith I had, kept working hard, the upbringing I had, just kept working hard and even though if that didn't look promising, you just go out there and play hard and see what happens." Johnson ended up having a fine career as a pinch-hitter for several years with the Expos. He was however absolutely certain that he would have been an adequate second baseman in the majors, had he had a real opportunity. "I always believed in myself. And I know that I could. I played against a lot of guys, like Steve Sax, we came up the minor leagues together. Yes, I really felt that over the course of time, I would have been able to do that. I believed that I was a quality infielder. I was known for my offense but I felt I was a middle infielder who knew how to play the game. It was an asset."[38]

The second-base merry-go-round was on its way and it was Frank Taveras' turn after Johnson's demotion. It didn't seem that bad a choice, given that Taveras had played on some solid teams with the Pirates and that speed was his main asset, even though he had never played second base regularly in the majors.

The Expos were back home on May 6 with a 12–9 record, three games behind the Cards. The Expos lost the first two games of that home stint against the Dodgers with the Expos being limited to four runs and 13 hits in these two losses. The third game on Saturday, May 8, was scheduled in the afternoon but one player wouldn't make it: Rodney Scott was told his services wouldn't be required anymore. Nobody around the team was really surprised as it was clear right from the beginning of spring training that Jim Fanning had no use for him. He had played only two games since April 24, one as a pinch-hitter and the other as a pinch-runner. He had started five games in April but his play didn't convince Jim Fanning to change his mind. His batting average was only .200 in 25 at-bats. But what really made the headlines was Bill Lee's reaction. Lee decided to leave the stadium and go to a nearby bar with cartoonist Terry Mosher, from *The Gazette*.[39] Lee wasn't a stranger to that kind of behavior. He had gone on a one-day strike in June 1978 when his friend Bernie Carbo was traded from Boston to Cleveland.

Before the Saturday game, Al Oliver, who didn't need anyone to prepare himself for a game, called a players-only meeting.[40] The players came out flat as the Dodgers took a 9–3 lead in the first four innings. As the Expos were getting pummelled, Bill Lee was playing billiards, drinking a couple of beers, while keeping an eye on a game that looked out of reach. But the Expos staged a comeback with five runs in the fifth inning, including three on Tim Wallach's home run. The Expos couldn't complete the comeback however against the Dodgers' relievers and the Expos lost for the fourth time in a row, including the last three at home. Before the game ended, Lee was back at Olympic Stadium and considered himself ready to go if needed. After the game, Fanning and Lee had a rather heated exchange where the pitcher reproached his manager the way Scott was treated and how his friend never had the chance to win his job back. Fanning counter-attacked by telling Lee that he failed in his obligations when he left the team. He told him also that John McHale wanted to see him on Sunday. Lee was then told that he would join Scott as a player with no job.[41]

All that controversy should have made the biggest sports headlines in Montreal but on that Saturday, when Scott was released, the Quebecers lost one of their local heroes when Formula One driver Gilles Villeneuve was killed in an accident in Belgium during the qualifying session. The media attention was brought almost exclusively on Villeneuve for many days, the accident, his legacy, etc., leaving the Expos on the back-burner for the time being.[42] But still, there were some reactions that unfolded during that weekend. Scott had known for some time that he was not in Jim Fanning's plans, ever since he took over from Dick Williams in September 1981. But it seemed as if their on-field performances were not the only consideration taken into account by John McHale, who said that both Lee and Scott had serious personal problems and were lacking discipline. He wouldn't go into details but said that with Valentine, Scott and Lee gone, "the problem was definitely resolved."[43] It was clear to everyone that McHale was alluding to drugs. Scott said that McHale couldn't prove that he took drugs and that if baseball wanted to get rid of every player who was on drugs, alcohol or amphetamines, there wouldn't be enough players left to play the game.[44] As for Lee, who considered himself as the link between the blacks and whites on the team, McHale replied that Lee self-nominated himself and that his pitcher and friends were getting the stuff from the same source anyway.[45]

Between Villeneuve's articles, some columnists found some time to react as well, writing about a real house cleaning, even though the two players involved were not important parts on the team anymore. Columnist Réjean Tremblay, from *La Presse*, wrote that the Expos were building a very neat and clean team, devoid of any negative influence, with players corresponding to the image of the GM and president, John McHale.[46]

After Wallace Johnson, Rodney Scott and Frank Taveras, Tim Raines then became the next second baseman in less than two months. On Sunday, the Dodgers completed the four-game sweep at Olympic Stadium, winning, 5–4, in Ray Burris's sixth loss in as many starts. Burris suggested that he be sent to the bullpen for some time and after one more start (another loss), Fanning obliged.[47] The Expos moved back in the standings, four games from first place, and were playing below .500 with a 12–13 record.

The Expos had ten more games to play at home, where they had been dominant in the last three years. But they couldn't do better than four wins against San Francisco, San Diego and Atlanta, a sequence where only one starting pitcher was able to garner a W, Steve Rogers against Atlanta. In the series against the Braves, Phil Niekro said he didn't recognize the same Expos he had faced the year before.[48] The same observation was made also by another Brave, Bob Horner.[49] Michel Blanchard, from *La Presse*, would add that Jim Fanning didn't have the respect of his players.[50] Woodie Fryman and Ray Burris couldn't help but notice a lack of concentration from the team.[51]

The team left Montreal for a six-game road trip to Cincinnati and Houston with a 16–19 record but against all odds, they swept both series. Charlie Lea started that week with a combined two-hitter with Woodie Fryman. Five days later, David Palmer made his first start in the majors since 1980, allowing only two hits and one run in six innings in Houston. He uncharacteristically gave up six walks but managed to hold the Reds to a single run, getting the win in the 6–1 decision. Palmer was taking Ray Burris' spot in the rotation.[52] Lea closed that trip with another superb outing, allowing one hit in nine innings in a 4–0 win over Houston in ten innings. In six games, the Expos allowed a total of five runs. The Expos kept it on with two more victories at home before losing 6–4 to the Astros. After yet another four-hit shutout to close the month of May by Charlie Lea, who just looked unbeatable, the Expos lost three times in a row against three different teams in three different stadiums in four days! They first lost, 6–4, to Houston. The day after, they lost again in Pittsburgh, 5–4, in ten innings in a game that made up for the opening series of the season when all three games were rained out. Then it was off to Atlanta where, after a day off thanks to a rainout, they ended up on the wrong side of a 2–1 decision. They won the last game of what became a two-game series before facing for the first time of the season the leaders in the NL East, the St. Louis Cards.

After the last victory over Atlanta, on June 6, the Expos were tied for second place with Philadelphia and the surprising New York Mets, four and a half games behind St. Louis. Whitey Herzog, after some successful moves before the 1981 season, added more ingredients to his team for 1982. He got defensive wizard Ozzie Smith from the San Diego Padres in a straight deal for incumbent Garry Templeton. Smith's bat was suspect but on the field he was already acknowledged as the best shortstop in the business. Templeton was extremely talented, with everything that could be asked from a shortstop, quickness, a strong arm and a quality bat from both sides of the place. But he had to leave St. Louis. In August 1981, Templeton made an obscene gesture towards the fans. Herzog promptly got him out of the game and a shouting match almost mounted to an physical altercation between them.[53] The Cards had acquired another Smith, Lonnie, from Philadelphia, and another speedy outfielder from the Yankees chain, Willie McGee. The latter was called up in early May but made an immediate impression as the new center fielder, hitting .352 before the series in Montreal. Herzog didn't have that workhorse on the mound, like Steve Carlton or even Steve Rogers. But he could count on some solid starters, like Bob Forsch and Joaquin Andujar, and what was probably the best bullpen in baseball, anchored by Bruce Sutter.

The Cards had been in first place since their 11-game winning streak in April. The Expos seemed to be settling themselves. In left field, Terry Francona was used regularly since Tim Raines' switch to second. Francona had raised his batting average from .261 to .315. For the first game of the series, Joaquin Andujar, who could almost beat the Expos in his sleep, was facing Scott Sanderson. Neither pitcher figured in the decision. Andujar allowed two runs in six innings but the Cards tied it at two in the seventh. Warren Cromartie, who was hitting only .220, won it for the Expos in the bottom of the ninth with a game-winning home run against Sutter.

The second game featured another pitcher duel between Steve Rogers and Dave LaPoint. The game went into extra innings when it was tied at two after nine. The Cards won it in the 12th on an RBI triple by McGee and a squeeze bunt by Ken Oberkfell, which proved important as the Expos scored once against Sutter, who had blown a save opportunity in the 11th. The Expos won the third game, 5–1, thanks to Gary Carter's home run and Bill Gullickson's solid outing. After that game, the Expos traded Bob James to the Detroit Tigers for a player to be named later. James had been used only seven times so far, never in a crucial situation. In nine innings, he struck out 11 batters and also allowed eight walks and ten hits for a 6.00 ERA. The pitcher who had been nicknamed the "Canadian Goose" in spring 1979 would have the chance to be a closer in Detroit.

After the Cards, the Expos swept the Chicago Cubs in spectacular fashion. They first won, 9–8, on an eighth-inning two-run double by Tim Raines. Then, Al Oliver broke a 5–5 tie in the seventh with yet another two-run double. Lastly, Tim Wallach's two-run home run made the Expos a winner in the tenth inning for a 5–3 triumph. The Expos picked up some ground and only two games separated both teams as the Expos headed to St. Louis. But this time, the Cards turned the table and won two out of three. The Expos had some chances in the first two games though. They lost the first game, 2–1, even after they got ten hits. In the last two innings, they couldn't score even though they had the bases loaded with no outs and one out, respectively. The Cards won the second game, 3–2, in 11 innings. The Cards had tied the game on an error by Tim Raines in the eighth inning. Only Charlie Lea got a win for the Expos in the last game, thanks to an eight-run outburst in the first three innings. In that game, though, Terry Francona left the game in the seventh when his knee got caught in the outfield padding on a long fly by Julio Gonzalez.[54] His season was over. Francona was hitting .321 at that point and had provided some spark with his infectious enthusiasm. The Expos called up second baseman Mike Gates from Wichita and installed him as the new regular second baseman, putting Tim Raines back in left field for good. A new pitcher was also acquired, left-hander Dan Schatzeder. Since his trade to Detroit after the 1979 season, Schatzeder never seemed at ease and in his own admission, it took him almost a half season to get comfortable in his new surroundings.[55] In 1981, the Tigers had almost no use for him towards the end of the campaign. Pitcher Mike Griffin was sent down to the minors, without pitching a game with the team during his one-week stay with the Expos.

The Expos then went on to sweep both the Cubs and the Mets for seven straight wins on the road. So after the June 23 games, which was when Quebecers celebrate their St-Jean-Baptiste national holiday, the Expos were tied for first place with the Cards. The Expos dominated in Chicago and New York as only one game was won by one run. Two of these wins were shutouts by Steve Rogers. In his two games before that, he had pitched nine innings without a decision. Rogers' shutouts were his eighth and ninth victories and lowered his ERA to 1.74. Offensively, Al Oliver, Gary Carter, Andre Dawson and Tim Wallach were as dangerous a foursome as there was in the National League. The first three had slugging percentages that hovered around .500. Wallach was named the Player of the Month in May. Tim Raines got his batting average up to .300 after a rough first month but he was still short of his spectacular self, at least short from his 1981 season.

Steve Rogers was one of the most consistent pitchers in the National League for almost a decade. He was the best pitcher in the National League in 1982 but wound up one win shy of the coveted 20-win plateau, which probably deprived him from winning the Cy Young Award.

But some players were not entirely happy. Chris Speier was left on the bench in Chicago when manager Jim Fanning decided to go with Frank Taveras. Speier told Fanning in no uncertain terms how he felt about his decision.[56] It was clear Speier wouldn't have voiced his displeasure in such a way to Dick Williams. Andre Dawson was summoned to his manager's office after some comments that were deemed inappropriate.[57] The players were not the only ones going after Jim Fanning; in an article penned by Bill James, Jim Fanning was rated the worst major league manager.[58]

The Expos didn't remain long in first place. After their seven-game winning streak, they were unable to win two in a row in the next three weeks, losing ten out of fifteen games prior to the All-Star Game. David Palmer won two of these games, including a complete-game three-hitter against Pittsburgh. On June 29, Tim Raines was out of the lineup in the first of a three-game series at home against the New York Mets. According to the official version, Raines had stomach problems, but something looked fishy. The day after, Raines met with both Jim Fanning and John McHale, which was quite exceptional for someone who only had an upset stomach.[59] Raines statistics were not bad up to that point, with a .289 batting average and a .363 on-base percentage. But the writers on the Expos' beat noticed a change in the outfielder's behavior, doubting the team's official version of his absence against the Mets. Serge Touchette wrote that Raines wasn't the same and was just going through the motions.[60] Jean-Paul Sarault, from *Dimanche-Matin*, went as far as comparing Raines' case to that of Ellis Valentine. Sarault wrote that even though there was no proof of anything, questions should be asked.[61] One didn't have to think long before concluding that drugs were implied by these writers. The Expos remained very discreet concerning Raines, who missed only one game.

Before the All-Star break, as the Expos were struggling at home against the West Coast teams, John Milner was given his walking papers. Before leaving, Milner said he would miss both Montreal and Crescent Street, one of the hottest nightspots in the city.[62] Wallace Johnson was called back, but there was no way he would be given the chance to play second base. The Expos just needed an extra bat on the bench.

Even if the Expos were far from being out of the playoff picture, their inconsistency really worried John McHale, who said the team was not jelling.[63] When the team faced San Francisco, veteran outfielder Reggie Smith added to some other comments to the effect that he didn't recognize the same Expos as the year before.[64] In such a context, the number one target is usually the manager and that was the case with Jim Fanning. *La Presse* columnist Réjean Tremblay questioned whether or not he should leave.[65] His colleague on the beat, Michel Blanchard, opined that the Expos were a ship without a captain.[66] Rumors were swirling as to the future of Fanning after the All-Star Game. Speier didn't help by saying that changes could occur if the team didn't begin to play better. He also concurred with John McHale as to the lack of unity within the team.[67] Al Oliver didn't go for that, however, saying that the players had their share of responsibility in the team's failed expectations up to that point.[68] In spite of all these criticisms, Fanning was assured to wear the Expos' uniform one more time, as he had been selected as a coach for the All-Star Game, which was scheduled to take place in Montreal.

The Expos had been in the majors since 1969, but they really became relevant only in 1979, the first season where they truly competed among the game's elite teams. The Expos' presence in the postseason in 1981 only added to the team's visibility. The All-Star Game couldn't occur in Montreal at a more opportune moment.

Expos marketing VP René Guimond was in charge of the event, organization-wise. He had to accommodate some 600 media members and as many technical staff. The demand for tickets was enormous, to such a degree that Guimond thought he could have filled two Olympic Stadiums.[69] Guimond virtually had to start from scratch, because he had no reference. The year before, Guimond didn't get much information from the All-Star Game in Cleveland: "Baseball had just been out on the strike and we didn't know yet whether we would have a game. It was very hard. Cleveland's reputation was not good as well. Usually, you take some information in events from years past but in that particular case, we didn't get much."[70]

Montreal had every intention to make it a first-class event and the whole media world and political brass were asked to contribute. Roger D. Landry, who became the boss of *La Presse* newspaper after leaving the Expos after 1980, came back as an honorary president. To Landry, that title was more that mere symbolic: "I was honored to be involved. I had to do some planning with the people already in place, to show the world that Montreal was special. I was friends with Mayor Jean Drapeau and I told him, 'You have to be involved.' It was a big party where everyone took part, the TVs, the radios, whether they were broadcasting the game or not, everybody joined in."[71] Landry was in charge of a big show at the Place des Arts, with international stars such as King Cole and Patsy Gallant (a famous singer from France), with Donald Sutherland, a huge Expos fan, as an anchor.

As it was the first time the All-Star Game was held outside the U.S., the emphasis was towards international baseball. Before the game, players from more than ten countries were introduced. The national anthems were sung beautifully by an international baritone, Montreal's Louis Quilico. His exceptional rendition caused ABC's star announcer Howard Cosell to say that that was the way the U.S. anthems should be heard.[72]

On the field, five Expos players were part of the game, including four in the starting lineup: Gary Carter, Andre Dawson, Tim Raines (all three selected by vote from the fans) and Steve Rogers. Al Oliver was picked by manager Tommy Lasorda. The National League won, 4–1, the eleventh straight time the senior circuit had gotten the upper hand. David Conception was named the game's MVP, thanks to his second-inning two-run home run against Dennis Eckersley. In fact, one would be able to see Concepcion hitting his home run in the Baseball Hall of Fame in Cooperstown on an enlarged picture of the front page of *Le Journal de Montréal*, with the caption: "L'Étoile des étoiles!"[73] (The biggest star among stars!). Steve Rogers got the win, when he threw three innings, allowing one run. Al Oliver got two hits, Gary Carter and Andre Dawson, one each. Raines got a walk and a stolen base.

Apart from the game, the organization around the event was a great success. René Guimond recalled with pride, that the Expos produced a document with the do's and how's that was a model for years to come for future All-Star Games: "It included everything, from the invitation cards to the printing of tickets, plans of theatres, etc. This document became a reference on how to organize an All-Star Game."[74]

After the euphoria of the All-Star Game, it was back to business and off to California with stops in San Diego, Los Angeles and San Francisco. That was the kind of road trip the Expos dreaded in the past. But in 1982, their road record was quite impressive with 23 wins and 16 losses. But inexplicably, the team just couldn't duplicate its past success at home, with only 20 victories and 26 defeats. It was true that the fans were far more demanding than before, as players were booed more often and more vehemently.[75] The Expos had to up their game a notch if they hoped to catch the Cards. As the second part of the season began on, the Expos' record stood at 43–42 in fourth place, four games back from St. Louis.

The Expos started on the right foot by sweeping Dick Williams' Padres, as all four starting pitchers—Charlie Lea, Steve Rogers, Bill Gullickson and David Palmer—ended up as winners. As the Expos had just arrived in Los Angeles on the night of July 18, reliever Jeff Reardon decided to voice his unhappiness over what he considered unfair treatment by veteran beat writer Ian McDonald, from *The Gazette*. At the hotel bar, Reardon blasted McDonald about his lack of impartiality, saying he never gave him credit. He also believed that relievers were subject to unjustified criticism.[76] Reardon was doing fine in his first full season as the team's closer. In 37 games and 53 and one-third innings, his ERA was 1.89. He had only one loss in four decisions, with 14 saves. Reardon, despite a rugged appearance, was very sensitive and, in fact, was very unhappy over being ignored for the All-Star Game.[77] And when he was with the Mets, he always felt he wasn't appreciated the way he should have been.[78] The verbal altercation with McDonald didn't have any sequel.

The Expos won once in both Los Angeles and San Francisco. They had another stop in Chicago where they won twice in two games for a very successful 8–4 road record in these two weeks away from Montreal. It was not enough to gain ground in the NL East race, as both the Cards and the Phillies were also playing well. The Expos would have the chance to climb in the standings as 16 of their next 19 games were scheduled against St. Louis and Philadelphia.

The Expos' first series back home was against the Cards for four games. The first two games were extremely spectacular with two Expos triumphs in extra innings. In the first one, the Cards' bullpen blew a two-run lead in the eighth with a bases-loaded walk to Gary Carter by Bruce Sutter and an RBI groundout by Warren Cromartie against Jim Kaat. Tim Wallach's sacrifice fly ended the game in the tenth. The scenario repeated itself in the second game as the Expos tied the game at five on Chris Speier's single off Sutter in the eighth inning. Andre Dawson drove in the winning run in the 11th with a single. That game featured another second baseman, Bryan Little. Mike Gates was hitting only .233 and had been blanked in six consecutive games for a total 21 at-bats. After a 10–1 clubbing by the Cards, the Expos won another comeback game, thanks to a two-run triple by Jerry White in the eighth. If White could play the hero, the Expos had to thank Tim Raines for that, as he showed up late for the game.[79] Raines still contributed to that seventh inning with a single.

The Expos were four games back but the Phillies were the news leaders as Philadelphia was the team's next destination for another four-game series. This time, the Expos were not as fortunate, losing three of them. They lost the first one, 2–1, stranding ten runners on base. The biggest news of the day on August 2, however, was the acquisition of veteran second baseman Doug Flynn from the Texas Rangers for future considerations, a transaction that would be settled with cash.[80] Flynn was known for being reliable defensively, a quality that was badly lacking at second base in 1982. But his arrival did nothing to help the team offensively, which was one of the reasons Rodney Scott lost his job. After 1981, John McHale insisted that the team couldn't afford two .230 hitters in the lineup[81] and that's why Wallace Johnson was given the job at second base. With Flynn, it was back to square one; he had no power, no discipline at bat and his batting average was mediocre at best. Pierre Ladouceur wrote in *La Presse* that the Expos should have found an adequate replacement before letting Scott go.[82] Mike Gates was demoted to the minors. He told the media he had no idea what the Expos had in mind, pointing out rightly that they wanted to improve the offense but acquired a defensive specialist. He said that the team was panicking and that the pressure was enormous, especially for the youngsters.[83] The irony of it all was that the Expos lost the first game Flynn played at second on an error ... by the new second baseman!

As the Expos were getting ready for the third game in Philadelphia, they got another new player, outfielder Joel Youngblood from the New York Mets, for a player to be named later, which turned out to be pitcher Tom Gorman. Youngblood had played a game in Chicago that same afternoon and arrived during the game in Philadelphia. He was inserted in the lineup in the sixth inning and in the seventh he hit a single, becoming the first player to get hits in two different cities the same day. Youngblood started the next game in right field and made his contribution in a 9–2 win with two hits, three RBIs and two runs. Warren Cromartie became the odd man out. At .248, his batting average was below what he usually hit, but since June 1, he was hitting .278 with a respectable .358 on-base percentage.[84] But more was expected from Cromartie.

The Expos then won two out of three games in St. Louis. In the first game, they at last got the best of Joaquin Andujar, who suffered his first defeat against the Expos after 10 wins. After that series, on August 8, the Expos were four games back in fourth place, behind Philadelphia, St. Louis and Pittsburgh. But they just couldn't get any momentum as they lost two out of three against the lowly Cubs before embarking in another all-important series against Philadelphia. While the Expos were facing the Cubs, it was announced that Bill Virdon had been fired by the Houston Astros. Virdon had led the team to the playoffs in both 1980 and 1981, but just couldn't get things going in 1982 with a 49–62 record, for fifth place in the NL West. Virdon was highly respected in baseball circles with stints as manager with both the Pittsburgh Pirates and New York Yankees. It didn't take long before speculation made its way to Montreal. In fact, Virdon's name had already surfaced in November 1981[85] when Jim Fanning had not yet been confirmed to return as manager. John McHale did nothing to try to quell these rumors, saying that he would talk to Virdon, but only as a friend.[86] Michael Farber, from *The Gazette*, was quite direct: the Expos had to get Bill Virdon.[87]

The series against the Phillies was highly expected, even more so than against the Cards. The Expos and Phillies had battled in both 1980 and 1981. The Expos had an ideal opportunity to make up some ground in the NL East. A doubleheader on August 12 was scheduled to start off things and the Expos prevailed. In the second game, the Expos blew a three-run lead in the eighth and a two-run lead in the ninth before Warren Cromartie put an end to an 8–7 effort with an RBI single. The Expos were four games back, but from the Cards. On Friday August 13, the Expos won a third straight from the Phillies, 3–2. Bryn Smith was the winner but the credit belonged to Jeff Reardon. He was summoned in the sixth with the bases loaded and one out with a 3–1 lead. Reardon coaxed Bo Diaz to hit into an inning-ending double play. But after the game, there were some dark faces in the Expos' clubhouse. David Palmer was removed from the game in the third inning when a ligament snapped on a pitch: "Pete Rose was hitting and I threw a pitch and it was like somebody shot me in the arm and the ball flew over Gary Carter's head. I thought I had broke my arm or something like that. Some pieces of ligament just ripped off my bone and my elbow, so I got Tommy John's surgery. I didn't feel 100 percent but it didn't feel like I would throw one pitch and have it snap like that either."[88] His season was over and many wondered whether they had seen the last of David Palmer in a big league uniform.

Saturday afternoon, Scott Sanderson and Steve Carlton were the starters. Sanderson had been inconsistent for the last two months. He had allowed four runs or more seven times in his last 13 starts and, like most of his teammates, he had more success that year on the road. On the other hand, Carlton was his old self. At 37, he was leading the league in several categories, including wins with 16.

The Expos exploded with four runs in the first inning, including a two-run homer by Gary Carter. But the Phillies tied the game with two runs in the second and two more in the seventh. Bryn Smith was called upon with a runner on second and no outs in the seventh, but retired Mike Schmidt, Bo Diaz and Garry Maddox in order to keep the game tied at four. Smith was the first batter due in the bottom of the seventh, Jim Fanning decided to let him hit and the pitcher reached second on an error by Schmidt. Four batters later, the Expos had scored four runs for what looked like a comfortable lead leading into the eighth inning. But to the surprise of most people, Smith was not back on the mound but rather Woodie Fryman. The veteran retired only one of the four batters he faced. Jeff Reardon, who had pitched five times in the last four days, didn't fare any better, allowing all three batters he faced to reach base. At that point, the Phillies were within one run of the Expos but had the bases loaded with only one out. Ray Burris was called upon to try to put out what looked like an uncontrollable fire. Burris walked the next two batters before yielding a grand slam to Bill Robinson. Dan Schatzeder put an end to that nightmarish inning by inducing Pete Rose to fly out. The Phillies added three more runs in the ninth for a 15–11 win.

After the game, there was only one question that had to be answered: why wasn't Bryn Smith on the mound to start the eighth inning, especially after letting him hit for himself in the bottom of the seventh? Jim Fanning was on the defense. No matter what position he had filled within the organization, he always had been very discreet regarding the team. He would never say anything that could trigger any controversy. According to Ian McDonald, even though Fanning had the appearance of being very open to the media, he rarely gave anything worthy to the writers: "When he was general manager and a player was traded, we would never know it and we could never see the player before he left. From the organization's standpoint, he was great but that was very hard for the media."[89] As a manager, Fanning was very discreet regarding injuries to the players. But this time, he was cornered by the journalists and had no choice but to explain his decision. Fanning told them that Smith mentioned that he wasn't 100 percent — he had pitched three innings the night before — but that he was good to go.[90] Fanning didn't want to take any chances and thus Fryman was sent to start the eighth, with the disastrous results that followed.

On Sunday, August 15, the Expos were counting on Steve Rogers to give the bullpen some slack but, as of late, the team's ace had not been his usual self, allowing ten earned runs in 17 and two-thirds innings in his last three starts. But Rogers was in top form that afternoon, limiting the Phillies to only four singles in the first seven innings. But Marty Bystrom was almost as good, allowing one unearned run on a double-play ball. The Phillies tied the game in the eighth on Garry Maddox's home run. In the ninth, Pete Rose led off with a single off Rogers. Manny Trillo moved him to second on a sacrifice and after a Garry Matthews pop-out to second, Mike Schmidt was due to hit. With two outs and first base open, play was stopped to decide whether Rogers would face Schmidt or not. But it was not Jim Fanning who came to the mound but rather pitching coach Galen Cisco.[91] He wasn't there to relay any decision but to ask Rogers if he wanted to face Schmidt or give him a free pass to first. Schmidt was, at that point, one of the best, if not the best, hitters in the majors. But Rogers had handled Schmidt fairly well in that game in three at-bats, including two strikeouts. Rogers gave it a try, but the decision backfired as Schmidt hit an opposite-field home run down the right-field line, silencing the more than 59,000 fans that had packed Olympic Stadium. With these very tough two losses, the Expos were five games back from St. Louis.

As one could expect the day after these disastrous two games, Jim Fanning's job as the team's manager was heavily criticized, more than ever. Serge Touchette wrote that Fanning couldn't manage a team[92] while both Michel Blanchard and Réjean Tremblay were questioning his leadership qualities.[93] Gary Carter said that the decision to face Schmidt should have been made by the manager.[94] He was not alone along those lines, as most critics agreed that Fanning should have made that decision.[95] Rogers, as a true competitor, would never back down from a challenge, especially since he was in the middle of his best season in the big leagues. If he wasn't convinced that he could get the best hitters out, he would not have been considered among the league's elite. Rogers thus acted in agreement with the mind of a true professional athlete.

There was more to that, however, in Rogers' decision to face Schmidt. Years later, Rogers, remembering very well that particular game, said that the situation wasn't that clear-cut as it seemed: "The first three times Schmitty came up, I had struck him out the first two times and I popped him up the third time. Then you got the hitter right behind him who was George Vukovich, who was 1-for-3 but he hit the ball on the nose three times. Two outs, Rose on second, I said, 'I'll pitch Schmitty tough. I am going to pitch him tough and if I miss, if I fall behind, I'll walk him. But right now, I want to give us a chance because Vukovich is swinging the bat well.' The first pitch was a ball, just missed outside, the second pitch was a slider for a strike. It was 1–1. As for the third pitch, I had not thrown Mike Schmidt a fastball inside the entire game, not one single sinker inside. I said, 'You know, it's time to show him that I will throw the sinker inside, but I'm not going to throw it for a strike.' So, I threw the ball a foot inside, about a foot off the ground when it got to home plate. He put an inside-out uppercut swing on the ball and hit the ball to the opposite field that went 341 feet; it just scraped the back of the wall, and went just inside the foul pole in right field for a two-run homer. I will tell you, you will never see Mike Schmidt, take that swing again, before or after. I don't know where it came from. He just simply beat me in what I would say was the most unlikeliest way. Had he hit that pitch and golfed it out, and hit a two-run dinger by pulling the ball, I would have called myself the most stupid SOB that ever hit the earth. But it was a good pitch, and he hit it the weirdest way possible."[96]

Jim Fanning completely accepted the responsibility for what unfolded: "I had a front-line pitcher pitching to a front-line hitter. If I had a second-line pitcher pitching to Mike Schmidt, there isn't any question what I would do. There's some things you really have to understand and writers don't understand. You put Mike Schmidt on first base and the next guy got a base hit, or whatever, and it was probably a left-hander hitter hitting behind Mike Schmidt, and that guy gets a base hit, and Steve Rogers can say to the pitching coach, you mean, he doesn't think I can't get Mike Schmidt out? Has Mike Schmidt yet hit .500 off of me? There's a lot of things to think about. I walked Mike Schmidt as a winning run in a playoff game. Now had we lost that game, I would have been chastised from coast to coast. Since we got the next guy out, nobody ever mentioned it." To his credit with his line of thought, Fanning was consistent in that George Vukovich, a solid lefty hitter, was the next batter. When reminded about the identity of the next batter, Fanning said: "Vukovich was a very fine hitter. He was hitting behind Mike Schmidt, that should tell you something."[97]

To try to make up for David Palmer's loss, the Expos acquired left-handed pitcher Randy Lerch from the Milwaukee Brewers in a straight cash deal. His eight wins were quite misleading though — thanks to Milwaukee's explosive offense — as his ERA was 4.97.

After the weekend debacle, the Expos had to regroup on the road for ten games in Atlanta, Houston and Cincinnati. Montreal won five of them. In Cincinnati, the Expos faced the Reds's new sensation, Brad Lesley.[98] His antics after getting a strikeout didn't earn him many accolades among his opponents — he would yell and show some exuberance like wrestler Hulk Hogan — but he was getting lots of publicity and became very popular in Cincinnati, whose fans badly needed some entertainment as the Reds, after more than a decade of excellence, were mired deep in last place in the NL West. Lesley had been called up from the minors in late July and when he faced the Expos his ERA was around 1.00. But his passage to the majors would be very brief, as he couldn't sustain that level of excellence very long.

Back in Montreal on August 26 for ten games, the Expos won seven of them against the same three teams they had just faced, Houston, Cincinnati and Atlanta. On September 1, Tim Raines showed up late again against the Reds, the third time it happened that season. Serge Touchette wrote that the Expos were just beating about the bush, comparing his case with that of Ellis Valentine,[99] as did Jean-Paul Sarault earlier that season.

The Expos had a very good chance again to gain some ground as the team headed for St. Louis. The Cards scored six times in the three-game series but ended up winning two of them, 1–0, thanks to complete-game efforts from Joaquin Andujar and Bob Forsch. But the Expos got back in the mix, winning five in a row in Chicago and New York while the Cards were splitting six games, reducing the gap to only two games with 18 to play, including two versus the Cards in Montreal. The hopes were quickly quashed, however, with a five-game losing streak that ended against the Mets in the second game of a doubleheader. With 12 games to play, the Expos were six games back and quite honestly, nobody thought the Cards would fold in the last two weeks of the season.

Since the start of the season, Raines' performances and especially his behavior were the subject of much innuendo and rumors. Raines' stats were not that bad by any means, including leading the league in stolen base. His batting average was hovering around .275 with a subpar but not bad .350 on-base percentage. These numbers were off compared to 1981, but many a times players have had problems adjusting in their second season after a successful rookie season, a phenomenon called the sophomore jinx. But in Raines' case, there was more than that. What many suspected became public knowledge on September 15 when CJAD aired an interview by anchor Bob Dunn with Raines, who acknowledged that he had taken drugs during the season.[100] The interview was reported the day after by Wayne Parrish in the *Toronto Star*.[101] But Raines denied that his play was affected in any way, giving as an example running back George Rodgers, the NFL leader in yards gained, even though he had admitted taking cocaine.[102] Raines said that he had stopped taking drugs in May after his bad start. But the real truth would come to light later.

It was in December that the real story would be made public. In a front-page article by Michael Farber in the *Montreal Gazette*[103] — a story that earned him a prize for the best sports report by the Canadian Newspaper Awards — Raines told him that he had taken drugs regularly for six months, from January to July, and in a more intermittent way thereafter until the end of the season. His habit cost him about $40,000 in his estimation.[104] Montreal broadcaster Jim Bay, who was close to Raines, said that his problems had begun in the winter of 1981–82. His new contract, which called for a $350,000 salary, more than ten times what he had earned in 1981, afforded him the means to enjoy his newest recreational activity.[105] Raines took drugs before games in his window-tinted car, in the toilets, and in his apartment with friends.

During games, some people, like broadcaster Dave Van Horne, noticed a lack of concentration by Raines. "I can recall a time, the Expos were playing the Braves, and Tim Raines drew a walk. When he drew the walk, he put the bat down and walked almost aimlessly toward first base. I wasn't sure he was ever going to get there. And it just struck me, something has to be wrong there, he's not right. And I remember shortly after, the team was struggling on the field, and I remember going to John McHale and saying, 'John, we've avoided being critical of Tim Raines' and pointed out what happened in Atlanta. I said, 'I think we have to say something about this because he's such an important part of the ballclub.' Now, when I was saying this to John, I wasn't meaning to indicate that Raines was on drugs. I didn't know what the problem was. All I knew was, there was a problem. He was not able to focus on the game and he was hurting the team. John McHale said, 'We're working on this, we'd just like this to stay in house until we make something public, if we make anything public.' Again, as I say, there was an attempt to protect the integrity of the game, and ensure the continuing support of the fans towards the game and the players. It wound up blowing up in the face of not just the Expos and their front office but also in all of baseball."[106]

The first time the Expos were confronted with Raines' problems was when he showed up late for a game on June 29. In the next few weeks, McHale drove Raines to Montreal General Hospital twice a week so that he could meet with Dr. Alan Mann, who was the head of the institution's psychiatry department. Shortly after the end of the season, Raines was on his way to a rehabilitation center in California, where he stayed for a month.[107]

John McHale involved himself personally. According to Jim Bay, there was no way the Expos' president and GM would lose another player to drugs after Ellis Valentine.[108] Said McHale: "We were started to get educated on that whole question of drugs. We were seeing one of our best, desirable players playing an unusual way. We knew something was wrong, so we started getting into it. I know, personally, I made a commitment that Montreal was not going to lose this great young player because guys were running around the street selling cocaine to him. We turned him over to a very high-class psychiatrist, a very excellent medical man in a hospital in Montreal. We got him on a program to go see him for the rest of that year. I think you probably know that I was a baby-sitter for his young son. I would take him in a car, Tim would go see the doctor and I would baby-sit young Rock. I certainly felt good that we were doing everything we could to try to get this fixed and at the end of

One of the most underrated players of the 1980s, Tim Raines was the most productive offensive player in the National League between 1983 and 1987.

the year we sent him out to Betty Ford. In the meantime, there was a very well-known doctor inside the airlines who was a very successful consultant and experienced in this whole question of drugs. We got Tim involved with him, and I think he did an excellent job working with Tim."[109]

Contrary to Tim Raines' assertion, McHale believed that his habit went way back to 1980, when he came in contact with Ron LeFlore: "Not that he (LeFlore) was the first one but he popularized it around on the team. I think he was eventually the guy who led Tim Raines into it." According the McHale, at least eight players who were with the team in 1982 were drug users.[110] But the Expos were far from being the only team to be hit by that culture of drugs. And they sure were not the only team to be slow in reacting. In his autobiography, Dick Williams said that the team's brass was told about some problems, especially after coach Ozzie Virgil found a bunch of doobies on a towel.[111] But the Expos, as most teams did, turned their heads the other way. There were some warning signs, however. In September 1980, Andre Thornton, the Cleveland Indians designated hitter and a very respected individual, said that a drug culture existed in baseball, in every team, and that alcoholism was prevalent in the majors. Some teams were having drugs problems and the regular use of amphetamines was common since the 1960s. Thornton believed that baseball leaders had the responsibility to be more active and tough in regard to drugs but were doing nothing.[112]

It was not the first time, nor the last, where professional organizations ignored some obvious problems, fearing the consequences of negative publicity. More than 20 years later, pro sports would have to deal with performance-enhancing drugs, years after the first hints of its use were quite clear. Outside pressure made the leagues move towards some form of self-regulation. At the beginning of professional sports, gambling was the main problem and major league baseball decided to seriously tackle it only after it became public knowledge that the 1919 World Series wasn't played fair and square by the Chicago White Sox. In each case, the situation worsened when nobody reacted, up to the point where it exploded in the face of everyone concerned. In the case of drugs, two big cases were brought to justice in Kansas City and Pittsburgh. Dozens of players had to testify and four of them ended up sentenced to three months in prison, Willie Aikens, Jerry Martin, Vida Blue and Willie Wilson.[113] More players had to give up ten percent of their salary while going through rehabilitation.[114] In all this, Montreal had the reputation of being a hot spot for drug and cocaine use in baseball circles.[115] True, Montreal was, and still is, an entertaining city. Not unlike most metropolitan areas, one could easily get drugs or whatever recreational substance one would be willing to use. Why was Montreal singled out? The answer: customs. Montreal was the only Canadian city in the National League and players traveling there from the U.S. were wary of being caught with drugs while going through customs; thus those who wanted their stuff had to buy it from local providers.[116]

In the case of Raines, it took the Expos some time to make it public. The first reaction to CJAD's interview and the *Toronto Star* story was to say that Raines had talked too much and that there was no problem.[117] As if that wasn't enough, during the five-game losing streak, Jim Fanning had to be driven to the hospital because he was suffering from strong migraines.[118] He missed five games and during his absence coach Vern Rapp was managing the team. Migraines were no stranger to Jim Fanning, as he suffered from that condition since childhood, but surely not that to that extent. While he was in hospital, Fanning was the subject of another story by Wayne Parrish in the *Toronto Star*. Parrish knew his way around the team, as he had been on the beat for the *Montreal Star* when it folded in September 1979. Fanning's qualities (or lack thereof) were questioned by his own players in the article. Woodie Fryman said he told Fanning he wished he wouldn't have been back in 1982 for his own good. Dawson added his own, adding that the players had no clue what to expect with Fanning as manager. Another Expo, who didn't want to be identified, was harsher in his comments, blaming Fanning for at least ten losses, a conservative estimate according to that player.[119]

Fanning was back on September 22 in an 11–4 win over Philadelphia, but it was clear that the game had no significance whatsoever. On Saturday, September 25, after a 9–4 victory over Pittsburgh, Fanning didn't meet the press. On Sunday, the Expos were blanked, 3–0. This time, Fanning met the media but was extremely irritated and sarcastic in his rather short and quick answers. When someone brought up his absence the day before, Fanning's reply was: "It's none of your business. I left right after the game and, quite honestly, I'd like to do the same today!"[120]

The Expos were officially eliminated from postseason consideration on September 27 at home after a 4–2 loss to the eventual NL East champions, the St. Louis Cardinals. The Cards won the way they knew best, with all their runs in the first inning, including three on Willie McGee's inside-the-park home run. For the first time since 1978, the Expos were out of the postseason picture before the last weekend of the season. They ended up with an 86–76 record, in third place in their division. On the last day of the campaign, it was announced that Jim Fanning wouldn't return for the 1983 season.

After the season, it was time for a major questioning session. How could a team with five bona fide stars (Carter, Oliver, Dawson, Raines and Rogers), an acknowledged solid starting rotation and a solid number one reliever for the first time in years fail so miserably? Without surprise, most eyes turned to Jim Fanning. Of course, Raines' drug problems were brought up when Fanning assessed his 1982 season years later: "I think I got a fair chance as a manager, sure. And the Montreal Expos, at that time, weren't the only club with these problems. Because there were other managers who told me that their situation was not much different than ours. The Expos were not different. When the drugs came in the game, none of us knew how to handle it, really. The union was so powerful, you might do the best you can to help some players but there wasn't much you can do. When Timmy Raines called me and said he had a problem, then you can go to work and help him." Being the subject of that heavy a scrutiny right from the start didn't bother Fanning a bit, he said. But he maintained that with a Tim Raines playing in his full capacity, it would have made a world of difference. "We finished six games out of first place. If I had had a healthy Tim Raines, one player, not anybody else who was involved in drugs, only one player that had kept himself healthy, we win the pennant."[121]

Problem is, Raines wasn't that bad in 1982. He had reached base 256 times, the highest number in the National League among leadoff hitters (and seven more than Ricky Henderson, who was viewed as the best in baseball). Raines led the league with 78 stolen bases in 94 attempts. Nonetheless, Raines didn't provide the Expos with the same quality of play of his rookie season or of his years to come. Using Bill James' win shares stats,[122] if Raines had been able to maintain the level he showed in 1981 and 1983 over a full season, he would have added two more wins for the Expos in 1982. The Expos finished six games back from the Cards. It would thus be grossly unfair to blame Raines and only Raines, for the team's failure in 1982.

Fanning for one, even after making the playoffs in 1981, could never gain the respect of his players.[123] In his September article regarding Fanning, Wayne Parrish had quoted a member of the team, according to whom the team was caught in a no-win situation: Fanning didn't have what it took to win, but if the players could pull it out, then they would be stuck with him as manager. Many players pointed out his hesitations to make decisions, due to a great sense of insecurity. Woodie Fryman said that he had to warm-up 150 times during the season.[124] Gary Carter started more than 150 games, which was far more than a catcher could sustain in the long run and one had to wonder whether he would be able to reach the end of his contract on both legs (he would, but barely). Fanning defended himself by saying his team had a better chance of winning with Carter behind the plate, which was quite obvious. But the Expos had signed free agent Tim Blackwell to give Carter a break now and then and to make sure he would be fresh come September. In 1982, Carter had, in fact, not the best of months with only two home runs and seven RBIs in September and October. Maybe a fresher Carter could have helped the team more. For the record, the Expos' record with Tim Blackwell as the starting catcher was four wins and six losses.

Fanning would say that the decision to go back to an office position was agreed upon mutually with John McHale: "That kind of happened in the last series of the season when we played in Pittsburgh. John and I were talking and it had been a very difficult year, with the drug situation and all that stuff. I said to John, maybe there is another way we can do all these things. He offered to think about it and I said that there are guys out there you might think about."[125]

Among players, especially those who had been there for some years, there was a consensus: the team made far too many changes.[126] When Bill Beacon, from UPI, asked Gary Carter what went wrong, the catcher took him by the arm and stopped at several lockers, telling the young reporter, "Was he here last year?"[127] The message was clear. Steve Rogers and Woodie Fryman also voiced such opinions.[128] During the season, several players remarked that the team's attitude wasn't the same anymore, that there was no spark on the field, contrary to years past. For that, the departure of three players contributed to that perceived change: Larry Parrish, Rodney Scott and Bill Lee.

Since Tony Perez departed for Boston after 1979, many had wondered who was the real leader on the Expos team. In the middle of 1979, when Perez was still with the Expos, Larry Parrish's name had been brought up. The tall third baseman saw his career derailed thanks to the wrist injury he sustained in May 1980. It was hard for him to assume a leadership role, considering he had to cope with his own problems. But he had redeemed himself with a solid second half in 1981 and was as a reason why the Expos made it to the postseason.

According to Steve Rogers, the team lost a very important part of what was the Expos' family: "What I truly believe, there was an element that was no longer there. Larry Parrish didn't put up .340 batting averages with 42 dingers and 140 RBIs. What he did was put up solid years every year, playing a very solid third base. In the family unit of the Expos' core of players from the system, LP was the focal point, he was the enforcer. The fact is he went out and taped up elbows, very much like Andre Dawson, taped up and went out to play. And squabbles in the locker room, it just didn't happen. I can't tell you whether LP got into our veins or something like that. He was just at the center of that family core. On the talent alone, it was a trade that made sense. On stats alone, Al (Oliver) certainly provided those stats. But it was more about the heart of that core that was gone. I think it made the family unit of that team a little weaker and that was probably one thing that we missed."[129]

That lack of team unity was voiced more than once during the 1982 season, from Chris Speier and John McHale most notably. Dave Van Horne also believed the Expos missed Parrish's intangibles: "In my opinion, the mistake was made not so much on baseball terms, because Al Oliver had a wonderful year and won a batting championship. He couldn't have done more for the club than what he was asked to do and what he delivered. But I think where the Expos underestimated Larry Parrish was with his leadership ability. He was the heart and soul of that team and he kept everything together. In that clubhouse, in the dugout and on the field. He was the one who could bridge the gap and keep other players in line and keep them focused with the job on hand and I think they underestimated his effect on that team. And so, the absence of Parrish, his passion and his heart, was greatly missed and I think that was one of the reasons why the Expos failed to get back to the playoffs."[130]

Beat writer Serge Touchette admitted that it took him some time to truly evaluate Parrish properly: "I didn't think he was that important. He was not a rah-rah guy but he brought an imposing and important presence into the clubhouse. His absence created a void. In pure talent, the Expos didn't lose per se as Oliver provided the team with a batting championship. But the Expos lost a huge leader that we had underestimated."[131]

Parrish himself hesitated some when asked about his place with the team, at the time of the trade at the eve of the 1982 season: "I ran into some players and they said it wasn't the same after I was gone. I know that John (McHale) said that was the worst trade he ever made. Those things, that makes you feel good. And I think the pitchers knew also. I would study their mechanics, I would look at them in the bullpen, I would listen to Jim Brewer, the pitching coach, and then we had Galen Cisco. I would try to pick up on their mechanics, what they were doing when they were throwing the ball right. I felt because of that, a lot of times I could come in from third and help a guy get through an inning and things wouldn't unravel for him and we wouldn't have to make a pitching change." Parrish would point out also at a sense of security he brought to his pitchers. "The pitchers talked about the fact that they just missed the fact that I wasn't at third. They knew if they threw at a guy they weren't worried about the guy getting to them on the mound!"[132]

Bill Gullickson also believed Parrish was a big asset in enforcement: "He was like the cowboy on the team. He was a big strong intimidating guy and I think not so much towards his own teammates but towards the opposing players. You knew he was going to be in your corner."[133] It is worth noting that the player who succeeded him at third base, Tim Wallach, did a very good job. But in his first year as a regular, Wallach couldn't take Parrish's place in the clubhouse.

The release of both Rodney Scott and Bill Lee also changed the atmosphere within the club. Their insolence, combined with Parrish's imposing presence, forced opponents to always be on their toes. The Expos obviously erred in giving the second base job to Wallace Johnson. All in all, seven candidates paraded at the second base position before the team traded for Doug Flynn. But nobody was better than Scott had been. Furthermore, the Expos could never find any kind of defensive cohesion during the season. As for Bill Lee, he was no more than a mop-up pitcher when he was let go. But still, he was a peculiar guy that brought some life to the team. To Richard Milo, from *Canadian Press*, Lee wasn't just a clown: "Bill Lee could really motivate his teammates. He was passionate about the game and it was infectious. We could talk to him and he would say funny stuff but that had no importance. He just loved baseball and it showed."[134]

In hindsight, the people involved in these two players' early exit, including the players themselves, remained with their respective positions. Scott still believed that Fanning didn't like him as an individual: "No doubt the team was deprived of its personality when I and Lee were let go. And they didn't win anything. They weren't as good as they were." Scott believed he was made the scapegoat and paid for others. As for the rumors of drug use, he said the team was making excuses to get rid of him.[135] Lee never made excuses, but he didn't expect to be released. He would have wanted to keep playing but remained convinced that he was blacklisted.[136]

Jim Fanning didn't make excuses either when recalling that episode: "First, one guy just wasn't doing anything and the second guy literally jumped the club, went to a tavern. He really released himself. If he were a very productive pitcher, I suppose we might have handled that a different way, or we might have released him anyway. He didn't win any favors with his teammates, I can tell you that." When asked if these moves were strictly baseball-related, the reply was short: "There were circumstances, let's put it that way."[137]

John McHale, the one who had to make the final decision, gave the context of where these players stood when the Expos acquired them: "Nobody wanted Bill Lee when he was finished with the Red Sox. There was no market for him. We picked him up, we signed him, we made him an awfully good contract and we repeated that after he had a good first year. He was a very good pitcher for our club in that first year and then we gave him a very strong contract the next year. I just thought he forgot to play baseball after that. Rodney Scott was a short-term guy any place he went to play. He gave you an increase in energy, working hard to keep his job. But the minute he got very satisfied, other things were on his mind." When asked directly whether these decisions were drug-related, McHale replied: "We had a heavy drug problem in our club going on at that time. We thought we could have won or should have won with what we had. I don't know for sure. I liked Rodney Scott. He did make a solid contribution to our club, was a colorful player, gave us good running speed and scored runs. He was a very difficult guy to manage over a period of time, but had a lot of value. A good guy, but I guess he was always frustrated being among big hitters where he couldn't produce the power that all the rest of the guys in the lineup did. It was a baseball decision because nobody knew for sure what was happening in the drug area."[138]

The team's overall record was certainly disappointing, but several players put up solid if not spectacular numbers, with Al Oliver getting the highest grades. Oliver led the league in many categories, including batting average (.331), hits (204), total bases (317), doubles (43) and RBIs (109). Serge Touchette said he never saw a player hit the ball with such authority for a complete season.[139] Oliver was a model of consistency in 1982.

Gary Carter showed again that he was the best overall catcher in baseball. Offensively, he hit 29 home runs with 97 RBIs, to go along with a .293 batting average and 78 walks, a personal best. He played 153 games and would have played even more had it not been for a minor eye infection. Without much fanfare, Dawson showed good numbers as well, even though he was not as spectacular as in 1981. He ended up leading the team with 107 runs, hitting .301 with 23 home runs and 39 stolen bases. In his second season, first as a regular, Tim Wallach didn't disappoint, with 28 home runs and an impressive

97 RBIs. He was still learning his craft defensively at third base but showed improvements as the season unfolded. Warren Cromartie's stats might look rather ordinary at first glance. He nonetheless established a career high with 69 walks and hit 14 home runs, even though he lost the right field job to Joel Youngblood in August. Youngblood never got untracked with Montreal with 0 home runs and a .200 batting average in 40 games.

On the mound, Steve Rogers clearly established himself as the best right-handed pitcher in the National League. His 2.40 ERA led the league and he finished with a career-high 19 wins. Some would say that Rogers benefited from playing at Olympic Stadium, but even when adjusted, Rogers' ERA was still the best in the league. The Cy Young Award was voted to Steve Carlton overwhelmingly, 112 to 29. But Rogers should have earned a lot more consideration from the voters. Yes, Carlton was still impressive with his 23 victories and leading the league in wins, innings pitched, complete games and strikeouts. But, in overall contribution, Rogers' season was better then Carlton's. When asked years later about the outcome of the vote, Rogers would still give credit to Carlton: "I appreciate people saying that. But the only thing that I beat Steve Carllton in, the only category I beat Steve Carlton in, was ERA. He had better everything else. You look at every other major stat for starting pitchers, Steve Carlton was ahead of me. Wins, fewer losses, higher winning percentage, more strikeouts and innings pitched. I'd like to say that I got robbed. I didn't get robbed. I had a Cy Young-type year. Only it was in the same league as Steve Carlton. I appreciate people's analysis. It was, for me, by far the best year I had."[140]

Bill Gullickson, Scott Sanderson and Charlie Lea all won 12 games, with Lea having the best ERA at 3.24. Ray Burris never could recover his confidence after losing his first seven decisions in eight starts to begin the season. In 15 starts overall, Burris didn't get a single win, as his four victories all came in relief. Jeff Reardon in his first full season as a closer was a success, with a 2.06 ERA in 109 innings and 26 saves.

The Expos still looked good on paper and most of its core was young. John McHale's next mission was to find a new manager. As soon as the season ended, speculation abounded about who would succeed Jim Fanning. Bill Virdon's name came up repeatedly and it looked as if he was the only serious candidate.[141] Pierre Ladouceur believed Virdon was going to be McHale's man, but that it would be hard to forgo a very solid man who had been a good organization employee for several years, Felipe Alou.[142] He had just completed his second season managing the Expos' AAA affiliate in the American Association. He had been with the Expos since 1976 and his qualities were acknowledged by every player who came into contact with him.[143] But McHale believed he needed an experienced man with a solid track record and in that sense Bill

Virdon looked like the perfect man.[144] Eight days after the end of the 1982 season, Bill Virdon was appointed the team's new manager, the fifth in the team's history. He took over a club that, according to many observers, had yet to reach its potential. Virdon's hiring was welcomed throughout Montreal.

Not much was expected from the Expos in the offseason. The lineup looked set as was the pitching rotation and the bullpen. But that was not the only reason why the Expos weren't active in the free agent market. John McHale insisted that the Expos become more responsible financially.[145] It was quite a change from past years as the Expos did everything to satisfy their own players and to lure all-star players with big money, namely Reggie Jackson and Don Sutton. McHale had said before that money wouldn't be an obstacle in the acquisition of a player who could make the difference.[146] The Expos were never a team to throw money around left and right. Financial controller Harry Renaud made sure the money was spent rigorously. They had refused to go after Nolan Ryan after 1979 because of what the Expos thought were extravagant demands.

McHale's comments meant that the team would be far more cautious in the future. The team, according to some reports, lost between $2 million and $3 million in 1982[147] and still had nothing to show for it, in terms of winning. A good portion of these losses, though, should be attributed to players who were released at some point. It was estimated that around $1.5 million was paid to Bill Lee, Rodney Scott, John Milner, Fred Norman, Rowland Office, Stan Bahnsen and others, players who were let go early in 1982 or even before that.[148] Substitute catcher Tim Blackwell was lured to Montreal with a $300,000 salary to take some slack from Gary Carter. He started ten games, including three in doubleheaders and five more because Carter had en eye infection. Blackwell was thus paid $30,000 per game while Carter was getting half that on a per game basis! All that money couldn't guarantee a title. Consequently, John McHale concluded that the goal from then on would be to be competitive, contrary to prior claims about winning championships, a subtle but significant difference.

With a set roster, the Expos made few noises before spring training. They traded for Jim Wohlford, who was with San Francisco, and re-signed Woodie Fryman, who was a free agent. Fryman had no intention of playing anywhere else anyway, especially after saying that the Expos would at last have a genuine manager in 1983 in Bill Virdon.[149]

In January 1983, brothers Paul and Charlemagne Beaudry, who had been limited partners since the Expos' initial days, sold their 20 percent shares to Charles Bronfman.[150] For years, both men didn't have much say anyway in how the team was run and the gap widened between Bronfman and the

Beaudrys. After 1976, *Montréal-Martin* published a series of articles, penned by Jean Aucoin, where the Beaudrys blasted John McHale and Jim Fanning after that disastrous campaign.[151] Charles Bronfman had tried to buy both out, without success until January 1983.

The eyes then turned to the man who was touted as the solution to all the aches that hit the Expos in 1982, Bill Virdon.

9

1983: They Blew Their Last Chance

Rigor and optimism: two words that fit exactly with the prevalent atmosphere in West Palm Beach at the 1983 Expos spring training camp. Nothing was left to chance with Bill Virdon and everything was set to prepare the players to play the new manager's way. Right from the start, Virdon stated that the emphasis would be placed on the basics.[1] According to Gary Carter, the camp was the hardest since the days of Gene Mauch.[2] Woodie Fryman, who certainly was used to hard work on his Kentucky farm, said that the schedule was quite busier than years before, "exactly the way I like it!"[3] And even though the players were working a lot harder, they were hard pressed to complain, considering many of them had no respect for previous manager Jim Fanning.[4] Since Fanning was held as mainly responsible for the 1982 fiasco by the players, the media and the fans, Virdon's presence had everybody believing that the Expos had all it took to go all the way to the World Series.

Even before the first official day of the camp, Virdon established a set of rules that players had to adhere to, including their language and a dress code. There would be no beer in the clubhouse nor in rides in training camp. Players would have to have their hair cut neatly, at an acceptable length that couldn't be longer than their shirt's collar. Facial hair was forbidden, but Virdon was open in this case.[5] Bryn Smith and Dan Schatzeder decided to conform by erasing their moustache, but Jeff Reardon pleaded to keep his thick beard, saying that it gave him a more combative look and a psychological edge,[6] arguments that Virdon didn't try to argue.[7]

Contract-wise, one player was quite unhappy: Bill Gullickson. He had lost his case in arbitration just prior to the reporting date to West Palm Beach. He wanted $365,000 but had to content with the Expos' offer at $275,000.[8] Gullickson tried to convince the arbitrator that his 12–14 record was due more to the lack of offensive and defensive support than to his own pitching. Gullickson reported with a vengeance, with the intention to prove the Expos wrong. Jeff Reardon agreed to a one-year $450,000 contract, which was most welcomed as the Expos' closer had most of his belongings stolen in the winter as he was moving to Florida.[9]

Camp opened officially on February 20 and the first surprise was Ray Burris, who showed up 35 pounds lighter, going from 230 to 195.[10] The main question marks were in the bullpen, where only Jeff Reardon and Woodie Fryman were assured of their spots. Bill Virdon wanted to add a lefty starter to the righty quartet of Steve Rogers, Bill Gullickson, Charlie Lea and Scott Sanderson. Bryn Smith, Ray Burris and lefties Dan Schatzeder and Randy Lerch were no sure thing, even though they had spent a good part of 1982 in Montreal.

The situation looked stable among position players but Bill Virdon left the door open at both middle-infield positions and in right field.[11] Doug Flynn, Chris Speier and Warren Cromartie would have to prove their worth to their new skip. Speier and Flynn were threatened by diminutive Bryan Little, a switch-hitter who was very confident, who would have every opportunity to win a spot on the roster. The Expos added some depth in the infield with Rennie Stennett, whom they invited to their minor-league camp.[12] Stennett hadn't played in 1982 after his release from the San Francisco Giants. His best days were with the Pittsburgh Pirates in the mid–1970s but since a broken leg suffered in 1977 (he was in the middle of his best season hitting .336), he had never been the same.

For Cromartie, having to justify himself was nothing new. Since his first day in Montreal, Cromartie had to do some adjusting in order to keep his job and survive. And up to then, he had prevailed. The Expos had a big prospect in Roy Johnson. In 1982, Johnson, a player with an imposing physique, had won the batting title in the American Association. Terry Francona was also in the mix, but the Expos wanted to be cautious after his knee injury in 1982. Francona was not very happy with the Expos' extreme cautiousness, getting almost restless at times.[13]

There was no doubt from the get-go that Bill Virdon was the boss on the field, which was enhanced in the first few days after a clash with Gary Carter.[14] The All-Star catcher became one of the best defensively after many hours working with Norm Sherry in his first few years. They both worked on every single aspect of the trade, including pop-ups around the plate. Carter became so good at catching these that he developed the habit of calling every single pop-up that was within reasonable reach, including those in play. But Virdon insisted that the pitcher was the one to call the defensive player who would catch the ball. Carter pleaded that he had always done it that way, to no avail.

In the meantime, Carter and Tim Raines got offers to pose for *Playgirl* magazine. John McHale didn't think it was a good idea but he didn't need to get involved as both players denied the invitation, especially image-conscious Carter.[15] As for Raines, he was geared up to regain the level of excellence of 1981 and show the world that 1982 was behind him. In the first week of March, Raines took part in a call-in radio show at CFCF radio, hosted by Jeff Rimer. The callers were backing him all the way, which was quite reassuring for the young outfielder.[16]

Andre Dawson also wanted to redeem himself, even if his 1982 season wasn't all that bad. But he had to battle hand and knee injuries, which curtailed his production.[17] In the first week, he had to get his knee drained after some inflammation that followed exercises on the basepaths, which were very hard for the joints.[18] Dawson was used to seeing needles in his knees since his days in college.

In the first week of exhibition games, the Expos and Charlie Lea got a big scare when the tall right-hander was hit in the face by a liner off Al Bumbry's bat against the Baltimore Orioles. But Lea was not seriously injured.[19] Randy Lerch was not injured but was not happy either and wanted to leave.[20] He was thinking about being a free agent, to which he was entitled to be on March 15, as he was acquired in 1982 in the middle of a multi-year contract. Lerch acknowledged that it took him some time to accept his trade from Milwaukee to Montreal.[21] But Lerch wisely decided to stay in Montreal,[22] as his value was not very high and most teams were in the middle of assessing their own organization.

In getting ready for the long season it was not unusual to have aches and pains left and right but the Expos were more and more concerned about Woodie Fryman's left elbow. For years, Fryman had been pitching without knowing whether "Arthur," the nickname for his arthritic left arm, would hold up from one pitch to the other. Fryman was used to pitching with pain but this time it looked more serious and he had to take cortisone shots.[23] He wasn't used at all until the end of the exhibition games, pitching two scoreless innings.

Bill Virdon decided to keep all the veterans from the year before on the mound, which meant that Lerch, Schatzeder, Smith and Burris would begin in the bullpen. The only new face worthy of a look was Bryan Little, who was named the best rookie in camp.[24] Virdon said he planned to use him on a regular basis, to the detriment of Chris Speier. The Expos would begin the season with three catchers with Gary Carter, Tim Blackwell and Roberto Ramos. The latter had no options left and the organization didn't want to lose him.[25]

While the Expos were in Florida, talks were on-going regarding a new lease for Olympic Stadium with the Montreal Olympic Park Board. Comments were heard via the media left and right and as was the case in 1977, though discussions were anything but smooth, at least publicly. But like 1977, both sides were bound to find an agreement as they needed one each other. The Expos originally wanted to lower their lease cost by $1 million while the provincial organization wanted the team to increase its payment by the same amount.[26] They finally reached an agreement that confirmed the status quo at $2.6 million a year.[27]

Before the season began, most pundits forecast the Expos to finish either first or second in the National League Eastern Division.[28] The absence of the left-handed starter and a weak bench were deemed as the Expos' weaknesses.[29]

The Expos opened the season the same way they did in 1982, with a complete-game shutout by Steve Rogers, in a 3–0 win in Chicago. Al Oliver looked as if 1982 never ended, with two home runs. The team jumped the gates with four straight victories, all in convincing fashion in Chicago and Los Angeles by a combined score of 25–8, with wins going to Rogers, Bill Gullickson, Scott Sanderson and Charlie Lea. In the fourth game, a very alert Tim Raines scored from second on a wild pitch. In the first four games, Raines got six hits, five runs and five RBIs. The Expos suffered their first loss to the hands of Fernando Valenzuela, who threw a shutout. Woodie Fryman pitched his first game, retiring the only batter he faced, but his arm was not sound and he would have to be placed on the disabled list on April 14.[30]

The Expos came back home on April 12 against the Cubs with a 4–1 record. When the team was introduced before the game, manager Bill Virdon was the subject of the biggest ovation.[31] But the Cubs and pitcher Steve Trout spoiled the party in a 5–0 Cubs win. After a Scott Sanderson triumph, the Expos flew to Houston where they had to content themselves with only one win, that of Charlie Lea, who came very close to pitching his second career no-hitter. Canadian Terry Puhl deprived Lea of that honor with two outs in the bottom of the eighth inning with a single. In the top of the ninth, Andre Dawson hit his third home run of the season, a shot that landed in the upper bleachers in left field, where very few balls were hit in the history of the Astrodome. The victim of Dawson's moonshot, Frank LaCorte, said after the game that he wished his golf tee shots were that impressive.[32] The Expos then were idle for three full days thanks to bad weather and they could play only one game against the defending World Series champions, the St. Louis Cards, the Expos prevailing, 7–6. It was only the Cards' second loss in eight games.

While the Expos were waiting for the rain to subside, the organization had to deal with another of their players who had off-the-field concerns. It was announced that Roy Johnson had some issues with drugs and that he would enter a rehabilitation center. It was Johnson himself who asked for some help. In the winter of 1982–83, he was scheduled to play winter ball in the Dominican Republic, but was sent home due to what was said to be lackadaisical play. In Florida during spring camp, he didn't seem alert, according to members of the organization.[33] Johnson would be back on the field before the end of the season, but he wouldn't ever again be considered a bona fide prospect.

On Wednesday, April 27, Olympic Stadium was the scene of a historic moment when Nolan Ryan, of the Houston Astros, got passed Walter Johnson as the all-time strikeout king. Ryan needed just five strikeouts to go past Johnson. Even though he was age 36, his fastball was still explosive and among the best in the majors. That day against the Expos, Ryan was in control but the strikeouts were not coming. By the eighth inning, he needed two more Ks to become the new strikeout monarch. The first batter, Tim Blackwell, became his 3,508th victim and then pinch-hitter Brad Mills was called out on strikes as Ryan punched his 3,509th strikeout.[34] Ryan would keep pitching for another decade, adding more than 2,000 victims along the way before finishing with 5,714 lifetime strikeouts.

That game against Houston was the second of a ten-game stay in Montreal, during which the locals couldn't do better than four wins. Jeff Reardon couldn't help his team, being sidelined most of that time with chronic back pain.[35] The Expos could have used him as they twice allowed three runs in the ninth for losses during that sequence in Montreal. The Expos were already without Woodie Fryman, so Bill Virdon had to turn to Bryn Smith and Dan Schatzeder as his two main men in the bullpen. The Expos in the meantime acquired lefty Chris Welsh from San Diego. Welsh was available after a fallingout of sorts with manager Dick Williams. On April 30 Padres coach Norm Sherry went to the mound to tell Welsh to not throw to first base as they were set for a trick play to get the runner. Welsh retorted that if Williams was not happy, he'd better find someone else.[36] That was Welsh's last inning with the Padres. Reardon wouldn't have to be placed on the disabled list but during his 10-day absence, no one recorded a save.

After the May 8 games, the Phillies were in first place with a 15–9 record, a game and a half ahead of the Expos, who were set for a seven-game road trip to Atlanta and St. Louis. The Expos won twice in Atlanta in three games, a series highlighted by a brawl in the second game. In the sixth inning, Claudell Washington, who had hit a home run in the second inning, didn't like a high and inside pitch by Scott Sanderson and immediately charged the mound as both dugouts emptied.[37] Less than a week before in Montreal, Sanderson had been spiked on a play at first by Washington.[38] After the game, Sanderson denied the pitch was retaliatory, insisting that he believed the spiking of the preceding week was his own fault.[39]

After Atlanta, the Expos were swept in a four-game series in St. Louis, losing twice in extra innings and once by a shutout. After thirty games, the team record stood at .500, 15 wins and as many losses, two and a half games behind both St. Louis and Philadelphia. The frustration was already palpable,

Bill Virdon was deemed the savior when it was announced he would succeed Jim Fanning as manager in 1983. But, to many, Virdon had already lost his passion for the game by the time he came to Montreal.

from players and coaches. The fans were less and less patient. Scott Sanderson noticed that the public had become increasingly demanding.[40] Manager Bill Virdon was not at all satisfied with his team's concentration on the field. In early May, Virdon blasted his team, insisting on a lack of execution, a situation that had been lasting for at least a week.[41] Al Oliver didn't like what he saw either. He hadn't been as solid as in 1982 and had no home runs since Opening Day and his batting average had yet to reach .300. He knew that 1983 was a very important year, not only for the Expos but for himself as well, saying, "I wouldn't be surprised to be traded if we don't win the title."[42] Doug Flynn was also concerned about his situation but, contrary to Oliver, it was the present and not the future that worried the second baseman. Bryan Little had started six straight games in early May. Flynn had repeatedly voiced his unhappiness about his tax situation and said he'd rather play regularly with an average team than to platoon with the Expos.[43] He wanted to meet John McHale. But the Expos' general manager wasn't impressed one bit by the way Flynn expressed himself via the media. "He didn't tell me why he was hitting .231," was McHale's terse reply.[44]

After that disastrous series in St. Louis, the Expos learned of the passing of coach Mel Wright, at age 55.[45] Wright was as close as one could be with Bill Virdon. In fact, Wright was Virdon's confidante everywhere he had managed, in Pittsburgh, New York and Houston.[46] Wright had been battling cancer for some time and it looked as if he was good to go in spring training.[47] But his health deteriorated thereafter and it was only a matter of weeks before cancer got the best of Mel Wright.

The Expos, back in Montreal, were first managed by Vern Rapp as Virdon was honoring his old friend.[48] The Expos split the first four games against Los Angeles and San Francisco before sweeping San Diego in three straight, including a Steve Rogers' shutout against his old manager, Dick Williams. The Expos were back in the NL East mix, only a half game from the lead.

John McHale was looking for ways to improve his bench and got two veterans, Mike Vail and Terry Crowley. Vail was acquired from San Francisco for Wallace Johnson, who had been up and down between the Expos and the minors for more than a year. Crowley, a pinch-hitting specialist, had been released by the Baltimore Orioles. Brad Mills was sent down to AAA. Another player was given his walking papers as Tim Blackwell was released, even though the Expos still owed him more than half of the three-year contract they gave him as a free agent after 1981, a move that would cost the team more than $500,000.[49]

After bringing the winning streak to five with a 7–4 win in Philadelphia on May 27, the Expos were involved in another altercation the following day. In the fifth inning, the Phillies had already scored once and, with one out, Charlie Lea threw a high and inside pitch to Gary Matthews who eventually reached first on a single, pushing Joe Morgan to second. After a second out, Von Hayes hit a single, driving in Morgan. After the relay from the outfield, Gary Carter tried to nail Hayes at second. Matthews, who had reached third, decided to sprint to home plate. Bryan Little's relay to Carter was well in advance to get Matthews, but the Phillies' runner charged the Montreal catcher with his elbows up high, sending both men sprawling. Carter didn't appreciate what he considered to be an unnecessary collision.[50] In the ninth, with the game tied at three, two outs and a runner on second, Bill Virdon decided to face Mike Schmidt. The Phillies third baseman was mired in one of the worst slumps of his career. He hadn't hit a home run in three weeks, and had only three singles in his last 40 at-bats, which was enlarged by Schmidt's tendency to over-analyze everything.[51] But that night against Jeff Reardon, Schmidt fell out of his lethargic period with a game-ending and game-winning two-run home run.

The Expos also lost the next three games, one more in Philadelphia and two in San Diego. In the second game against the Padres, the Expos lost on a bases-loaded walk in the ninth inning by Steve Rogers. The Expos pitcher was so mad after the fourth ball that he threw his glove in the direction of umpire Ed Montague.[52] But the Expos redeemed themselves with four wins in the last five games of that road trip. Chris Speier missed the whole California ride when his name was added to the disabled list due to some discomfort in his right elbow.[53] With a 26–22 record, the Expos were just one game behind the Cards.

After June 7, the Expos embarked on a month-long schedule in which they would face exclusively NL Eastern Division foes, right to the All-Star break. In the first seven games, they won only twice, including Randy Lerch's first win in his first start of the season. Lerch was summoned to the mound to replace Scott Sanderson, who was really struggling. Sanderson's record of four wins and four losses was quite misleading as his ERA was 5.74. In ten starts, he had pitched less than five innings per outing since the beginning of the season.

Sanderson was not the only one who was playing below expectations. Gary Carter's production was not up to the standards he had established in the past few years. His batting average stood at .219 with seven home runs and 17 RBIs in 37 games. On June 9, Carter was ejected after being struck out by Pittsburgh. After the game, Carter, who usually was very polite, had very harsh words towards umpire Jerry Davis, assessing him as being incompetent.[54]

Despite their inconsistencies, the Expos remained in the hunt for first place as nobody else seemed interested in taking advantage of the division favorites' struggles, including the Cards and Phillies. On June 13, the Expos had a very average record of 26–25 but were nonetheless only a game from first place. The Phillies, at .500, were only a game back from the Cards. It was then that the Expos launched their most successful sequence of the season with nine wins in eleven games, including four out of five against the Phillies at Olympic Stadium. Ray Burris set the tempo with his first shutout since 1981 against Steve Carlton. After splitting a doubleheader, the Expos won a very emotional game that was decided in the ninth inning. Both teams were scoreless in the ninth, thanks to pitchers Charlie Lea and Marty Bystrom. In the bottom of the ninth, Bystrom retired the first two batters and it looked as if extra innings would be required to settle that game. But Joe Morgan mishandled a ground-ball by Jerry White and after a walk to Chris Speier, Charlie Lea was due up. But Bill Virdon sent Andre Dawson as a pinch-hitter. Dawson had been the most consistent hitter in 1983 up to that point, with a .327 batting average and 13 home runs. The day before, Dawson had won the second game of the doubleheader with a home run in the bottom of the 12th inning. Dawson had a night off following what had been a long day, but with the real possibility of winning the game in the ninth, Virdon couldn't resist the temptation to use Dawson as a pinch-hitter. Dawson never got the chance to hit as he was hit by the first ball thrown by Bystrom, which was high and inside. Dawson was very upset and got up menacingly, which led both teams to rush to the field, but calm was restored with no further damage. The Expos then had the bases loaded and Al Holland was called upon to end the inning once and for all against Tim Raines. Holland's night was very short: on his first pitch, Tim Raines launched the ball over the left-field wall for a game-winning grand slam.[55]

After that 9–2 run, on June 24, the Expos found themselves in first place with a three and a half games lead over the Cards and five and a half over the Phillies. Ironically, during that stretch, Hugh Hallward, a team minority owner, said that the team was lacking a sparkplug, like Rodney Scott.[56] At the same time, many writers reported that the team had no spirit or energy.[57] Before the June 19 game, Bill Virdon once again addressed his players, blaming them for costly mental miscues.[58] One player who was hearing more and more boos was Gary Carter.[59] The Expos tried to get some help in the bullpen before the June 15 trading deadline, with Kent Tekulve as their main target, but the Pirates considered themselves still in the hunt for first place.[60]

The Expos managed to increase their lead to four and half games while splitting four games with Chicago at home, which included yet another bench-clearing brawl. This time, Keith Moreland, who had the physique of a line-backer, charged Chris Welsh, whose body had nothing to do with a football player, after being hit by a pitch. Nobody was injured and after the game Moreland said he made a mistake in charging the mound when there were two runners on base and a 4–3 Cubs lead in the fifth inning.[61] The day after, Tim Raines was ejected by umpire Bob Davidson in the fifth inning after being picked off first by Chuck Rainey.[62] Raines swore afterwards that he would never be ejected ever again (he would be once more, in 1989).[63]

As the Expos were in first place, the team was considering the possibility of signing Rodney Scott! The former second baseman was without a job and looked in good spirit. John McHale seemed open and on July 7, Scott signed a minor league contract.[64] Shortly after his arrival in Wichita, the Expos' main affiliate, Rennie Stennett retired,[65] given the evidence that he wasn't in the team's plans.

After the Cubs, the Expos had nine games left before the All-Star Game, four in Philadelphia and five in Chicago. The first game, which was scheduled to be the first of a doubleheader, ended in a 5–5 tie after 11 innings because of rain. The next day a doubleheader was played to make up for at least one game, which ended in a split before the Expos lost the third one. Then the Cubs, who had just swept the Pirates, won three in a row and unexpectedly saw themselves only two games back. But the Expos won both games in a doubleheader. In the second game, Scott Sanderson was solid, allowing only three hits and one run in six innings. But in the top of the seventh inning, he sprained badly his right thumb when he fell while running along the first-base line.[66] Some thought his season was over but he would be back in September.

At the break, the Expos were first place with a 41–36 record, one and half games over Philadelphia and two games over St. Louis, which was quite satisfying considering their inconsistency up to that point. The All-Star Game was held in Chicago's Comiskey Park in 1983 and the Expos were represented again with five players, including four starters: Gary Carter, Al Oliver, Tim Raines and Andre Dawson. Steve Rogers was the fifth player chosen. Every year, the stars' selection left some players very unhappy over being left out, which was the case with Jeff Reardon for a second straight year.[67] Reardon was leading the league in saves and had blown only two missions but he was off from his 1982 season. Gary Carter would have rather stayed home to take care of some nagging injuries, especially his right elbow. But John McHale insisted his catcher — and everyone of his players picked — had to go to Chicago.[68] Andre Dawson seemed to be back at the level he showed in 1981. He had been named the Player of the Month for June with 27 RBIs in 28 games and an impressive .634 slugging percentage. According to a poll among the players published in the *New York Times*, Dawson had become the number one player in the majors, ahead of shortstop Robin Yount of the Milwaukee Brewers.[69] As for the All-Star Game, the American League shook off the dominance of the National League, with a 13–3 blow-out, triggered in great part by Fred Lynn's grand slam against Atlee Hammaker in the third inning.

The return back to the regular schedule was not a pleasant one as the Expos lost three out of four at home against Atlanta. The fourth game featured the return of Woodie Fryman on the mound. Fryman was summoned to protect a two-run lead in the eighth. But Rafael Ramirez ruined the party with a three-run home run on a pitch low and inside, a quality pitch by most standards, but the veteran lefty said after the game that the pitch wasn't where he wanted to throw it.[70] That loss also meant the Expos were no longer in first place, being overtaken by the Phillies who had won their last four.

The return of Fryman also triggered the departure of Jerry White. Bill Virdon almost had no use for him and had started him only once since the beginning of the season. In fact, White was seventh on the depth chart in the outfield, behind Tim Raines, Andre Dawson, Warren Cromartie, Terry Francona, Mike Vail and Jim Wohlford. One must have wondered why a team would need that many outfielders. White wasn't a bit surprised by the Expos' decision. Virdon thought White didn't have enough power, an evaluation with which White wouldn't agree: "His thinking was he wanted some power from the bench and I think I had the most home runs of anybody who had come off that bench in the Expos' history, other than Hal Breeden. I don't know how he would come up with that. I think the whole year, no one hit a home run off the bench."[71] White was absolutely right: nobody hit one out from the bench in 1983. He was also second on the team's all-time pinch-home runs list with four, tied with Breeden, but behind Jose Morales. He would eventually end up playing two years in Japan, hitting 27 home runs in his first year there.

The last loss against Atlanta was the first of six straight for the Expos, including three in Houston. Even Charlie Lea, who had the habit of handling the Astros at will, was hit hard at the Astrodome, being sent to the showers in the second inning. While in Houston, the Expos called up a familiar face from the minors: Bob James. Yes, the same Bob James who was sent to Detroit one year before for a player to be named later. When it came the time to complete the transaction, the Expos got James himself. So James was basically traded for himself. What was left to know was who had the better of the deal. In his last 13 innings in Wichita, James had struck out 20 batters.[72] Everybody knew he had a major league fastball. But he allowed only one walk, which was quite unlike everything he had shown up to that point, with an average of seven walks per nine innings in the minors.

Right before the next series against the Braves in Atlanta, Virdon had told his players that they were the luckiest bunch of athletes in the world being in contention while being so inconsistent.[73] They were one game out of first place, with Philadelphia and St. Louis tied for first. The Expos were still lifeless in a 9–3 loss, the team's seventh in eight games. After the game, Warren Cromartie, who had had enough, knocked over the table that held the food for the traditional postgame snack.[74] Such a reaction would surely have pleased Dick Williams. Not Bill Virdon, who voiced his displeasure over such a reaction, reminding Cromartie that he was the one leading the team.

Cromartie's season wasn't to his liking, even though his batting average wasn't all that bad at .282, but expectations had always been higher from everybody, including himself. He struggled some defensively, which didn't endear himself with his manager. It was true that one couldn't help but not notice Cromartie's presence, anywhere: he liked to talk, loudly, and was a master at trash-talking, to the point where he could really annoy his teammates, leading to some near-physical confrontations with Larry Parrish.[75] But nobody could question his work ethic. He had worked very hard to become an adequate left fielder.[76] In his first year in 1977, everybody and his grandmother would be sent home from second on a single to left. In 1980, he was moved to first base to accommodate Ron LeFlore and in 1982 went to right field, a very unfamiliar position for him. And for the record, Cromartie had gotten two hits before he flipped the table over. Some would be satisfied with their own personal success, no matter how the team was doing. Cromartie, despite his sometimes unpleasant ways, was playing to win.

The Expos avoided a second straight sweep on the road in Atlanta in a 3–1 win, thanks to rookie Greg Bargar in his first career start in the big leagues. But the team, which had a comfortable four and a half games lead a few weeks earlier, was now battling not only the Cards and the Phillies but also the Pittsburgh Pirates, which were in the middle of an incredible run that would lead them right to the top of the division before the end of July.

As the team was heading home after that disastrous road trip to Houston and Atlanta, the Phillies announced the firing of their manager, Pat Corrales, on July 18, even though the team was in first place, tied with the Cards. But their place in the standings was more a testament to the divisional ineptitude than their own success, as their record was 43 wins and 42 losses. After they had lost four of their last five games, Paul Owens replaced Corrales. The Expos were only one game back, behind the Pirates who were only a half-game out. Even the Cubs were in the mix at four and a half games behind the co-leaders.

Philadelphia was not the only place where the pressure was high. In Montreal, fans were becoming more and more impatient and restless. Tim Wallach, for one, wanted to be left alone. "I don't boo people at their work," he lamented.[77] In the meantime, columnist Jerry Trudel, from *Dimanche-Matin*, a baseball lover and big Yankees fan, began publishing a series of articles about John McHale's tenure with the Expos. Trudel, who never hid his dislike for McHale, blamed him for his trades, the way he handled his managers, and his lack of commitment towards the Quebec community, especially the French-speaking fans. According to Trudel, McHale had to leave.[78]

On July 19, the Expos were hosting Cincinnati and the game was delayed for more than two hours. The weather was terrible but it was decided that the game would start anyway. In the bottom of the fifth, another rain delay forced an interruption. Two hours later, the players were back on the field and when the game ended, 5–2 for the Reds, it was almost 3 A.M. After the game, Steve Rogers, the loser, even after allowing only four hits in seven innings, noticed a lack of intensity within the team. Rogers added that the team's attitude was a heritage from Dick Williams' passage with the team: "With Williams, it was more important to say that we didn't cause the loss than to say that we contributed to a win."[79]

While the Reds were in Montreal, the Expos honored Johnny Bench on July 20, who was playing the last year of a Hall of Fame career.[80] Bench was used as a pinch-hitter and was struck out by Charlie Lea, a game won by the Expos, 6–4. After a split of that two-game series, the Expos won three out of four against both Houston and Cincinnati, leaving them a half-game behind the Pirates, who had not lost consecutive games since the end of June.

After July 28, the Expos embarked a three-week stretch where they would face NL East foes, including St. Louis and Pittsburgh twice in separate series.

The Expos in fact began that run at home with a double header against the Cards. More than 50,000 fans showed up at Olympic Stadium as Steve Rogers and John Stuper were scheduled to open the hostilities in the first game. It was still tied at two when Woodie Fryman began the tenth inning. He had pitched only once in the last two weeks, allowing four runs in one-third of an inning against Houston. The first batter, Andy Van Slyke, hit a single but was erased when he was caught stealing. Floyd Rayford was the next batter. The count was two balls and two strikes when Fryman threw a third ball. That pitch would be the last of Woodie Fryman's career, as a ligament in his left elbow just gave out.[81] Fryman was never one to complain, but as he was grimacing on his way to the dugout, it was obvious that the injury was serious and that it was likely the last time Fryman, then age 43, would be seen pitching on a major league field. Reardon was asked to replace Fryman and was greeted by boos. Reardon had had his part of problems, especially in Atlanta when he allowed all five runners he inherited to score. His first pitch against the Cards was a ball, which allowed Rayford to get on base with a walk. Three batters later, with the bases loaded, Reardon allowed another walk to Tom Herr, giving the Cards a 3–2 lead, which would be the final score.

Between games of that doubleheader, Pierre Marcotte, who was the host of a very popular TV talk-show in Quebec, came onto the field for a special presentation. Marcotte was accompanied by Phoebe Reardon, Jeff's wife. The Expos' reliever had strongly suggested to her not to go on the field, but as it was for a cause for the needy she didn't expect any problem.[82] But even though she had nothing to do with her husband's pitching struggles, she was booed vehemently, to the point where she left the field in tears. She insisted that the incident be kept secret from her husband, which was impossible. Jeff Reardon was furious and asked to be traded.[83] In the following days, Phoebe Reardon received many flowers and letters from appreciative fans. In the next few days, writers in Montreal were blasting those fans who booed Phoebe Reardon.[84] In the second game, the Expos were absolutely lifeless in a 10–1 loss to the Cards. The Expos won two of the next three against the Cards, including Bryn Smith's first victory as a starter.

As July turned to August, the Expos were barely over .500 with 52 wins against 50 losses, one and a half games behind division-leading Pittsburgh. Both Philadelphia and St. Louis were also ahead of the Expos. The incident involving Phoebe Reardon just revived the already existing tension among the players. Doug Flynn said he never saw a public so demanding and uncompromising.[85] But Woodie Fryman, in what appeared to be an end-of-career interview he gave to Tim Burke, thought that the whole organization was at fault and was looking for excuses, be it the players or the executives. As for the fans, Fryman said that they were promised a winning team and they had been waiting for some time already. The lefty opined that the offensive leaders had to step up their game for the team to win.[86]

As the Expos were getting set to play the Mets in New York, they called up left-handed reliever Dave Tomlin. But he had to go through waivers and the Pirates, also involved in the NL East race, decided to claim him.[87] The Expos had to settle instead for rookie Dick Grapenthin, for whom it was a second call-up in 1983. Montreal could do no better than one win in three games in the Big Apple, falling three and a half games behind Pittsburgh, which was precisely the next destination for the Expos. Since June 20, the Pirates had won 30 of their 41 games, thanks to the excellence of their pitchers. Rick Rhoden, Larry McWilliams and John Candelaria were the leaders among the starters and Jose DeLeon had been their equal since being called up from the minors. The bullpen was also superb with ageless Kent Tekulve, with strong support from Rod Scurry, Cecilio Guante and Manny Sarmiento. But against all odds, the Expos scored 20 runs in three convincing 7–1, 7–3 and 6–0 triumphs for a complete sweep. With that close a race, the Pirates were ousted from first place by the Phillies, winners of their last four. The Cards slid to fourth place, thanks to a seven-game losing streak. The Expos then won two out of three against the Mets to remain one game back from the Phillies. But all that fine work was almost completely erased when the Pirates turned the tables and swept the Expos at Olympic Stadium.

The last game against the Pirates on August 7 was a special day, as the Expos commemorated their fifteenth year in the National League. Many members of the very first edition were invited, including Ron Hunt, Mack Jones, Coco Laboy, Bill Stoneman, Ron Brand, Dan McGinn, Boots Day and Quebecers Claude Raymond and Ron Piche. More than 50,000 people were on hand to applaud their first-year heroes. Gene Mauch, the first manager in team history, was also present. Each of these former Expos had kind words for Montreal, especially Mack Jones. The outfielder became an instant star by hitting the first-ever home run in Jarry Park in an 8–7 victory. When asked whether April 14, 1969, was the best day of his life, he smirked back: "When we consider the night that followed, yes, that was probably my best day!"[88] The former Expos were scheduled to face the Old-Timers, including Bill Mazeroski, Bobby Thomson and Don Larsen, all famous for their World Series heroics. After that exhibition game, Gene Mauch attended the Expos' loss in a suite with John McHale and Charles Bronfman. Mauch was still an employee of the California Angels and had been their manager in 1982, leading them to a division championship. Mauch at first left the door open, as the Expos were openly interested to bring him back into the organization.[89] But, in September, Mauch decided to stay in California.[90]

In August 1983, baseball commissioner Bowie Kuhn decided to leave his position amid high pressure from a group of owners, who were very unhappy about the way he had handled the labor relations. Since taking over the baseball's highest job, every single collective bargaining negotiation had gone in the players' favor, according to these owners. In 1972, 1976 and 1981, a work stoppage had disturbed either the regular season or training camp. Kuhn just couldn't mobilize the owners the way Marvin Miller, the executive director of the Players Association, could. Kuhn saw himself as the guardian of the sport's integrity while, in truth, he was merely the owners' employee.[91] Among his potential successors, John McHale was mentioned. It was not the first time his name was brought up. In fact, he had been considered when Kuhn was named in 1969, but had decided to turn down the opportunity, opting instead to join the Expos.[92] Peter Ueberroth, the CEO of the 1984 Los Angeles Olympic Games, would eventually replace Kuhn in 1984.

Bill Virdon was concerned about his team's lack of consistency and had been so since almost the beginning of the season. As the team embarked on a ten-day four-city trip, Virdon told Réjean Tremblay and Brian Kappler, from *La Presse* and *The Gazette*, respectively, that the team wouldn't win if the players couldn't perform in pressure situations.[93] The first stop was St. Louis and that's where the Expos acquired veteran second baseman Manny Trillo from the Cleveland Indians for minor-leaguer Don Carter and cash. Trillo was available since the Indians, as was their custom during these years, were going nowhere. Moreover, Trillo had no intention to stay in Cleveland after the last year of his contract.[94] At the beginning of the season, he had already stated so, naming Montreal as one of his preferred destinations.[95] Trillo had been traded to Cleveland from Philadelphia along with four players for outfielder Von Hayes. Trillo felt deeply humiliated to be part of such a trade for someone who had only one complete season in the majors and had yet to prove anything yet, even though Hayes was considered to be a blue-chip prospect.[96]

As had been the case since the beginning of the season, there was some moaning from players. Gary Carter thought the team's sluggers were disadvantaged at Olympic Stadium because of the long distances to the fences, going as far as to suggest that these fences be closer to home plate.[97] It was true that the alleys were rather vast in Montreal. But Olympic Stadium was far from being the worst offensive ballpark in the majors. Shea Stadium in New York, Dodger Stadium in Los Angeles, Busch Stadium in St. Louis and Jack Murphy Stadium in San Diego were all places where pitchers always had the upper hand in a far more obvious manner than at Olympic Stadium. And during Carter's first complete season as the full-time catcher, Carter had hit 22 of his 31 homers at Olympic Stadium. These complaints were just a way to deflect blame for the team's lack of offense.

In St. Louis, Chris Speier tried to call a team meeting but Bill Virdon refused to let him.[98] Speier was again relegated to the bench for Bryan Little at that point and the arrival of Manny Trillo seemed to push him back deeper on the depth chart as Doug Flynn was moved from second to shortstop. Speier would start only one more game until the end of the season. Another unhappy customer was Al Oliver, who was pretty upset that he was left on the bench in a game in San Francisco. When informed that the decision was made to give him some rest, his reply was: "When I'm tired, I go to bed!"[99] And just to add some spice to that road trip, days before the Expos were scheduled to play in San Diego, Padres' manager Dick Willams said in an interview to a Philadelphia radio station that the Expos would never win anything because Steve Rogers would again fold under pressure.[100]

On the last leg of that road trip in Los Angeles, the Expos were involved in a third bench-clearing brawl that season in the second game when Bryn Smith hit Mike Marshall in the seventh inning.[101] Smith had just allowed a two-run homer to Ken Landreaux that had given the Dodgers a 2–1 lead. Marshall also had been hit on the head earlier that season by Jeff Reardon. The following day, Smith was extremely harsh towards some teammates, without naming them. He said that some Expos were only playing for themselves, remarks that were backed by Ray Burris.[102] It was only Smith's first complete season in the majors, but his role had increased steadily since the start of 1983. Smith also never had it made, as he spent seven complete seasons in the minors before getting his first chance.

The Expos ended that trip with only three wins in seven games, but were still able to gain a game from the Phillies in the standings, two and a half games behind Philadelphia, with both St. Louis and Pittsburgh in between. On August 26, the Expos launched their longest stay at home with 16 games in 17 days against San Diego, San Francisco, Los Angeles, Chicago and New York. The Expos responded, winning 12 of these games to climb back to first place on September 11, a half-game over the Phillies, one game and a half over the Cards and two games over the Pirates. Bill Gullickson and Charlie Lea both got three wins, Steve Rogers and Charlie Lea threw shutouts and Ray Burris, back in the rotation as the fifth starter, was solid in two Expos victories, even though he wasn't involved in the decisions. In the bullpen, Jeff Reardon got two saves but it became more and more evident that Bob James was getting his manager's confidence in important situations, especially during that homestand, while he was used mostly in mop-up situations until then.

It was on September 1 that Bill Virdon summoned Bob James for the first time with the game on the line. In the sixth inning against the Dodgers and the Expos leading, 4–2, he was called in after Charlie Lea loaded the bases with no outs. James first struck out Ken Landreaux and then induced Mike

The last year the Expos were real contenders was 1983 and it was more by default as no team played consistently until the Phillies pulled it out in the last three weeks of the season. Seated in first row (left to right): Tony Araujo, Tino Di Pietro, Robert Araujo, Sotiris Athanasiou; first row (left to right): Al Oliver, Woodie Fryman, Vern Rapp, Billy DeMars, Bill Virdon, Galen Cisco, Joe Kerrigan, Steve Rogers; second row (left to right): Chris Speier, Tim Wallach, Randy Lerch, Scott Sanderson, Ray Burris, Charlie Lea, Bill Gullickson, Andre Dawson, Gary Carter; third row (left to right): Ron McClain, Jerry White, Doug Flynn, Jeff Reardon, Bryn Smith, Terry Francona, Warren Cromartie, Tim Raines, John Silverman; fourth row (left to right): Mike Kozak, Bobby Ramos, Tim Blackwell, Dan Schatzeder, Dick Grapenthin, Brad Mills, Jim Wohlford, Bryan Little, Mike Phillips.

Marshall to hit an inning-ending double play. James allowed a run in the seventh and Reardon would record the save but everybody agreed that the game was won in the sixth. Three days later, James struck out four batters in two innings in an extra-inning victory. On September 5, James struck out Leon Durham in the eighth inning with two men on and two outs to preserve a 4–3 Expos lead. The fact that James got Durham with a breaking ball instead of his trademark fastball didn't go unnoticed. Not too shabby for a player whose return to the club during the summer was welcomed with skepticism, at best.

Offensively, it looked as if everything seemed back on track. But that stay in Montreal wasn't without some controversy. Al Oliver, whose season was barely a shadow of the year before, attributed most of his failure to not getting good pitches to hit due to Gary Carter's bad season.[103] Of course, Carter wasn't very happy about these comments.

The Expos spent only a few days in the NL East Division top spot with only three wins in eight games in Chicago, Philadelphia and Pittsburgh. That included only one win in three games in both of the latter cities. In Philadelphia, the Expos were swept in a doubleheader. In the first game, Bryn Smith was sent to the showers in the third inning, allowing eight straight batters to reach base. Smith would admit that he didn't react very well to the pressure of that particular game.[104] Smith would be used in the second game for two scoreless innings. After that road trip, on September 18, the Expos were two and a half games back.

Before the last homestand of the season, which was against St. Louis, Philadelphia and Pittsburgh, respectively, Bob James was named the National League Player of the Week. In ten and one-third innings, James allowed only three hits and three walks, no runs and 15 strikeouts. In his last 16 and two-thirds innings, he struck out 27 batters. Jeff Reardon was not really happy with the situation, but to his credit he was the one who helped James the most since he was called up.[105] It took some time, more than the Expos' brass would have hoped for, but at last it looked as if James had finally arrived. And even if James acknowledged that Jeff Reardon was of great help, it was James himself who was mostly responsible for his success.

In an interview with the author, James was the first to admit to some maturity issues in his first few years in the organization. An incident in spring training 1979 was very indicative of these maturity problems. James was having some fun in a Bradenton bar and, after having a couple of beers too many, decided to take his chance in a contest where people were asked to do Elvis Presley impressions. Those kinds of contests were extremely popular everywhere, not only in the United States but in Canada as well. The following morning, a hungover Bob James showed up and was asked to do some running under a very hot sunny day.[106] Many times the Expos were worried about Bob James' weight, which was never an issue according to the burly reliever: "That's always been an issue and, as I look back now, I see guys who were a lot bigger than I was. But back then, it was more of an issue than it is today. I was always overweight, according to the Expos, but it was just something I didn't agree with, to this day. They thought I had a weight problem, and, by my thinking, that's one of the reasons I had a very rebellious side to me."[107] Many observers believed James might have had too much of a liking for beer. James would later be very candid about other likings: "One of my maturity things was that I was smoking lot of marijuana back then. And I probably drank too much. Unfortunately, alcohol was legal and marijuana wasn't. And that was a big part of my maturity thing. It was quite prevalent, but players have the individual choice to do that or not."[108] In his first game with Detroit in 1982, the first batter he faced for the Tigers was Bobby Murcer, with the game on the line. Murcer hit a three-run home run in the eighth, the deciding blow in an 8–7 Yankee victory. Two days later, James lost in extra innings in Toronto. He was never a big factor again with the Tigers. The Expos got him back in 1983. After seven years and several personal and professional bumps along the way, James was becoming an important part of that Expos run for the title in 1983.

With two weeks to go, one at home and one on the road, nothing was decided. One couldn't ask for a better scenario, not unlike what Montreal went through from 1979 to 1981. The Expos began by sweeping the Cards in their three-game series. The Cards had lost six of their last seven prior to their visit in Montreal. They were the first to fold among the top four leaders. After the Expos' third win, Gary Carter was quoted: "It's between us and the Pirates!"[109] There was only one problem though: the Phillies, not the Pirates, occupied first place and Philadelphia was precisely the Expos' next opponent at Olympic Stadium for a crucial two-game series. It was the ideal situation for the Expos as they were in fact two games behind the Phillies.

But Carter's comments made headlines more than he would have wished for. Montreal's sports fans didn't have to go way back to find some comments that backfired badly. In spring 1981, the Montreal Canadiens were facing the Edmonton Oilers in the first round of the NHL playoffs. Canadiens goalie Richard Sevigny told the press before the first game that Guy Lafleur would put Wayne Gretzky in his back pocket during the series.[110] Gretzky had yet to achieve the incredible numbers he would gather in the next several years. But even that season, Gretzky had broken the single-season point scoring record and he was barely 20 years old. Against the Canadiens, he had three goals and six assists as the Oilers swept the Canadiens in three straight games. Lafleur was limited to one assist.

For the series against the Phillies, the Expos could count on both Charlie Lea and Steve Rogers. John Denny and rookie Charlie Hudson were scheduled for the Phillies. The first game on September 21 was postponed due to rain, so a doubleheader was scheduled for the day after, which didn't sit well with many Expos fans, who thought that doubleheaders were made to be split. Before the first game, Tim Burke had a chance to talk to Joe Morgan. Burke wanted to talk to him because Morgan seemed destined to play elsewhere in 1984, possibly in the American League, and the columnist saw a last occasion to talk to a future Hall of Famer. Of course, Morgan talked about the upcoming series against the Expos and the veteran second baseman, never one to shy away from an opinion, however controversial it might be, told Burke that the Phillies would win both games. To Morgan, the Phillies had players who were just waiting and relishing the moment they will make the difference for their team. With the Expos, Morgan said he noticed an attitude that told him that the players didn't want to be in these situations. "Why me?" was the prevalent thinking with the Expos.[111] Morgan was never more right. The Phillies won decisively, 9–7 and 7–1. Lea and Rogers allowed a total of eleven runs in ten innings. Andre Dawson, Gary Carter and Tim Wallach managed to get a single hit in 23 at-bats. Carter was made the scapegoat by the fans, as he was booed vehemently.[112] Only Tim Raines and Al Oliver were able to do some damage offensively with nine of the team's combined 17 hits in the twin bill. As for Morgan, he contributed heavily in this demolition night with five hits, including three doubles, and two walks.

That September 22 night knocked the Expos down and put them four games out of first place. And it took them a while to recover as they scored only once in their next two games, both losses at home against Pittsburgh, 10–1 and 1–0. The Expos won the next game, 5–3, the last of the season for the Expos at home and, ironically, the day they were officially eliminated from postseason contention as the Phillies won their tenth straight. The day after in St. Louis, Bob Forsch threw his second career no-hitter against a lifeless squad. The Expos ended their season with three straight losses to the Mets in New York, in third place with an 82–80 record, eight games behind the division-champion Phillies.

If one had to characterize the 1983 season from the Expos' standpoint, it could easily have been labeled "the year of the complainers." Just to confirm that assessment, in the last home game of the season John McHale blasted a journalist from *Dimanche-Matin*.[113] McHale had reasons to be upset over a number of things, including the five-article series penned by Jerry Trudel in August and the complete collapse of his team in the last ten days of the season. Owner Charles Bronfman, who was usually rather discreet, voiced his deep disappointment over how the season unfolded. He went back to the Gary Carter contract, saying it was a mistake.[114] He lamented the lack of passion on the team, adding that indifference was worse than pure hate.[115]

Among those who were quite unhappy, one could count Warren Cromartie and Chris Speier. Cromartie could leave, as he was a free agent, and there was very little chance he would be back, as he and Bill Virdon never connected. In September, Cromartie barely played. In the offseason, only the San Francisco Giants showed any interest. He would continue his career in Japan.[116] Like Cromartie, Speier was not a favorite of Virdon. He knew it and asked to be traded during the season.[117] In September, he played some games at third base. In the last week of the season, Virdon used at shortstop young prospect Argenis Salazar, from Venezuela, which didn't bode well at all for Speier's future in Montreal.

Another matter that was brought up during the season was the high taxes paid in Montreal. Doug Flynn was certainly the most vocal about the situation that professional athletes had to face in Montreal.[118] The Montreal Canadiens were not immune to that in hockey either. Before the 1982 season, they had to trade away a young defenseman, Rod Langway, an American who wanted out of Montreal.[119] Langway would win two Norris Trophies, as the top rearguard of the league, not with the Canadiens but with the Washington Capitals. It was acknowledged that the taxation was higher in Quebec than almost everywhere else in North America. But what was the real situation for an American athlete earning a living in Montreal?

Former Expos financial controller Harry Renaud was involved in negotiations with players and agents during his time with the Expos from 1969 to 1981. He had to deal with fiscal, immigration and law specialists. Often the situation was complicated by multiple jurisdictions. From one state to another, a player's situation could differ. But Harry Renaud was formal about one thing: a professional athlete plying his trade in Canada and Quebec was not penalized when compared to those in U.S. markets. He explained that players in Canada were taxed on the money made in the country, while in the U.S. their overall earnings were counted, no matter where that money was earned. Harry Renaud added that the players could get a credit in the U.S. for taxes paid in Canada.[120]

If there was a player who most probably knew how to take advantage of the best of both worlds, it was Gary Carter. Nobody was better organized than Carter, both professionally and personally. Nobody could see a neater locker than his. About his time in Montreal, Carter would say that he was backed by competent people who took care of his business. In his case, he bought a place to live in Montreal to have permanent-resident status, in order to get all the fiscal advantages that Quebec had to offer, without all of the inconveniences.[121] When Steve Renko was traded away to the Chicago Cubs in the middle of the 1976 season, he said that the best way to not be hit too harshly by taxes was to buy a house and live there long enough to make sure he was a permanent resident, but Renko just didn't want to do that.[122] Chris Speier and Steve Rogers were two players who also elected to buy a place to live in the Montreal area.

That being said, Doug Flynn's tax problems, along with Warren Cromartie and Chris Speier situation, didn't account for the lack of consistency in 1983. At the end of the season, Woodie Fryman repeated that the team lack unity,[123] a problem that was brought up in 1982 and was expected to be handled by Bill Virdon. In 1982, all these problems fell on Jim Fanning's shoulders. He had been an easy target, due to his inexperience as a major league manager. And because he didn't have the physical presence of Dallas Green (who also went directly from the farm system department to the manager's position), he couldn't command the same kind of respect. Virdon, like a saviour, was supposed to right the ship. At the end, 1983 looked like 1982 and at least showed that Fanning was far from the only problem hitting the team, indicating that maybe the problem was far deeper.

Offensively in 1983, only two players responded: Tim Raines and Andre Dawson. Raines, with a renewed energy, led the National League in runs (133), stolen bases (90) and times reaching the bases (282). Dawson led the circuit in hits (189), total bases (341), and extra-base hits (78) and was among the league leaders in several categories. But his production tailed off again in September, when the Expos needed him the most. Again, his eagerness to make the difference hurt him, as he got only 26 non-intentional walks in the entire season, one of the worst ratios in the National League. To his defense, Dawson's left knee gave him trouble all season long. Four times from the start of spring training, his knee was drained to allow him to play.[124]

The other big guns, Gary Carter, Tim Wallach and Al Oliver, all produced below expectations. Overall, they hit 44 home runs, 35 fewer than in 1982. It was true that the overall offense declined in the majors in 1983, but that didn't explain the stiff power drop-off. Carter was most targeted mostly because of his huge contract. Wallach was going through some obvious growing pain, even though his defense showed consistent improvement. Oliver showed an exact .300 batting average, but that was misleading as his power and on-base percentage had declined. Oliver repeated what he had said earlier that season, that he thought he wouldn't be back.[125]

Otherwise, Warren Cromartie, despite everything Bill Virdon didn't like about him, was the only other hitter with some sort of contribution. His on-base percentage was second on the team to Tim Raines. John McHale had wanted to improve the mid-infield offense for two years. It was almost back to square one. Chris Speier, Doug Flynn, Bryan Little and even Manny Trillo didn't bring much to the table. In fact, Little was the only one who wasn't that bad, thanks to his 50 walks in 106 games which lifted his on-base percentage to .352. The bench was equally awful as the pinch-hitters displayed a slugging percentage of .287.

On the mound, no trio won more games than Steve Rogers, Bill Gullickson and Charlie Lea. They finished with 50 wins. Scott Sanderson's injury forced the team to reshuffle the rotation for the last two spots. Only Bryn Smith showed any consistency, throwing three shutouts in the last five weeks of the season. In the bullpen, Jeff Reardon wasn't able to repeat his solid 1982 season, but still couldn't be faulted for the Expos' overall failures. Bob James and Dan Schatzeder did a fine job out of the bullpen.

Since 1979, John McHale's mission had been to add bits and pieces to a machine that didn't seem to require much alteration. But after a 82–80 showing, the task looked rather different: to bring the team back into contention.

His main priorities were a lefty reliever and a better bench. Southpaw Dan Schatzeder was already in the bullpen but, for whatever reason, lefty batters were hitting .314 against him, while the righties were limited to a .237 average. McHale insisted that nobody was untouchable. Manny Trillo wouldn't be offered a long-term deal and there was no intention to renegotiate Andre Dawson's deal.[126] Trillo wanted $4 millions for five years. Dawson wanted some adjustment to his treatment,[127] especially in light of Gary Carter's deal, which called for a salary twice that of Dawson's.

Among the four Expos who became free agents, only Schatzeder stayed, agreeing to a three-year deal. Cromartie and Jerry White left for Japan and Trillo headed for San Francisco. At the winter meetings in early December, the Expos acquired from San Diego the lefty reliever they had been seeking, Gary Lucas. In a three-team deal, Scott Sanderson was sent to the Chicago Cubs while Carmelo Martinez went from Chicago to San Diego. Within the next week, in an interview with Michel Blanchard from *La Presse*, Sanderson said that the problem with the Expos was not on the field but rather in the clubhouse. According to the former Expo, some players just hated each other and jealousy was rampant. He found it weird that he was traded away while he was among the only few who wanted to play in Montreal. The problem was too deep to be cured by the arrival of Lucas.[128] Sanderson didn't name anybody, but it was clear that Gary Carter was at the core of these observations. Towards the end of the season, baseball columnist Peter Gammons, from the *Boston Globe*, wrote that Carter was among the most hated players within his own team.[129]

The interview by Blanchard provoked many reactions and Sanderson tried to temper his comments.[130] But it was obvious there was some truth in his assessment of the reality that was the Expos in both 1982 and 1983. A lack of leadership was said to be a major problem and in that sense, the Expos had their eyes set on one player: Pete Rose.[131] He had just spent his last five seasons with the Philadelphia Phillies after a brilliant career with one of the most powerful offenses in modern baseball history, the Cincinnati Reds. As a leadoff hitter, Rose was the perfect table-setter and had the temperament for that role. His attitude was that of a man who was playing every game as if it was his last. He was a free agent and available. But he was age 42 and coming off his worst season, with a paltry .245 batting average with the Phillies. The demand for his services was non-existent.[132] He had slowed down some, his arm also was suspect and since he had no more power, his .245 average did nothing to impress anyone. But the Expos were curious about what he could bring in terms of leadership. Rose, with his three World Series titles and eight participations in the post season, seemed to fit with what John McHale was looking for. Rose wanted to stay in the National League but didn't really have many options. He wanted to keep playing in his quest for the all-time hit record of Ty Cobb, which stood at 4,191. Rose was ten hits away from 4,000. Rose signed a one-year contract with the Expos in January.[133]

As it became more and more likely that Rose would sign with Montreal, Andre Dawson was concerned that Al Oliver would be the one paying the price. The Expos would take a step back in doing so, according to Dawson. The star outfielder stated also that Gary Carter's contract wasn't the cause of any problem in the clubhouse. But he thought that the Expos' catcher was too concerned about his own stats and should show more maturity. When asked to comment on Scott Sanderson's take on what ailed the Expos, Dawson acknowledged that the Expos lacked unity and that it was up to the players to settle the situation.[134] Owner Charles Bronfman thought that Sanderson's comments did the Expos a favor.[135]

Among those who also departed, Ray Burris was sent to Oakland for minor-league outfielder Rusty McNealy. Two more players were added in the offseason via free agency, speedster Miguel Dilone, an outfielder, and super utilityman Derrel Thomas. Both were signed to add depth to the bench, fulfilling what John McHale deemed a priority after the 1983 season.

10

1984: The End of an Era

The concept of a savior had been pretty popular around the Expos since 1981. First it was Jim Fanning, who took over for Dick Williams as the team's manager and led the Expos to the playoffs. In 1982, Al Oliver was supposed to add that last ingredient, an experienced left-handed hitter, to an already strong team. In 1983, Bill Virdon was expected to cure all that ailed the team under Jim Fanning in 1982. For 1984, it was Pete Rose's time to settle what looked more and more like a dysfunctional family.

Gary Carter was the subject of harsh criticism during and after the 1983 season. If he thought it was over when 1984 began, he was in for a big unpleasant surprise. In early February, Charles Bronfman invited him to Florida. Carter thought the owner wanted to share some thoughts about the upcoming season. That was far from what was awaiting Carter. Bronfman blasted his catcher, blaming him for his lack of clutch-hitting and lack of commitment towards the community, even though Carter was one of the most generous Expos ever with the fans. He also saddled Carter with the responsibility of not being able to bring a championship to Montreal. Carter could barely say a word during that meeting and left with a bitter taste in his mouth, an encounter which the All-Star catcher detailed in his autobiography.[1]

Contrary to 1983, Bill Gullickson didn't have to go to arbitration as he and two other players, Jeff Reardon and Charlie Lea, agreed to multi-year deals. Gullickson and Reardon signed for four years at $3 million while Lea agreed to a three-year deal at $2.1 million.[2] Gary Lucas was also signed for three years. Tim Wallach went to arbitration, but lost his case and had to content himself with a $300,000 salary. His demand was $500,000.[3]

In his second camp, Bill Virdon didn't waste time showing his cards regarding the shortstop position. In the first few days, he announced that Argenis Salazar would be his everyday shortstop.[4] Salazar was acknowledged as a fine defender and with Wichita in 1983 he had hit .302 after skipping the AA level. In 1981, he was playing in a rookie league, the lowest rung in professional baseball. His progression was nothing short of spectacular. Salazar seemed to be surprised as well, as he said in 1983 that he didn't think getting a regular job was likely before 1985.[5] Of course, that decision did nothing to improve Chris Speier's relations with his manager. Speier had in fact asked again to be traded.[6] Bryan Little believed that his chances to play second base were better with Salazar in the lineup. Little, who had a cocky side, wasn't shy to assess that with Salazar, Doug Flynn and the pitcher, the Expos would have three automatic outs in the lineup.[7]

Another big decision was announced early on: Andre Dawson would play right field while Tim Raines would move from left to center.[8] Bill Virdon was addressing the media people in his office, discussing the status of both Pete Rose and Al Oliver, when at the tail end of the media session, as the writers were backing out, Virdon told the writers and broadcasters: "By the way, gentlemen, Dawson will play right field and Raines center." To most people, that was THE news of the day and maybe of the whole training camp. When Serge Touchette came back to his typewriter to write his story, he was still fuming that Virdon didn't first address the media with that important change, repeating to himself between curse words: "By the way, gentlemen!"[9]

As for the status of Al Oliver, it didn't take long for everybody to find out. On February 27, he was traded to San Francisco for pitcher Fred Breining and reserve outfielder Max Venable. Oliver's departure left the door wide open for Pete Rose and also Terry Francona, who was projected to play regularly. Oliver expected to be traded but the Expos really blew how the trade was handled. The day before the transaction became official, Oliver and his wife, Donna, were present in John McHale's house, in West Palm Beach where the team's president had invited players and wives. McHale never said anything to Oliver but told Francona that he would be a happy man very soon.[10] The trade had already been agreed upon with the Giants but the Expos had planned to announce it the day after. But the news leaked out of San Francisco. When Oliver came back home, he then learned from a friend in the wee hours of the night that he was an Expo no more. Donna Oliver was really upset and didn't really appreciate the way the Expos treated her husband, saying that he was treated like an animal.[11] McHale tried to do some damage control, saying that it was the Giants who were at fault for not respecting the embargo. He acknowledged, however, that players who are traded should be informed properly.[12] It might be true that McHale had no intention to hurt Oliver. But to hint something to Terry Francona before informing Oliver, a 15-year major league veteran, was tactless from an organization which was known for being first class.

Oliver had a good idea he wouldn't be back and had said so as early as in the first few months of 1983, especially "if the team didn't win the title."[13]

McHale was rather severe when asked to assess Oliver's contribution to the team. "If he was a leader, we never saw it," he said.[14] These are harsh words for a veteran who had put up a solid career in the majors, a true professional who never needed a pushy manager to be ready to play. Oliver tried to mold himself with the team early on, even though he was more of a loner outside the white lines. He had tried to shake things up by calling a meeting in his first few weeks in 1982 when things were not going the way it should have been, to his liking at least.[15] In his autobiography, Oliver quoted his teammate Steve Rogers regarding his perceived lack of leadership. According to the pitcher, it was very unfair to ask Oliver to provide leadership to a new team full of home-grown players in a new league.[16] Oliver loved it in Montreal and was in fact a fan favorite during his two seasons there. In reaction to Oliver going west, Andre Dawson, who had already voiced his concerns about the possibility of losing Oliver, said that the team looked nothing like the year before.[17]

Bill Virdon was expecting improvements in the bullpen in 1984. Jeff Reardon, Bob James, Gary Lucas and Dan Schatzeder were assured of a spot and looked like a solid foundation. Steve Rogers, Bill Gullickson, Charlie Lea and Fred Breining were the first four starters in the rotation. Another right-handed pitcher would be inserted very soon as well: David Palmer. After a second elbow surgery in 1982, he had pitched in the fall of 1983 with interesting results.[18] Many thought his career was over when he left an August 1982 game at Olympic Stadium. The outlook on the mound looked bright but that was on paper and not counting on possible injuries, which was exactly what happened to Fred Breining and Steve Rogers. Rogers' struggles dated back to the end of the 1983 season.[19] In seven starts in September and October, his ERA was 4.73 with only one win. In the first few days of March, it became obvious that Rogers wouldn't be ready for the beginning of the 1984 season.[20] Breining's case was even worse: he just couldn't pitch and the Expos filed an official complaint to get some kind of compensation.[21] These two injuries opened the door for both Palmer and Bryn Smith, who had wished to be traded to Atlanta (he was from Georgia) after the Expos acquired Breining.[22] Smith's number on the depth chart went from no spot in the rotation to number three. Palmer's challenge was merely to prove that his arm was sound and good to go when the season would open.

Training camp was shook up by an article penned by Murray Chass for *Inside Sport*. Chass wrote, in that special baseball preview edition for the 1984 season, that talent was not the problem with the Expos on an individual basis, but that they just couldn't win because of their individualism. According to the article, Andre Dawson was too concerned about his own stats when things wouldn't go his way. Joe Torre, then the manager of the Atlanta Braves, said that he chose the Expos year after year to finish first in the NL East. But Torre was quick to add that the Expos reminded him of the Philadelphia 76ers in the NBA, a team full of stars who just couldn't win it all.[23] Dawson was involved in another controversy in March when he was quoted in the *New York Post* asking how many white players hitting .300 had been traded away to free a spot for a black player.[24] The reference to the Al Oliver trade was obvious. John McHale was quick to defend Dawson: "If there's a team player with the Expos, it's Dawson." And Dawson had earned the respect of his teammates and opponents throughout baseball, whether they were blacks or whites.[25] Dawson was stunned by all this attention. He was a man of few words and was already annoyed by the trade of Al Oliver and by his own knee problems. He said he had never been a trouble-maker and had no intention in becoming one.[26]

With Steve Rogers on the shelf to begin the season, the starting assignment had to go to another pitcher for the first time since 1975. Charlie Lea was picked by Bill Virdon. He had been one of the best starters in the National League in 1983 with 16 wins and a 3.12 ERA. He was also one of the toughest pitchers to hit against, as the opponents' batting average in 1982 and 1983 were .222 and .238, respectively.

At second base, Bryan Little won his battle over Doug Flynn.[27] Bill Virdon decided to play Pete Rose in left field and Terry Francona on first base.[28] Francona seemed completely recovered from his knee injury. In Venezuela, in the winter of 1983–1984, Francona had hit .320 and, more importantly maybe, had 12 stolen bases.[29] Also, Raines not only was moved to centerfield but also became the new number three hitter in the lineup.[30] In 1983, Raines had driven in 71 runs, a rather high number from the leadoff spot. Bill Virdon thought that Raines' clutch hitting would improve the Expos' offense. At the tail end of the camp, the Expos got pitcher Andy McGaffigan from the Giants in compensation for the Fred Breining fiasco. He became de facto the fifth man in the rotation. There were two surprises: Mike Stenhouse, who led the team in homers in exhibition games, and pitcher Greg Harris also made the team.

Even though the Expos had failed to make the postseason in the last two years, they were still picked in some circles to finish first in 1984 in their division, *Baseball Digest* and *The Sporting News* among them.[31] It was true that Raines, Dawson, Carter and Wallach formed a solid core of players who were in their prime. On the other hand, some were concerned about the lack of production from the two middle-infield positions. For that reason, *Sport* magazine placed the Expos fifth.[32]

The season began on April 3 in Houston where the Expos won, 4–2, thanks to a three-run eighth inning. Charlie Lea, who had been almost unhit-

It took some time for Expos fans to truly appreciate Tim Wallach. Heavily booed in 1983 and 1984, Wallach went on to be a fixture at third base for the Expos and eventually became captain of the team.

table at the Astrodome, was the winner with Jeff Reardon getting the save. After splitting the two games in Houston, the Expos played three games in Atlanta. In the second game of the series, David Palmer made his first start in more than a year and a half, limiting the Braves to one run and four hits in five innings. He also hit his first major-league homer in a 7–2 victory. They finished that first road trip in Cincinnati, getting one win in three games there, for a 4–4 record, not too bad for a road trip to begin the season. The last game in Cincinnati was not without some controversy. Pete Rose was one hit away from 4,000 and the Reds were highly promoting the event. But the Reds' pitchers refused to cooperate, issuing four walks to Rose, in a game the Expos won, 9–3. Frank Pastore was heavily booed when he issued the last walk. In that game, out of 22 pitches, Rose saw only two strikes.[33]

The first local game at the Big O was on April 13 against the Philadelphia Phillies, with Charlie Lea and veteran Jerry Koosman on the mound (and Céline Dion signing the two national anthems).[34] Rose was still one hit from

4,000 and in the first inning he hit a soft grounder to first base. In the second, Rose reached on an error by Koosman. It was the second miscue of the inning for the Phillies, which led to two unearned runs for the Expos. In his third time at bat, in the fourth inning, Rose hit a solid liner down the right-field line for a double for the 4,000th hit of his career. He would eventually score on a two-run single by Tim Raines. The Expos won the game, 5–1, and had to be content with only two home games, thanks to inclement weather, before embarking on another road trip to New York and St. Louis. In New York, the Expos managed to win only one game out of three, with Bryn Smith's first shutout. In these three games, the Expos also faced a 19-year-old flamethrower, Dwight Gooden. In 1983, he had pitched in single-A ball, striking out 300 batters in less than 200 innings. Against the Expos, he pitched five innings, striking out seven, allowing four runs, but none earned. While the team was flying from New York to St. Louis, the airplane had to land in Indianapolis when Jeff Reardon was hit by a violent allergic reaction. Fortunately, Reardon was all right thereafter.[35]

In St. Louis, the Expos were idle on Friday, May 20, thanks to continuing rain, and a doubleheader was scheduled for Saturday, even though rain was expected as well. In the first game, Steve Rogers won his first start of the season, pitching six and two-thirds innings, allowing three runs on six hits. His teammates made it easier by scoring three times in each of the first two innings. In the second game, David Palmer got the starting assignment when rain began falling again in Busch Stadium. The Expos scored three times in their first time at bat. The Expos added another run in the third on a home run by Tim Wallach. In the meantime, it became increasingly difficult to play as the rain was stronger and stronger. David Palmer did his best by retiring the Cards in order in each of the first five innings. The Expos came to bat in the sixth and led off with two hits but enough was enough as it was decided to send both teams to their dugouts in the hope that the rain would subside. Play would not resume, which meant that David Palmer was credited with a five-inning perfect game![36] Only one ball left the infield, a fly out by George Hendrick in the fifth inning. The Expos completed the sweep on Sunday on Bryn Smith's fourth win of the season.

After 16 games, the Expos had a very respectable record of nine wins and seven losses, considering that they had played only two games at home at that point. Even though things looked pretty good, there were reasons for concern with Andre Dawson, whose left knee was acting up.[37] His batting average, while below his usual standard, was still an acceptable .288 but he had only one home run and two stolen bases. Bob James was another one whose performances were cause for some worries. He had been used only once since April 10. In his first four outings, totalling four innings, James allowed 11 hits and four walks, leading to an ERA of 15.75. Doug Flynn was quite unhappy with his situation and the Expos allowed him to try to negotiate a deal with another team.[38]

The Expos were back in Montreal for a week where they won two out of five against the Mets and the Cards before winning two in Philadelphia in a three-game series. The Expos were still in the mix in early May but the inconsistency that plagued the team in 1983 seemed to be back in full course in 1984. In a *Sports Illustrated* feature story penned by Jim Kaplan, Bryn Smith thought the team was maybe too stiff: "Chemistry is everything and we don't have enough togetherness. Maybe it's because all but two of our players are married. They go home instead of out drinking. I think we need someone crazy — a guy who'll sit on birthday cakes."[39] It was a rather interesting observation by Smith. Since 1983, the players' wives could accompany the players on the road so some players would rather spend time with their families instead of talking baseball or hanging around with each other.[40]

Also in May, Pete Rose was involved in a controversy when quotes attributed to him in *La Presse* by beat writer Michel Blanchard were printed, in effect that Bill Virdon wasn't communicating enough with the players.[41] Rose did in fact voice his opinion in that regard to Pierre Rinfret, who was covering the team for CJMS radio station. But it was part of a conversation that was off the record and Rinfret had never identified Rose in his report. But Blanchard concluded — correctly — that Rose was the source of the information.[42] Rose was quite embarrassed by the situation and asked repeatedly to hear the taped interview, which of course never existed. Virdon retorted that nobody would tell him how to run the team.[43] It was worth noting that Rose wasn't really happy at that time, as he was used only twice in a two-week period between May 2 and May 15.

On May 24, the Expos played their annual exhibition game against the Toronto Blue Jays, for the Pearson Cup, in what had become a bad burlesque show. Players from both teams had no interest whatsoever for that game and would have rather taken a day off. Chris Speier had voiced so in 1981.[44] And the 1984 edition in Toronto just reinforced that feeling. The game was tied, 1–1, in extra innings but the Expos were short of pitchers — or, rather, long on pitchers they were adamant not to use! So, bullpen coach Joe Kerrigan, a former Expos pitcher who had last pitched professionally in 1982, was summoned to the mound. The first batter he faced was left-hander Rick Leach, who was hit in the middle of his back. Kerrigan apologized heartily to Leach. Minutes later, the Jays won the game, 2–1.[45] That denouement was the logical continuation of an event that was played in an almost completely indifferent atmosphere. In 1983, just to enliven to atmosphere, Warren Cromartie had decided to don the uniform of the team mascot, Youppi, on a day more appropriate for a football game. Some thought Cromartie's initiative amusing, but surely not René Guimond, the team's VP of marketing, who insisted that the image of Youppi not be tarnished, especially with the young fans.[46]

Those kind of anecdotes would be quite funny had it not been for the fact that the Pearson Cup cost the Expos a bona fide prospect and a pitcher whose career never got untracked after being injured. In 1978, Canadian reliever Bill Atkinson scored the winning run while sliding home but injured himself in doing so. He was sent down to the minors some time after that and was never able to get a regular job in the majors again.[47] Worse, in September 1982, the Expos started Darren Dilks on the mound against the Blue Jays. Dilks was the Expos' first-round pick in June 1981 after leading Oklahoma State to the College World Series finals, where he was also the team's designated hitter. Dilks was solid for six innings, but the game was played in cold weather, causing the pitcher some discomfort in his shoulder. He would never be the same thereafter and decided to end his career in 1984. The Expos tried to convince him to take a shot at being a first baseman, but Dilks saw that the team had a talented young Venezuelian in their system named Andres Galarraga.[48] As for the Pearson Cup, that masquerade of a baseball game would be played for the last time in 1986.

The Expos could have used that day off in 1984 to regroup, as they just couldn't get things going, being limited to playing .500 ball with a 24–24 record at the end of May. John McHale became more impatient and promised to make important changes if the team didn't right itself.[49] The first to go was Argenis Salazar. The rookie shortstop seemed completely lost, both on the field and at the plate. His batting average was a pitcher-like .143 with only two walks. He was sent down to Indianapolis, the Expos' new AAA farm team in the American Association.

A former Expo was also trying to get his bearings right. Warren Cromartie was struggling mightily with the Yomiuri Giants in Japan. He was blanked in 25 straight at-bats and was complaining that he was seeing a steady diet of breaking balls. He was not impressed as well about the quality of umpiring. That didn't stop Cromartie from having opinions. In the *Globe and Mail*, Canada's main national newspaper, Cromartie said that the Expos should have won in each of his seven seasons in Montreal. He thought too many changes were made in the last few years and that there was no chemistry on the team, adding that the players were not playing as a team.[50] As for Cromartie, he would eventually adjust to Japan, where he would spend seven successful seasons, before ending his career as a pinch-hitting specialist with Kansas City in 1991.

Concerns about Andre Dawson were growing and some wondered whether he would be able to finish the season.[51] He wasn't close to his usual self. In May, he couldn't even hit .200. He had a week off at the end of May but there was no guarantee for the rest of the season.

The Expos began June with a four-game series in Pittsburgh. The Pirates were dead last in the NL East. In 1983, they had been able to climb to first place with a big mid–season surge, but that didn't look promising in 1984. The Expos couldn't take advantage of the Pirates, winning only one game, thanks to Charlie Lea's ninth win of the season. In the third game, the Pirates were leading, 1–0, in the seventh. With one out and nobody on, Bryan Little, a master in the art of bunting, tried to reach first via another bunt. But he was ruled out as the umpires, after a complaint from Pirates manager Chuck Tanner, who argued that Little was out of the batting box when he made contact with the ball, an argument that was accepted by the umpires.[52] Before the fourth game, Little was seen showing Tanner his bunting technique and how the umpires were wrong. Tanner was listening but it was too late for Little as the Pirates' manager had gotten his man out in an important situation.

The Expos were the same in June and Bill Virdon, trying to shake things up, decided to give Derrel Thomas a chance at second base for six games. On June 9, David Palmer and the Expos lost, 5–3, against the Mets in Montreal. It was Palmer's second loss in four decisions but also was his first loss ever at home in his 21st start at Olympic Stadium. No other player had such a home streak to begin his career in the previous 50 years.[53]

Five days later, again in Montreal, Terry Francona suffered another major knee injury. In the third inning against the Pirates, Francona hit a soft grounder that was fielded by pitcher John Tudor, but in trying to avoid a collision at first base he tore up his left knee.[54] Francona was then hitting .346 and had been named the team's Player of the Month in May.[55] Francona would never have the chance to play on a regular basis again. The Expos lost that game, 3–2, when the Pirates scored two unearned runs in the ninth after two errors by Doug Flynn and Derrel Thomas.

After the game, Pete Rose said that there was just too much negativity around the team, especially by the fans and the media.[56] The boos were part of the team's problems, according to Rose. CFCF radio anchor Jeff Rimer was very critical of Rose's comments, saying that he was aiming at the wrong target. Rimer also thought Rose should know better than that, having played in Philadelphia, a city with fans whose reputation was to be a lot harder on its players than Montreal's. Rose took the phone and called in himself, demanding an apology from Rimer, saying that the radio anchor was trying to ruin a reputation he took years to build. Both men stuck to their respective positions. It is worth noting that Rimer was very vocal promoting Rose's hiring by the Expos before the official signing. For weeks after the 1983 season, Rimer was praising Rose's leadership qualities and how positive his presence would be for the Expos. Nobody was happier than Rimer when the Expos announced his signing.[57]

On Saturday, June 16, the Expos won, 3–2, in extra innings against longtime nemesis Kent Tekulve. After that victory, Rimer entered the clubhouse with his tape recorder to discuss what happened the day before. As Rimer later recalled: "After the game, I went to the clubhouse. When you walk in the clubhouse, there is a first set of doors. Standing there were Chris Speier and Jim Wohlford, and again these guys were my buddies, who were making light of all this and were wearing boxing gloves and making fun, as a joke. I told the guys this was not the time. So I walked into the clubhouse and went over to see Pete Rose and the players were making fun of this! Pete, Pete, Pete, Rimer, Rimer, Rimer! I walked over to Pete's locker and Pete was sitting on his chair, removing his cleats. I said, "Let's discuss this as men." I've got the cassette tape on my hand, and he pushed the cassette tape out of my hand and, the next thing I know, he's standing up. I'm not going to let him hit me, so I tried to hit the ground. He grabbed me by the shirt, ripped my golf shirt, so that I had a nice big scratch on the neck. The next thing I know I hit the ground and everybody in the clubhouse got involved. Doug Flynn came over and started kicking me. Gary Carter saw it, came over, picked me up and loosened me away and pushed Doug Flynn out of the way. At this time, John McHale, president of the team, came in, saw what was going on and went nuts! He started yelling at the players, and yelling at manager Bill Virdon about why he allowed this to happen in the clubhouse."[58]

The stage, in fact, had been set before the game, as Steve Rogers and beat writer Michel Blanchard were involved in a heated verbal altercation. Rogers was very unhappy that Blanchard wrote about the possibility that the team's veteran could be sent to the bullpen if things didn't get better soon. The article quoted pitching coach Galen Cisco.[59] Rogers was having a nightmarish season with a 5.50 ERA and only two wins against five losses. His pitches had less zip than before; only once did he get more than two strikeouts and seven times he had allowed more walks than strikeouts. Rogers was going through a rough time and Blanchard was the one who paid for it, verbally, as the confrontation never got physical. Had it been physical, it was far from certain that Rogers would have had the upper hand; Blanchard had played professional lacrosse and was known for his rugged play in a sport that was very physical.

On Sunday, John McHale held a meeting where Pete Rose apologized to Jeff Rimer.[60] Rose would tell the media that it was one of the most stupid thing he had ever done in his career, justifying his outburst by wanting to shake up and regroup the team.[61] It looked as it might have worked as the Expos won four of their next six games, including two against the resurgent

New York Mets. Bill Virdon again changed his middle-infield combination, with Bryan Little at second and Doug Flynn moving to shortstop. But shortly after that, Argenis Salazar was back with the team as the number one short-stop, with Flynn at second in a merry-go-round which was not easy to keep up with. But the experiment didn't last, as the Expos went back to their yoyo ways.

Chris Speier was impatient to leave Montreal. He wasn't playing any-more, with only four starts since the beginning of the season and none since May 2. He wanted out and asked the Expos to release him if they had no use for him. On June 27, Speier had had enough. The veteran shortstop and Bill Virdon got into a heated verbal exchange regarding Speier's status, something Virdon insisted he had no control over.[62] Speier was so desperate to leave that he showed up with a tan that would have made a California surfer jealous, even though players were forbidden to expose themselves to the sun during the day.[63] On July 1, Speier was sent to St. Louis for utility infielder Mike Ramsey. The Expos also acquired from Houston outfielder Tony Scott, a for-mer Expos prospect in the mid–1970s. Bill Virdon knew him well from his time managing the Astros. Scott was inserted in the starting lineup for four games, but was useless shortly thereafter.

Even though the Expos showed no sign of getting out of their irregular performances, to the point where the attendance was suffering greatly, four players were still picked for the All-Star Game: Gary Carter and Charlie Lea, both as starters, plus Tim Raines and Tim Wallach. For Lea and Wallach, it was a first-time experience. At the break, Lea had already 13 wins with an ERA of 2.91. In 18 starts, he threw seven innings 15 times. Carter's stats were more Carter-like than in 1983. Raines was keeping his good work from 1983 going, while Wallach, while not the flashiest player, was getting accolades for his solid play, both offensively and defensively. The game was played in Hous-ton where the National League won, 3–1. Carter was chosen the game's MVP after hitting a tie-breaking home run in the second inning against Dave Stieb of the Toronto Blue Jays. Charlie Lea got the win, allowing one run in two innings. Both Tim Raines and Tim Wallach were hitless in their lone at-bat.

At the break, the Expos were at 41–43, seven games out of first place which was held by the young and arrogant New York Mets. The Chicago Cubs were second, a half game back and the Phillies followed, three and a half games back. The Mets were led by two immensely talented players in pitcher Dwight Gooden and outfielder Darryl Strawberry. In 1983, they had acquired veteran first baseman Keith Hernandez, which helped solidified their infield. The Cubs were built via shrewd trades by general manager Dallas Green, as no position player was groomed in the team's farm system. On the mound, only closer Lee Smith was a true Cub. But it was a veteran team that knew how to win, with several former member of the Phillies, Green's former team.

The Expos began the second part of the season with five wins in their first six games, gaining only one game on the Mets. It was from that point that everything fell apart for the Expos in 1984. They won once in seven games and, after a brief three-game winning streak, they lost eight of their next eleven games for a combined record of seven wins and fourteen losses during this period, which left them thirteen and a half games from first place on August 7, in fifth place. One would have to go back to that terrible 1976 season to see the Expos that far back from the top spot in early August. Bill Virdon tried yet again a new double-play combination with Derrel Thomas at shortstop, as Argenis Salazar was sent back to the minors for the second time. The Expos were greatly exposed offensively, with almost no production from the middle infield, first base and left field. And that didn't take into account Andre Dawson's struggles in the first three months of the season, when he just couldn't play at full speed because of his left knee. In late July, the Expos got some help, acquiring veteran first baseman Dan Driessen from the Cincinnati Reds for Andy McGaffigan and minor-leaguer Jim Jefferson. On the mound, Steve Rogers was demoted to the bullpen, which had been expected for some time. Dan Schatzeder, who had won his three spot-starting assignments, was promoted into the rotation.

With a double-digit deficit, the Expos had no time to lose. On August 2, they were facing the Cubs in Wrigley Field for the first of a four-game series. The Cubs had just over taken the Mets for first place. In the opener, the Expos were trailing, 3–2, in the top of the ninth when Tim Wallach and Mike Stenhouse were on first and second with one out. Pete Rose was next as a pinch-hitter against closer Lee Smith. A single would be enough to tie the game with speedster Miguel Dilone, running for Wallach. Rose connected solidly with Smith's offering, a solid liner that was hit directly through the mound. But the ball caromed off Lee Smith's back and was deflected directly to the hands of shortstop Dave Owen who threw immediately to first to double-up Stenhouse, thus ending the game for a 3–2 Cubs win. After the game, the Expos looked dejected and Bryn Smith, the loser even though he threw a complete game, said: "That gives you an idea the kind of season we have!"[64]

While the team was in Chicago, David Palmer's name was placed on the disabled list. Nothing serious in his case, contrary to his serious elbow problems of years before. Steve Rogers came back to the rotation, and, to fill Palmer's place on the roster, young lefty Joe Hesketh was called up. Hesketh, arguably the best pitching prospect in the Expos' system, was summoned for his major league debut in relief of Bryn Smith with a runner on first on August

7 in the first game of a doubleheader against Philadelphia at Olympic Stadium. Hesketh was known for his very deceptive move to first base. The Expos were already trailing, 4–0, and speedster Jeff Stone was at first. Before throwing his first pitch to Von Hayes, Hesketh tried to pick off Stone but his move was ruled a balk. Hesketh managed to keep the Phillies scoreless in another Expos loss. The Expos won the second game, 7–6, to trigger the most successful run of 1984 for the team, with 12 wins in the next 15 games, including a superb 10-inning performance from Dan Schatzeder on August 9 in a 1–0 victory over the Cubs in Montreal.

During that stretch, the Expos traded Pete Rose to Cincinnati, where he became a player-manager. The Reds were even worse than the Expos and Cincinnati believed that Rose, who not only was the sparkplug of the Big Red Machine of the 1970s but also was from Cincinnati, would bring some new life to the team. His departure from Montreal was not a surprise, as rumors were swirling that he might be merely released at some point.[65] Also, Bill Virdon never asked to have Rose with the team and almost had no use for him.[66] In Houston, Virdon could count on versatile players with obvious athletic qualities, and in that sense, Rose didn't fit the mold at all, especially at age 44. Rose's hiring was John McHale's initiative as he thought he could bring some leadership to the Expos.[67] But Bill Virdon was never one to delegate responsibilities to his players. One just had to go back to 1983 when he refused to hold a team meeting or when he reacted negatively after Warren Cromartie turned over a table after another loss.

Rose's departure had very little, if any, impact on the field. But the reactions were not all that kind in the clubhouse. Gary Carter didn't hide his feelings, saying that he was relieved to see Rose leaving for Cincinnati.[68] In 1984, Carter was used a little more at first base to give his knees a break from his normal catching position. The Expos still wanted his bat in the lineup, thus his use at first base. According to Carter, Rose also wanted to play first base, which created problems.[69] Rose had begun the season in left field but he just couldn't make the long throws from the outfield after hurting his right elbow. Carter went further, saying that Rose kept playing only to break the Ty Cobb all-time hits record, to the detriment of the team. Carter opined that Rose never took any leadership role and that, quite the contrary, his presence had a rather negative impact on the team. Because of his addition on the team, said Carter, the Expos were forced to trade Al Oliver, provoking a negative reaction from black players on the team, leading to the bad start in 1984.[70]

Carter's comments triggered another reaction, not from Rose himself, but from his buddy on the team, Doug Flynn, whom Carter had touted as the non-official spokesman of Rose. Flynn didn't like at all being linked to that story. The infielder was particularly miffed that an incident that took place on July 29 in Philadelphia was made public. The day after, Carter and Flynn had had a rather heated verbal exchange. Carter was playing first base and Flynn was trying to tell Carter how to play in certain situations. The exchange became public knowledge only after Rose left for Cincinnati. Flynn said that Carter's alleged inexperience at first base was just an excuse to justify his poor play at this position.[71]

In spite of their 12–3 run in August, the Expos were too far away back to catch the Cubs, who were running away with the NL East title. It was time to think about 1985 and changes were certainly coming. But already, it looked like these changes would be far more important than just on the field. The pressure had been extensive on the Expos for some years, especially on John McHale. The 1984 team resembled nothing like the spectacular editions of 1979 to 1981 and it was time to rebuild with new foundations. Since Bill Virdon's two-year contract was expiring at the end of 1984, when McHale asked him about his plans for 1985, Virdon told him he wouldn't be back.[72] Considering the context — the Expos were already out of the playoff picture in 1984, September would be a time to assess the team, and knowing that Virdon wouldn't be around in 1985 — McHale thought it was best to give the team to somebody else to manage for the rest of the season. Virdon was thus fired on August 30, after a sixth consecutive loss, which placed the Expos under .500 for good. Jim Fanning would lead the team for the rest of the season, but it was already clear this time that Fanning was there only to finish the season.[73]

When John McHale met the media for the managerial announcement, weirdly, Bill Virdon himself was there. Both men even shook hands for photographers. Virdon was smiling, something nobody had seen since he took over the Expos in 1983.[74] According to many media members who followed the team, Virdon had lost his passion even before accepting the job in Montreal.[75] At the beginning of his first training camp, Virdon had already said that there would be no more baseball for him after the Expos.[76] In fact, while he was still in Houston, he had already stated in December 1981 that he had enough of all the travel and that he expected to retire after two more years.[77] And days before the official announcement of his hiring by the Expos, he hinted that he was contemplating retirement.[78] Jim Fanning would say that Virdon was the right man but at the wrong time.[79] Broadcaster Dave Van Horne remembered that a long-time scout told him that Virdon looked lifeless, asking if something was wrong with him.[80] At the end of the season, even John McHale would say that his manager had lost his enthusiasm.[81] As for Virdon himself, he would associate the team's failures in his two years with the injuries to Gary Carter (1983) and Andre Dawson (1984).[82] He admitted that he had erred in giving the everyday shortstop job to Argenis Salazar right from the first day in camp, adding that he would kick his butt if he could.[83]

Few players were surprised by Virdon's firing. Reliever Gary Lucas thought he was often outmanaged and that he rarely tried to shake things up offensively during a game, even though it was obvious the team was struggling.[84] Dan Schatzeder remarked that Virdon was not really a motivator.[85] Charlie Lea thought that Virdon had nothing to do with the Expos' problems and, like Scott Sanderson had said the year before, that the problem was in the clubhouse and that the players accepted losing too easily.[86] Again, Gary Carter's name was brought up but Lea insisted that his contract had nothing to do with the situation.[87]

In early September, the Expos announced a yet bigger change: John McHale would no longer be the general manager of the team, while he would remain as the Expos' president.[88] It was the logical sequel of the long soap opera of 1984. At 63 years old, McHale knew that the team was due for a complete overhaul and that a huge task was at hand for the general manager.[89] The team needed a fresh start and a new identity. The team he had built was no more and, quite frankly, from 1982 to 1984, the team's success at the gates—notwithstanding the steep decline in 1984 — was due more to their performance in the three preceding years and to high expectations. It was time to pass the torch and, on September 5, Murray Cook was announced as the team's fourth general manager, following in the footsteps of McHale, Charlie Fox and Jim Fanning. Cook had been in charge of scouting and player development with the New York Yankees. But Yankees' owner George Steinbrenner had demoted him after his team lost pitcher Tim Belcher to the Oakland A's in the free-agent compensation pool draft. Cook was held responsible and was removed from his position.[90] Cook's hiring was a turning point in Expos history as it marked the first time that the team had filled such an important position from the outside. Moreover, it was felt that the John McHale-Jim Fanning era was coming to an end.

It didn't take much time before another controversy hit the Expos after Cook took over as the new GM, even though Cook himself was not involved. In an article published in the *Globe and Mail* in mid–September and penned by Montreal freelance writer Ian Halperin, the Expos' organization was depicted as being racist. On September 6, Derrel Thomas was sold to the California Angels and he was told so during batting practice. Thomas didn't really appreciate how the Expos acted and thought it should have been handled differently, and would have had he been white. He thought that the Expos wanted to keep the minorities invisible. Felipe Alou, who had been part of the organization for several years, was also quoted in the article. "Just look at my situation," Alou said. "I've been a minor-league manager, coach and outfield instructor in this organization but they wouldn't give me a chance to manage the Expos. The Expos would rather lose with a Bill Virdon than try a Felipe Alou. Maybe one day the Expos will hire a black as manager but I won't live to see it. Maybe it will happen in the next century or the century after." Fortunately for Alou and the Expos, the future would prove him wrong, as he would lead the team from 1992 to 2001, becoming one of the most popular figures in team history. Halperin's story also highlighted the lack of chemistry within the players' ranks. Thomas said that few players hung around themselves, and only with people they considered their own, whether they were blacks, whites or Latin-Americans. According to Thomas, Rose didn't like his time in Montreal, especially because of the privileged treatment afforded to whites. Thomas named Gary Carter as the player to whom the Expos did everything to please, while the organization should have been more careful with Andre Dawson when his knees were killing him in the early weeks of 1984. Dan Driessen was also quoted, saying that even though he didn't think he had been with the Expos long enough to make a sound judgment, he noticed that the sense of unity was lacking, comparing to the Reds' championship teams of the 1970s.[91] The Expos tried to discredit both the story and the writer, saying it was a set-up by the writer, but the *Globe and Mail*, after hearing Halperin's side, supported its journalist.

It was not the first time the Expos were involved in some kind of racial controversy. In the early 1970s, Mack Jones hinted that racism might have been at the root of his benching by manager Gene Mauch.[92] In 1978, Rudy May had his car vandalized and wondered whether it was because he was married to a white woman.[93] In April 1979, the blacks were quite unhappy after Dave Cash lost his everyday job to Rodney Scott.[94] In 1982, Jerry White and Andre Dawson were humiliated when policemen confronted them at gunpoint in the middle of a shopping mall looking for two black suspects.[95]

Were the Expos guilty of racism? In most teams, it was and is still normal to see players hanging around mostly with players from the same cultural background, whether blacks, whites, Latino-Americans, or Japanese. Prior to the 1983 season, as Tim Raines was preparing to make up for his 1982 drug-induced season, Gary Carter was asked about his leadership role in the team. His answer depicted this racial reality, when he said that he just didn't see himself telling Tim Raines to go full speed because he (Carter) was white.[96] Of course there were exceptions. Bryan Little was seen with everybody.[97] Bill Lee could be at ease in any surrounding. But generally speaking, the social behavior of the players was just not different from that of society as a whole. But the Expos were at fault in some instances, especially when Dawson and White were questioned by police. The least the organization could have done was to ask for a public apology.

The Expos ended the 1984 season with almost complete indifference. In their last ten games, they barely averaged 10,000 fans per game, with only

2,803 showing up on September 27 against the St. Louis Cardinals. Their final record was 78–83, their worst since 1978. For September, the Expos' Player of the Month was Jim Wohlford. Yes, he deserved the award, hitting .429 with four home runs and 12 RBIs. But with all due respect to his work, when Jim Wohlford is your Player of the Month, that means that you have deep problems.

Among position players, only Gary Carter and Tim Raines hit up to expectations. Carter was picked as the Expos' Player of the Year for the fourth time, after leading the league in RBIs. Raines led the National League in stolen bases for the fourth consecutive season. He was also among the league leaders in hits and walks. Tim Wallach continued his progress defensively but his bat tailed off for the second successive year, ending with 18 home runs, 72 RBIs and a slugging percentage of only .395. He had a miserable month of September with no home runs and a .137 batting average. Andre Dawson finished with a second half more indicative of his talent, hitting 14 of his 17 home runs in the last three months of the season, driving in 53 in the same period of time. The middle-infield was just pathetic offensively. Collectively, the second basemen and shortstops hit no home runs and showed a combined slugging percentage below .300! The shortstops also managed to walk only 20 times, only six more times than the pitchers. John McHale would say that the Expos had spent the season with three automatic outs in the lineup.[98]

Overall, the pitching staff did its job, finishing second in runs allowed and fourth overall, taking into account the pitcher-friendly Olympic Stadium. Charlie Lea was by far the most consistent performer among the starters. He had a legitimate shot at winning 20 games, with 13 victories at the All-Star break, but he got almost no support thereafter, ending with a still team-leading 15 wins. Bill Gullickson and Bryn Smith each won 12 while Dan Schatzeder and David Palmer were adequate. On the other hand, 1984 was the worst season of Steve Rogers' career, with only six wins and a 4.31 ERA, one of the worst among the qualifiers for the ERA title. His strikeout-to-walk ratio was also the worst in the majors. The bullpen was one of the best in the National League. Jeff Reardon was again the closer and finished with an 88 percent save percentage, the highest among the league's closers.[99] Bob James, after a rough start, redeemed himself and was a solid set-up man.

It was clear that new GM Murray Cook had to revamp a very suspect offense. Cook stated that nobody was untouchable,[100] but before making any move he first had to find someone to manage the team. Earl Weaver's name was mentioned, even though he had retired after the 1982 season.[101] Roger Craig was also named.[102] Felipe Alou was a candidate, not in Montreal but rather in San Francisco.[103] The Giants said they were impressed[104] but decided to go with Jim Davenport. It was a blessing in disguise for Alou, as the Giants went on to lose 100 games in 1985. Cook decided to stay within the organization by picking Buck Rodgers, who had led the Expos' AAA affiliate in Indianapolis to a solid 91–63 record in 1984. Rodgers, a former catcher with the California Angels in the 1960s, had also managed the Milwaukee Brewers from 1980 to 1982. He had an excellent reputation at handling the pitching staff. The media would also come to know a man who was a very good story-teller and communicator, a drastic change from Bill Virdon.

No major announcement was made in November, but things were brewing inside the organization. Murray Cook was preparing the landscape for the December annual winter meetings. Everybody could be traded, including Gary Carter, who had become the face of the franchise. Carter didn't ask to go, but he had heard the rumors about his possible departure since the end of the season. He was also well aware of the fact that his name was at the center of every discussion when team unity — or lack thereof — was brought up. After several attempts, Carter managed to contact John McHale, who told him that the Expos would trade him due to a decision from the Expos' board of directors.[105] But Carter had a right to veto any trade, with his status as a ten-year veteran having played the last five with the same club. He insisted in staying in the National League, with Los Angeles and Atlanta as his two preferred destinations.

As the major league teams executives were gathering in Houston for the winter meetings in December, Pete Rose looked absolutely great, representing the Cincinnati Reds. He had been rather discreet about his time in Montreal since leaving the Expos. But in Houston, his mood was jovial and Rose couldn't refrain himself from commenting about what happened in Montreal. "There's not enough players who were concentrating to win," Rose said about the Expos. He had tremendous respect for Andre Dawson, Tim Raines and Tim Wallach. The same couldn't be said of Gary Carter. "His nickname The Kid is appropriate because that's what he is. He'll become an asset to his team when he'll forget his own person."[106] Carter retorted again that Rose was thinking about one and only one thing: Ty Cobb's hits record. He insisted that Rose was offered the manager's job in Montreal, but that Rose refused because he wanted to keep playing.[107]

On December 7, Murray Cook completed a transaction with the Chicago White Sox, trading reliever Bob James and infielder Bryan Little for infielder Vance Law and Bert Roberge, a tall reliever who was from Maine and who could speak French. Law had played mostly at third base with the White Sox, but was expected to move to second base to provide some much-needed offense. In 1984, Law hit 17 home runs.

December 10 was the date the association ended between Gary Carter and the Expos. Carter was traded to the New York Mets for four players:

infielder Hubie Brooks, catcher Mike Fitzgerald, outfielder Herman Winningham and minor-league pitcher Floyd Youmans. Brooks, a former first-round pick, had been a third baseman since being a regular with the Mets in 1981, but was moved to shortstop in the last few weeks of 1984. That's where the Expos intended to use him. Fitzgerald would take over the everyday catching duties from Carter. Winningham was expected to patrol center field. The Expos were given the choice between him and Mookie Wilson.[108] The Expos opted for Winningham because he was younger and also after his strong showing in September, hitting .407 and playing a very solid defense. Youmans had yet to pitch in the majors, but there was no doubt about the quality of his arm.

That Carter trade was one of the most important in the team's history and, of course, triggered lots of reaction. The following day, John McHale said that Carter going to New York would improve the overall atmosphere of the team.[109] It was clear that Carter and Dawson were never able to provide some common leadership to the team. The schism couldn't be better depicted by what Dawson said in January 1985 in the Expos' annual promotional Expos tour in Quebec and Canada. As Dawson was in Hawksbury, Ontario, about a one-hour drive west of Montreal, he told Bob Elliott of the *Ottawa Citizen* that Carter was hustling only on Wednesdays and Saturdays, the days when the Expos were aired nationally on CBC. Some people around the team tried to cover the story and add Dawson among the club of the misquoted. But in the next few days, as Dawson was in Hull, Quebec, he was asked whether his comments were accurate or not. Dawson didn't try to hide anything and acknowledged that he was quoted adequately by Bob Elliott.[110]

Even though Dawson could barely stand Carter, both had very much in common. They had both worked very hard to become not only accomplished hitters but also to improve their craft defensively. After his coaching career was over, Galen Cisco, who had worked with dozens of catchers, said that Carter was the most-prepared he had ever worked with.[111]

But Carter's extrovert personality and his sense of self-promotion rubbed many teammates the wrong way. To his defense, Carter's way was legitimate. He was very generous with his time towards the media, whether it was radio, TV or the newspapers.[112] Many athletes would show up with their best smile when the camera lights were on but wouldn't care much about anything else related to the media. That was not Carter, who would be as generous with a young regional writer as he would with a nationally syndicated baseball columnist. His enthusiasm for the game was real and that's why he was so popular with the fans.

Even though John McHale said that the team atmosphere would be better from then on, he was very reluctant to submit himself to the board's decision to trade the star catcher. More than twenty years later, he would have a hard time trying to justify this transaction: "I'm not sure it was a good trade, losing your catcher and your fourth hitter. But nevertheless, I met with Gary down here in Florida. The key to making a deal for Gary Carter was for him to accept a trade. So we had to get that behind us first. I pointed out to Gary his great desire to be more than just a ballplayer, to be a personality and all that that incorporated. That the Mets would be the perfect place for him, because that's where the media is, that's where the television is and all that. And he bought that. He said, 'That's right, that's exactly how I would feel.' That's how he accepted being traded to the Mets. And Gary was his own man. I don't think his agent was very happy about that, Gary taking over and deciding what he's going to do. Many of these agents want to be on the ground floor, so to speak, on any of these important decisions."[113] Commenting on Carter's lack of popularity in his own clubhouse, McHale also defended his former catcher: "I guess I've been reading stories about Bench, great players who are the number one attraction on their team. There's always a group of people who're going to resent that attention. And Gary was aggressive about being popular. He almost dominated the entire marketing area by himself. I think several of the players had concerns that they didn't get anything and Gary got everything. But Gary worked for it. He would go spend all winter visiting, attending meetings, making speeches and doing stuff in order to get those endorsements. The others weren't that good or weren't capable of doing that."[114]

On a strictly marketing standpoint, Carter's trade was a big blow for the Expos and the fans. René Guimond, the team's marketing VP, would acknowledge that he had to adjust, even though he knew Carter had to go: "For the fans, it was hard, as Gary was one of the most popular players ever in Montreal. He was an important asset. But for the sake of the team, he had to go and many players were happy to see him out. But from a marketing standpoint, his loss represented a problem. He was our best spokesman. He was always available to meet the fans, generous with his time, unlike some players who didn't care. After Carter's trade, we had to readjust out publicity campaign, focusing on the young players and the team in general."[115]

For owner Charles Bronfman, who no doubt instigated the board decision to trade Carter, it was a big relief as he had always thought that his signing was a big mistake.[116] It was the second time in the team's short history that a franchise player was traded. On April 5, 1972, Rusty Staub was sent to the New York Mets for three players who became instant regulars, Ken Singleton, Tim Foli and Mike Jorgensen. Like Carter, Staub was one of the most popular Expos when he was traded. But to Bronfman, the similarities ended there. "The Staub trade was a lot harder," he confided in January 1985.[117]

For Carter, it was a new start with an up-and-coming team. He would have ended his career in Montreal, but it became a no-win situation for him. He would eventually end his career with a final season in Montreal in 1992. The trade was the most important of a series of changes that overhauled the whole organization. Billy DeMars and Galen Cisco, respectively, the batting and pitching coaches, left for Cincinnati and San Diego to join buddies (Pete Rose and Dick Williams, respectively). Larry Bearnearth, who would become an accomplice and good friend of Buck Rodgers, became pitching coach while Rick Renick succeeded DeMars.

Very few players would last more than a few years after 1984. Steve Rogers would be released in May 1985. Bill Gullickson and Jeff Reardon would both be dealt for multiple players after 1985 and 1986, respectively. Charlie Lea's 1984 season was his last as a first-rate pitcher. Thanks to shoulder problems, Lea didn't pitch in the majors in both 1985 and 1986. He made a start in September 1987 in the middle of the NL East race when the Expos were desperate for pitching help. But he lasted only one inning, his last in an Expos uniform. He pitched in 1988 with the Minnesota Twins and was getting better as the season went along. But again, shoulder problems occurred and curtailed a promising career. David Palmer left bitterly as a free agent after 1985. Dan Schatzeder was traded in 1986 for infielder Tom Foley. Terry Francona was released at the end of 1986 spring training. Andre Dawson would leave after 1986 to sign his famous one-year contract with the Cubs, when he asked the team to fill in whatever salary they wanted to pay him.

In 1987, only Tim Raines, Tim Wallach and Bryn Smith were still with the Expos among those who had played significantly in 1984. Buck Rodgers, Hubie Brooks, Vance Law, Mike Fitzgerald, Tim Burke, Andres Galarraga, Dennis Martinez and Pascual Perez would become the faces of the team of the late 1980s, which made two interesting runs for the NL East title in 1987 and 1989.

The Expos, who had the advantage in the early 1980s to be the number one sports team in Canada, were not supreme anymore. The Montreal Canadiens were back in the news in 1984 after three years of early playoff exits, reaching the conference finals. Another Canadian team, the Edmonton Oilers, were just beginning their run of excellence by winning the first of five Stanley Cups in seven years. In fact, Canadian teams would win the Stanley Cup seven straight years from 1984 to 1990. On the baseball landscape, the Toronto Blue Jays, after five years of mediocrity, were getting more and more relevant from 1982 on, showing constant improvement up to winning their first AL East title in 1985 and eventually two World Series titles in 1992 and 1993. At that point, they had become the country's number one baseball team for some years already.

The year 1985 was also the last of that five-year $35 million deal with the

O'Keefe Brewery. The Expos would be able to get about the same kind of money in their next deal with another brewery, Labatt.[118] But what was in 1980 the most lucrative deal in the majors was merely average in 1986, thanks to the rampant inflation in player salaries during those five years. O'Keefe was involved in another costly sports war in hockey pitting the owner of the Quebec Nordiques against Molson's Montreal Canadiens. One of O'Keefe's executive, Ed Prévost, said that the Expos were no more than a regional team, thanks to the baseball commissioner's decision to limit the territory over which the Expos' games could be broadcast.[119] There's good reason to believe that the money announced at the press conference to confirm the new Labatt-Expos agreement was exaggerated, in order to give the impression that it was not less than the former deal, especially in light of Labatt being one of the few organizations interested in getting involved.[120]

So what happened to that Expos team that was so spectacular and talented from 1979 to 1981, which had became almost an afterthought only a couple of years later?

After 1982, the lack of chemistry was cited time and again by people within the organization, players and executives. Many players said that the void left when Larry Parrish was traded was never filled. He had a presence that could be hardly replaced, especially from a player who had been part of the organization from his first professional contract. In their blind chase for that experienced left-handed batter, the Expos gave away a big part of their heart and soul. John McHale would admit that he misunderstood the importance of Parrish on the team and that he wouldn't make the trade again.[121] Al Oliver did everything that could be asked of him, but he just couldn't replace Parrish's quiet presence.

Defensively and offensively, the Expos were completely lost in the middle infield, getting no production whatsoever by the numerous combinations that were used from 1982 to 1984. The release of Rodney Scott triggered that merry-go-round at second base and shortstop, even though Scott's offensive production was below average at best. But even if his release wasn't entirely baseball-related, his cocky demeanor left everybody on his toes. Scott's release wouldn't have been that costly had the Expos been prepared to replace him. And they had the assets to fill his departure in the early stages of the 1980s. But their lack of a long-term plan made the situation worse. Throughout their history, the Expos have been praised as being an example in player development. It was especially true for outfielders and pitchers. But they had to wait until 1990 to get a bona fide regular infielder from their own ranks, Delino DeShields. Not that they didn't have any before who could have made the jump. In 1980, the Expos had at least four potential future major league second basemen in their system: Tim Raines, Tony Bernazard, Tony Phillips and

Wallace Johnson. Bill Almon, who did a creditable jobs with the White Sox, could be added as well. It had been already established late in the 1980 season that Ron LeFlore wouldn't be back in 1981 and that Raines would move to left field. Phillips, who was in AA, was traded away in 1980 as was Bernazard after the season. Of course, there was no way Rodney Scott would lose his job as long as Dick Williams was the manager. But that left Wallace Johnson as the only alternative at second base when 1981 began and Dick Williams was already on the hot seat with only a one-year contract. As for Johnson, it was obvious to most in 1982 that he wasn't yet ready. By promoting him far too soon, they lost a player who could have provided them with a solid bat in the long run if he had a little seasoning in AAA. Maybe Scott had to go, but better planning from the direction of the team wouldn't have left the Expos with a huge void in the middle infield that took three full years to take care of.

In 1977 and 1978, the Expos were looked at as a team on the rise, whose potential would lead them to pennant contention, which happened in 1979. Scouts and observers were in awe of this young crop of players, Valentine, Dawson, Carter, Parrish and Cromartie. But with all due respect to these players, it was the pitchers who carried the team through all those years. When you add along the way Tim Raines, Tony Perez, Al Oliver and Ron LeFlore, one must wonder how they didn't fare better offensively. The answer is simple: their on-base percentage was not on par with their more-publicized statistics. Thanks to Bill James and the book *Moneyball*, it is better known today that the on-base percentage is a far better tool to evaluate a player and a team than mere batting average. At the time, walks were not viewed at a weapon. From 1979 to 1983, the Expos' on-base percentage was at best number four in the league, and that was in 1983. In their best overall season (1979), the Expos finished eighth. From 1979 to 1984, only three Expos players finished among the top ten in walks, Rodney Scott (1981), Gary Carter (1982) and Tim Raines (1983). It must be noted, however, that these were years when walks were not praised. Bob Bailey, who played for the Expos from 1969 to 1975, remembered a meeting with then general manager Jim Fanning to discuss a new contract. When Bob Bailey brought up his high walk total, the reply was very indicative of the mentality of the times: "Who cares about walks?"[122] Bailey was the perfect *Moneyball* player in that he had both power and discipline at the plate.

The player development system had been the Expos' forte throughout their entire history. It was especially true from the moment Valentine, Dawson, Carter, Parrish and Cromartie became regulars in 1977. But from 1982, the Expos changed their ways, trading away prospects for the potential of immediate rewards, to the point where in 1984 they had to rebuild the whole farm system. The Expos also lost an opportunity to give a chance to some players who could have helped them, if only given a chance, most prominently first baseman Ken Phelps, who had both power and discipline. Acquired from Kansas City for Grant Jackson in spring 1982, Phelps spent only one year in the Expos' organization, destroying the American Association with a .333 batting average, 46 home runs, 141 RBIs and 108 walks, leading the league in both on-base percentage and slugging percentage. Phelps would become a solid major league hitter for several years in the American League. In the out-field, there was one player who should have been given a better chance, Mike Fuentes. He had been chosen the Collegiate Player of the Year in 1981 and had put up solid numbers in the minors in his first three years, with both power and discipline. He only got eight at-bats in two September call-ups. First-baseman-outfielder Mike Stenhouse was a walk machine in the minors and even in the majors, but again the Expos grew impatient with him, with the team opting to go with veterans who either didn't have any sense of belonging with the organization (for example, Joel Youngblood) and were just over the hill (Pete Rose). The Expos were in a position where they had to develop that family atmosphere in the organization when they knew they would have to overpay to attract free agents.[123] In some cases, even overpaying was not enough (Don Sutton, Reggie Jackson). In the early years of that run, from 1979 to 1981, the Brad Mills, Bob Pates and Tony Bernazards were more than adequate when called upon to replace injured or struggling players. In trying to get so-called experienced players, the Expos ignored their farm sys-tem, which was their strength.

The Expos also had to face solid opposition in those years, especially from 1979 to 1981. In 1979, the Expos were beaten by a very experienced Pitts-burgh club led by Willie Stargell. At age 38, Stargell probably knew it was his last chance at winning it all and he made the most of it. The Pirates were a very balanced team and in the course of the season made a couple of acqui-sitions (Tim Foli and Bill Madlock) that served them well. In 1980, the Phillies, a team considered as an underachiever for some time, pulled it off under Dal-las Green, a manager who shook up the way of doing things in Philadelphia. And in 1981, another underachiever, the Los Angeles Dodgers, got the best of the Expos in the only time Montreal made it to the playoffs. In all three instances, the teams that got the best of the Expos went on to win the World Series.

The Expos would have some interesting seasons thereafter, especially in the early 1990s under Felipe Alou. But even then, they were never able to gar-ner the level of popularity and passion they had from 1979 to 1981, when the Montreal Expos were truly the toast of Canada.

Chapter Notes

Chapter 1

1. www.baseball-reference.com.
2. *The Sporting News Baseball Guide*, 1977.
3. *Sports Illustrated*, June 14, 1976.
4. Personal interview with Larry Parrish.
5. *Montréal-Matin*, September 14, 1976.
6. *Montreal Gazette*, October 4, 1976.
7. Personal interview with Jim Fanning.
8. www.retrosheet.org.
9. Multiple sources.
10. www.espn.com.
11. *The Sporting News Baseball Guide*, 1977.
12. *La Presse*, September 21, 1976.
13. *La Presse*, November 11, 1976.
14. *La Presse*, November 18, 1976.
15. *Montreal Star*, November 15, 1976.
16. *La Presse*, November 18, 1976.
17. *Montreal Star*, November 18, 1976.
18. *La Presse*, November 2, 1976.
19. Personal interviews with Harry Renaud and John McHale.
20. *The Gazette*, November 20, 1976.
21. Personal interview with Harry Renaud.
22. *The Gazette*, November 24, 1976.
23. *Montreal Star*, November 20, 1976.
24. *The Gazette*, November 30, 1976.
25. *Montreal Star*, December 1, 1976.
26. Reggie Jackson and Mike Lupica, *Reggie*.
27. *Montreal Star*, December 3, 1976.
28. *Journal de Montréal*, December 9, 1976.
29. *La Presse*, December 7, 1976.
30. Personal interview with Harry Renaud.
31. *La Presse*, several dates in February and March 1977; personal interviews with Harry Renaud and John McHale.

Chapter 2

1. *La Presse*, February 22 and 23, 1977.
2. *The Gazette*, January 12, 1977.
3. *Journal de Montréal*, February 20, 1977.
4. *Journal de Montréal*, December 12, 1976; *The Gazette*, January 6, 1977; *La Presse* January 7, 1977.
5. *The Gazette*, February 21, 1977.
6. *Journal de Montréal*, February 25, 1977; *The Gazette*, March 1, 1977.
7. *The Gazette*, January 6, 1977.
8. *The Gazette*, January 21, 1977.
9. *Montréal-Matin*, February 20, 1977.
10. *Journal de Montréal*, February 25, 1977.
11. *Montréal-Matin*, March 12, 1977.
12. Jim Russo and Bob Hammel, *Super Scout*.
13. *The Gazette*, March 9, 1977; *Journal de Montréal*, March 3, 1977.
14. *Journal de Montréal*, April 30, 1977.
15. Warren Cromartie and Robert Whiting, *Slugging It Out in Japan*.
16. *La Presse* and *The Gazette*, March 19, 1977.
17. *La Presse*, March 19 and 25, 1977.
18. *Montreal Star*, March 25 and 31, 1977.
19. *Journal de Montréal*, April 3, 1977.
20. www.retrosheet.org.
21. *Journal de Montréal*, April 6, 1977; *Dimanche-Matin*, March 27, 1977; UPI, April 4, 1977; *Montréal-Matin*, April 8, 1977; *The Gazette*, April 5, 1977; *Montreal Star*, April 9, 1977; multiple sources.
22. www.retrosheet.org.
23. Several sources from Montreal papers.
24. *Montreal Star*, April 30, 1977.
25. Personal interview with Chris Speier.
26. *Journal de Montréal*, October 10, 1976.
27. *The Gazette*, February 9, 1977.
28. www.baseball-reference.com.
29. *Dimanche-Matin*, June 26, 1977.
30. www.retrosheet.org.
31. *The Gazette*, May 25, 1977.
32. Gary Carter and Ken Abraham, *The Gamer*.
33. *La Presse*, June 14, 1977.
34. Personal interview with Wayne Twitchell.
35. Personal interview with Wayne Twitchell.
36. Personal interview with Warren Cromartie.

37. *The Gazette*, April 21, 1977.
38. Personal interview with Don Stanhouse.
39. *La Presse*, February 27, 1979.
40. *The Gazette*, May 14, 1978.
41. Personal interview with Roger D. Landry.
42. Personal interview with John McHale.
43. *Journal de Montréal*, August 8, 1977.
44. *Montreal Star*, August 19, 1977.
45. Personal interview with Dan Schatzeder.
46. *The Gazette*, March 21, 1977.
47. *Montréal-Matin*, September 9, 1977.
48. Personal interview with Don Stanhouse.
49. Personal interview with Larry Parrish.
50. Personal interview with Mel Didier.
51. *The Sporting News Baseball Guide*, 1978.
52. Rich Gossage and Russ Pate, *Goose*.
53. *Journal de Montréal*, March 28, 1979.
54. *The Gazette*, December 2, 1977.
55. *Journal de Montréal*, April 4, 1978.

CHAPTER 3

1. *Journal de Montréal*, August 28, 1977.
2. *The Gazette*, December 5, 1977.
3. *Montréal-Matin*, February 2, 1978.
4. *The Sporting News*, January 21, 1978.
5. Personal interview with Norm Sherry.
6. www.baseball-reference.com.
7. *Dimanche-Matin*, October 30, 1977.
8. Personal interview with John McHale.
9. *Dimanche-Matin*, October 30, 1977.
10. Dick Williams and Bill Plaschke, *No More Mr. Nice Guy*.
11. *The Gazette*, February 28, 1978.
12. *The Gazette*, March 23, 1978.
13. Personal interview with Dan Schatzeder.
14. Multiple sources from Montreal dailies.
15. *The Gazette*, March 29, 1978 and personal interview with Jean-Paul Sarault.
16. *The Gazette*, June 12, 1978.
17. *Journal de Montréal*, April 8, 1978.
18. *Journal de Montréal*, February 2, 1978.
19. *The Sporting News*, April 29, 1978.
20. Personal interview with Wayne Twitchell.
21. Personal interview with Ellis Valentine.
22. *Journal de Montréal*, June 1, 1978.
23. Multiple sources from Montreal dailies.
24. Multiple sources from Montreal dailies.
25. *Montreal Star*, May 20, 1978.
26. Personal interview with Woodie Fryman.
27. *The Gazette*, January 27, 1978.
28. *Journal de Montréal*, July 4, 1978.
29. www.retrosheet.org.
30. Personal interview with Chris Speier.
31. Personal interview with Steve Rogers.
32. *Journal de Montréal*, December 9, 1984.
33. *Journal de Montréal*, July 28, 1978.
34. *Journal de Montréal*, July 31, 1978.

35. Warren Cromartie and Robert Whiting, *Slugging It Out in Japan*.
36. Personal interview with Warren Cromartie.
37. *Los Angeles Times*, July 20, 1979.
38. Personal interview with Scott Sanderson.
39. *Montréal-Matin*, August 16, 1978 and *Journal de Montréal*, August 23, 1978.
40. Personal interview with Bob James.
41. *Journal de Montréal*, September 8, 1978.
42. Several sources from Montreal dailies.
43. *Journal de Montréal*, September 9, 1978.
44. Author's personal recollection.
45. *Journal de Montréal*, September 26, 1978.
46. *La Presse*, January 31, 1979.
47. *Journal de Montréal*, September 28, 1978.
48. *Montréal-Matin*, October 2, 1978.
49. *The Sporting News*, October 21, 1978.
50. www.baseball-reference.com.
51. Multiple sources from Montreal dailies and other publications.
52. Gary Carter and Ken Abraham, *The Gamer*.
53. Personal interview with Ross Grimsley.
54. Personal interview with Warren Cromartie.
55. Personal correspondence with Warren Cromartie.
56. *The Sporting News Baseball Guide*, 1979.
57. Personal interview with Roger D. Landry.
58. *Journal de Montréal* and *La Presse*, March 14, 1981.
59. *Dimanche-Matin*, October 15, 1978.
60. Personal interview with John McHale.
61. Personal interview with Darold Knowles.
62. *The Sporting News Baseball Guide*, 1979.
63. Personal interview with Bob Bailey.
64. Numerous sources from Montreal dailies.
65. *The Gazette*, January 6, 1979.
66. Nancy Marshall and Bobbie Bouton, *Home Games*.
67. Personal interview and correspondence with Mike Marshall.
68. *Journal de Montréal*, January 9, 1979.

CHAPTER 4

1. *Journal de Montréal*, January 31, 1979.
2. *Journal de Montréal*, February 15, 1979.
3. www.baseball-reference.com.
4. *The Sporting News*, February 24, 1979.
5. Personal interview with Paul Arsenault.
6. *La Presse*, January 17, 1979.
7. *La Presse*, January 28, 1979.
8. *The Gazette*, December 29, 1978.
9. *La Presse*, March 1, 1979.
10. *The Gazette*, February 28, 1979.
11. *Journal de Montréal*, January 25 and 26, 1979.

12. Personal interview with David Palmer.
13. *La Presse*, February 24, 1979.
14. *The Gazette*, February 24, 1979.
15. *La Presse*, March 1, 1979.
16. *Journal de Montréal*, March 5, 1979.
17. *Journal de Montréal*, March 4, 1979.
18. Numerous sources from Montreal dailies and Bill Lee and Richard Lally, *The Wrong Stuff*.
19. *The Sporting News*, March 24, 1979.
20. *La Presse*, March 16, 1979.
21. *La Presse*, March 16, 1979.
22. *The Gazette*, March 21, 1979.
23. *Montreal Star*, November 18, 1976.
24. *Journal de Montréal*, April 4, 1979.
25. *Journal de Montréal*, April 4, 1979.
26. *Journal de Montréal*, April 4, 1979.
27. *Montreal Star*, April 4, 1979.
28. *La Presse*, April 5, 1979.
29. Personal interview with Tom Hutton.
30. *La Presse*, March 23, 1979.
31. Personal interview with Bob James.
32. Personal interview with Bob James.
33. *La Presse*, February 23, 1979.
34. *Journal de Montréal*, April 1, 1979.
35. *La Presse*, April 2, 1979.
36. *Houston Post*, April 1, 1979.
37. *Montreal Star*, April 4, 1979.
38. Personal interview with Steve Rogers.
39. *The Gazette*, April 9, 1979.
40. *Journal de Montréal*, April 12, 1979.
41. *La Presse*, April 23 and 26, 1979.
42. www.retrosheet.org.
43. Personal interview with Serge Touchette.
44. *Journal de Montréal*, May 13, 1979.
45. *Journal de Montréal*, May 13, 1979.
46. *Montreal Star*, May 17, 1979.
47. *Montreal Star*, May 17, 1979.
48. *Montreal Star*. May 17, 1979.
49. *Journal de Montréal*, May 30, 1979.
50. *La Presse*, June 1, 1979.
51. *The Gazette*, June 1, 1979.
52. Personal interview with Scott Sanderson.
53. Personal interview with Norm Sherry.
54. *Journal de Montréal*, June 12, 1979.
55. Dick Williams and Bill Plaschke, *No More Mr. Nice Guy*.
56. Personal interview with Serge Touchette.
57. Personal interview with Norm Sherry.
58. Personal interview with Rodney Scott.
59. Personal interview with John McHale.
60. *The Gazette*, March 20, 1978.
61. *Montreal Star*, June 6, 1979.
62. *La Presse*, July 16, 1979.
63. *Journal de Montréal*, June 16, 1979.
64. www.retrosheet.org.
65. www.retrosheet.org.
66. *Montreal Star*, June 30, 1979.
67. *Montreal Star*, June 30, 1979.
68. *Dimanche-Matin*, July 8, 1979.
69. *Journal de Montréal*, September 27, 1977.
70. Dick Williams and Bill Plaschke, *No More Mr. Nice Guy*.
71. *Journal de Montréal*, February 14, 1979.
72. *The Gazette*, July 31, 1979.
73. Personal interview with John McHale.
74. *Los Angeles Times*, July 20, 1979.
75. *Los Angeles Times*, July 20, 1979.
76. *The Gazette*, July 24, 1979.
77. Multiple sources from Montreal dailies.
78. *Journal de Montréal*, July 30, 1979.
79. *La Presse*, July 30, 1979.
80. *The Gazette*, March 21, 1979.
81. *La Presse*, July 30, 1979.
82. Personal interview with David Palmer.
83. *Journal de Montréal*, August 15, 1979.
84. *Journal de Montréal*, August 6, 1979.
85. Personal interview with Steve Rogers.
86. *Journal de Montréal*, August 11, 1979.
87. www.retrosheet.org.
88. Personal interview with John McHale.
89. Personal interview with Galen Cisco.
90. Personal interview with David Palmer.
91. Personal interview with David Palmer.
92. Personal interview with Dave Cash.
93. *La Presse*, August 30, 1979.
94. Personal interview with Dale Murray.
95. *Journal de Montréal*, September 16, 1979.
96. Multiple sources from Montreal dailies and personal interviews.
97. Personal interviews with Jacques Doucet and Monique Giroux.
98. *La Presse*, September 12, 1979.
99. Personal interview with Pierre Durivage.
100. Personal interview with Wayne Parrish.
101. *La Presse*, September 19, 1979.
102. Personal interview with Dale Murray.
103. Personal interview with Dan Schatzeder.
104. *The Sporting News*, August 25, 1979.
105. Willie Stargell and Tom Bird, *Willie Stargell: An Autobiography*.
106. www.retrosheet.org.
107. Multiple sources from Montreal dailies.
108. *The Gazette*, September 18, 1979 and personal interview with Steve Rogers.
109. Personal interviews with Mike Boone and Wayne Parrish.
110. Multiple sources from Montreal dailies.
111. www.retrosheet.org.
112. Personal interview with Jim Fanning.
113. Personal interview with Jacques Doucet.
114. *La Presse*, October 1, 1979.
115. *La Presse*, October 1, 1979.
116. Andre Dawson and Tom Bird, *Hawk*.
117. *Journal de Montréal*, July 17, 1979.
118. *Dimanche-Matin*, October 7, 1979.
119. *The Gazette*, October 24, 1979.
120. *The Sporting News*, November 10, 1979.
121. *La Presse*, December 3, 1979.
122. *La Presse*, October 24, 1979.

123. *The Sporting News*, March 29, 1980.
124. Personal interview with Steve Rogers.
125. Personal interview with Dan Schatzeder.
126. Red Murff and Mike Capps, *The Scout*.
127. Personal interview with Tony Perez.
128. Personal interview with Dave Cash.
129. *Journal de Montréal*, December 8, 1979.
130. Ron LeFlore and Jim Hawkins, *One in a Million*.
131. *The Sporting News*, December 22, 1979.
132. *Journal de Montréal*, December 7, 1979.
133. *The Sporting News*, December 22, 1979.
134. Personal interview with Eddie Robinson.
135. *The Sporting News*, December 29, 1979.
136. *La Presse*, December 21, 1979.

CHAPTER 5

1. Personal interview with Larry Parrish.
2. *The Gazette*, March 3, 1980.
3. *La Presse*, February 13, 1980.
4. Personal interview with Michel Lajeunesse.
5. *The Sporting News*, February 2, 1980.
6. Personal interview with Galen Cisco.
7. *Journal de Montréal*, February 20, 1980.
8. *La Presse*, March 10, 1980.
9. *Journal de Montréal*, March 17, 1980.
10. *Journal de Montréal*, March 15, 1980.
11. Personal interview with David Palmer.
12. *La Presse*, March 18, 1980.
13. Personal interview with David Palmer.
14. Personal interview with Bill Gullickson.
15. *The Gazette*, April 1, 1980.
16. *Journal de Montréal*, March 30, 1980 and *The Gazette*, March 24, 1980.
17. Multiple sources from Montreal dailies.
18. *Journal de Montréal*, April 1, 1980.
19. *The Sporting News*, April 19, 1980.
20. *The Sporting News*, April 19, 1980.
21. *Journal de Montréal*, April 2, 1980.
22. *The Gazette*, April 4, 1980.
23. *La Presse*, April 11, 1980.
24. Personal interview with David Palmer.
25. *La Presse*, April 11, 1980.
26. *The Sporting News*, April 26, 1980.
27. *The Sporting News*, April 26, 1980.
28. *Journal de Montréal*, April 7, 1979.
29. Personal interview with Larry Parrish.
30. *Journal de Montréal*, April 28, 1980.
31. www.retrosheet.org.
32. *Journal de Montréal*, May 4, 1980.
33. *La Presse*, May 9, 1980.
34. Personal interview with John McHale.
35. Personal interview with Larry Parrish.
36. Multiple sources from Montreal and national dailies.
37. *The Sporting News Baseball Guide* 1981.
38. *La Presse*, May 24, 1980.

39. *The Sporting News*, March 22, 1980.
40. Multiple sources from Montreal dailies.
41. *The Gazette*, May 29, 1980.
42. *Journal de Montréal*, June 3, 1980.
43. *La Presse*, June 9, 1980.
44. *La Presse*, June 9, 1980.
45. *La Presse*, June 4, 1980.
46. *Journal de Montréal*, June 15, 1980.
47. Bill Lee and Richard Lally, *The Wrong Stuff*.
48. Personal interview with Charlie Lea.
49. Personal interview with Charlie Lea.
50. *Journal de Montréal*, June 13, 1980.
51. *Journal de Montréal*, July 3, 1980.
52. *Journal de Montréal*, July 5, 1980.
53. Personal interview with Ross Grimsley.
54. *The Sporting News*, August 2, 1980.
55. *The Gazette*, July 6, 1980 and *La Presse*, July 26, 1980.
56. *La Presse*, July 24, 1980.
57. *Journal de Montréal*, August 1, 1980.
58. *Journal de Montréal*, August 10, 1980.
59. *La Presse*, August 11, 1980.
60. *La Presse*, August 5, 1980.
61. Personal interview with Tim Burke.
62. *The Gazette*, September 2, 1980.
63. *The Sporting News*, September 20, 1980.
64. *The Sporting News*, September 20, 1980.
65. *Inside Sports*, September 30, 1980.
66. *Journal de Montréal*, September 10, 1980.
67. *Journal de Montréal*, September 11, 1980.
68. *La Presse*, August 30, 1980.
69. *The Gazette*, September 13, 1980.
70. *La Presse*, August 21, 1980.
71. Personal interview with Bill Gullickson.
72. Personal interview with Ron LeFlore.
73. Personal interview with Ron LeFlore.
74. *The Gazette*, September 22, 1980.
75. *The Sporting News Baseball Guide*, 1981.
76. Hal Bodley, *The Team That Wouldn't Die*, and Frank Fitzpatrick, *You Can't Lose Them All*.
77. Hal Bodley, *The Team That Wouldn't Die*.
78. Hal Bodley, *The Team That Wouldn't Die*.
79. *The Trenton Times*, July 8, 1980.
80. Personal correspondence with Jayson Stark.
81. Personal interview with David Palmer.
82. Personal interview with David Palmer.
83. Personal interview with Woodie Fryman.
84. Hal Bodley, *The Team That Wouldn't Die*.
85. Hal Bodley, *The Team That Wouldn't Die*.
86. Hal Bodley, *The Team That Wouldn't Die*.
87. Author's recollections.
88. *La Presse*, August 7, 1980 and personal interview with David Palmer.
89. Personal conversation with Dallas Green.
90. Personal interview with Woodie Fryman.
91. www.retrosheet.org.
92. Gary Carter and Ken Abraham, *The Gamer*.

93. *La Presse*, October 6, 1980.

94. Hal Bodley, *The Team That Wouldn't Die*.

95. Personal interview with Larry Parrish.

96. *The Gazette*, October 8, 1980.

97. *The Gazette*, August 27, 1980.

98. *The Sporting News Baseball Guide*, 1981.

99. www.milb.com.

100. *The Sporting News Baseball Guide*, 1981.

101. *The Sporting News*, August 30, 1980.

102. *The Gazette*, February 26, 1980.

103. *The Sporting News*, April 11, 1981 and personal interview with Roger D. Landry.

104. *The Sporting News*, October 18, 1980.

105. *The Sporting News*, December 20, 1980.

106. *Journal de Montréal*, November 28, 1980.

107. Personal interview with John McHale.

108. Personal interview with Ron LeFlore.

109. *La Presse*, September 20, 1980 and *Journal de Montréal*, September 23, 1980.

110. *The Sporting News*, November 15, 1980.

111. *The Gazette*, October 30, 1980.

112. *The Gazette*, October 9, 1980.

113. *The Gazette*, February 4, 1981.

114. *The Gazette*, October 16, 1980 and *The Sporting News*, December 6, 1980.

115. *The Sporting News*, December 6, 1980.

116. *Journal de Montréal*, December 6, 1980.

117. Personal interview with Charles Bronfman.

118. *Journal de Montréal*, December 6, 1980.

119. *The Sporting News*, April 26, 1980.

120. *The Sporting News*, December 13, 1980.

121. *The Sporting News*, January 10, 1981.

112. www.retrosheet.org.

123. Personal interview with Serge Touchette.

124. *La Presse*, February 5, 1981.

125. *La Presse*, February 6, 1981.

126. *La Presse*, March 13, 1980.

127. *Journal de Montréal*, January 17, 1981.

128. Author's recollections.

129. *Journal de Montréal*, February 6, 1981.

130. *Journal de Montréal*, February 4, 1981.

131. *La Presse*, February 20, 1981.

132. *La Presse*, December 24, 1980.

Chapter 6

1. Multiple sources from Montreal and U.S. dailies.

2. *The Sporting News*, January 24, 1981.

3. Personal interview with Rodney Scott.

4. *The Sporting News*, February 14, 1981.

5. *Journal de Montréal*, March 7, 1981.

6. *The Gazette*, March 7, 1981.

7. *The Sporting News*, December 13, 1980.

8. Author's knowledge of the Quebecers' habits.

9. *Journal de Montréal*, February 4, 1981.

10. *The Gazette*, September 13, 1980.

11. *The Sporting News*, March 7, 1981.

12. *The Sporting News*, March 7, 1981.

13. *La Presse*, March 1, 1981.

14. *The Gazette*, February 21, 1981.

15. *La Presse*, December 5, 1980.

16. *La Presse*, December 8, 1980.

17. *The Gazette*, February 25, 1981.

18. *The Gazette*, February 26, 1981.

19. *Journal de Montréal*, February 26, 1981.

20. *The Sporting News*, March 7, 1981.

21. *The Sporting News*, March 14, 1981.

22. *The Sporting News*, February 21, 1981.

23. *The Gazette*, February 27, 1981.

24. *The Gazette*, March 3, 1981.

25. *La Presse*, March 7, 1981; *Journal de Montréal*, March 7, 1981; *The Gazette*, March 4, 1981.

26. *The Gazette*, March 5, 1981.

27. Personal interview with Roger D. Landry.

28. *The Gazette*, March 5, 1981.

29. *The Gazette*, March 12, 1981.

30. Personal interview with John McHale.

31. Personal interview with René Guimond.

32. *Chicago Tribune*, March 13, 1981.

33. *Journal de Montréal*, April 1, 1981.

34. *The Sporting News*, April 25, 1981.

35. *The Gazette*, April 1, 1981.

36. *La Presse*, April 3, 1981.

37. *The Sporting News*, April 18, 1981.

38. *The Sporting News*, April 4, 1981.

39. *La Presse*, April 8, 1981; *The Gazette*, April 8, 1981; *Journal de Montréal*, April 4, 1981.

40. *La Presse*, April 8, 1981.

41. *The Gazette*, April 27, 1981.

42. www.retrosheet.org.

43. *La Presse*, May 4, 1981.

44. Personal interview with Charlie Lea.

45. Personal interview with Charlie Lea.

46. *Journal de Montréal*, May 19, 1981.

47. Personal interview with Larry Parrish.

48. *La Presse*, May 25 and 26, 1981.

49. Multiple media sources.

50. *Journal de Montréal*, May 30, 1981.

51. Multiple sources and interviews.

52. Personal interview with Mel Didier.

53. Personal interview with Jim Fanning.

54. Personal interview with Larry Parrish.

55. Personal interview with Wayne Twitchell.

56. Jim Russo and Bob Hammel, *Super Scout*.

57. Personal interview with John McHale.

58. Personal interview with John McHale.

59. Author's recollection of the event.

60. *Montreal Star*, October 18, 1977.

61. Personal interview with Jim Bay.

62. Personal interview with Jean-Paul Sarault.

63. Warren Cromartie and Robert Whiting, *Slugging It Out in Japan*.

64. Personal interview with Larry Parrish.

65. Personal interview with Dave Van Horne.

66. Personal interview with Ellis Valentine.
67. Multiple sources from interviews.
68. Personal interview with Ellis Valentine.
69. Personal interview with Gary Roenicke.
70. Personal interview with Ellis Valentine.
71. Personal interview with Serge Touchette.
72. Personal interview with Jim Bay.
73. Personal interview with John McHale.
74. Personal interview with Ellis Valentine.
75. Personal interview with Ellis Valentine.
76. Personal interview with Michel Lajeunesse.
77. Personal interview with Pierre Ladouceur.
78. Personal interview with Claude Raymond.
79. *Sportsmania*, March 1980.
80. Personal interview with Ellis Valentine.
81. Personal interview with Serge Touchette.
82. *The Gazette*, May 30, 1979.
83. Personal interview with Serge Touchette.
84. *La Presse*, August 27, 1981.
85. Personal interview with Ellis Valentine.
86. Personal interview with Ellis Valentine.
87. www.bad.org (Baseballers Against Drugs website).
88. Personal interview with Jeff Reardon.
89. Brodie Snyder, *The Year the Expos Finally Won Something*.
90. *La Presse*, June 2, 1981.
91. *La Presse*, June 6, 1981.
92. *The Gazette*, June 9, 1981.
93. Personal interview with David Palmer.
94. *Journal de Montréal*, June 10, 1981.
95. Personal interview with Harry Renaud.
96. Personal interview with René Guimond.
97. Multiple sources from media.
98. *The Gazette*, June 13, 1981.
99. *The Gazette*, June 17, 1981.
100. *Journal de Montréal*, June 14, 1981.
101. *Journal de Montréal*, July 5, 1981.
102. Bill Lee and Richard Lally, *The Wrong Stuff*.
103. *La Presse*, June 20, 1981.
104. *La Presse*, June 24, 1981.
105. *La Presse*, June 23, 1981.
106. *La Presse*, July 7, 1981.
107. www.mlb.com.
108. *The Gazette*, August 1, 1981.
109. *Journal de Montréal*, August 1, 1981.
110. *The Sporting News*, August 22, 1981.
111. *The Sporting News*, August 22, 1981.
112. Multiple media.
113. *Pittsburgh Press*, August 10, 1981.
114. *The Gazette*, August 11, 1981.
115. Personal interview with Jeff Reardon.
116. *La Presse*, August 20, 1981.
117. *The Sporting News*, January 31, 1981.
118. *Journal de Montréal*, August 11, 1981.
119. *The Gazette*, September 1, 1981.
120. *La Presse*, September 18, 1981.
121. *La Presse*, August 31, 1981.
122. *The Gazette*, September 1, 1981.
123. *Journal de Montréal*, September 5, 1981.
124. *Journal de Montréal*, September 3, 1981.
125. *Journal de Montréal*, September 7, 1981.
126. *La Presse*, September 8, 1981.
127. Personal interview with Bob Elliott.
128. " Dick Williams and Bill Plaschke, *No More Mr. Nice Guy.*
129. *The Gazette*, September 9, 1981.
130. Personal interview with John McHale.
131. *Journal de Montréal*, September 10, 1981.
132. Dick Williams and Bill Plaschke, *No More Mr. Nice Guy.*
133. *Journal de Montréal*, September 12, 1981.
134. Personal interview with Steve Rogers.
135. *Journal de Montréal*, September 12, 1981.
136. *La Presse*, September 9, 1981.
137. *The Gazette*, September 10, 1981.
138. Personal interview with David Palmer.
139. Personal interview with Steve Rogers.
140. Personal interview with Galen Cisco.
141. *Sports Illustrated*, September 21, 1981.
142. *Journal de Montréal*, September 11, 1981.
143. *La Presse*, September 12, 1981.
144. *La Presse*, September 14 and 15, 1981.
145. *La Presse*, September 18, 1981.
146. Whitey Herzog and Kevin Horrigan, *White Rat.*
147. www.retrosheet.com.
148. Personal interview with Wallace Johnson.
149. Author's recollection.
150. Personal interview with Wallace Johnson.
151. Author's recollection.
152. *The Gazette*, October 5, 1981.
153. Personal interview with Larry Parrish.
154. Personal interview with Warren Cromartie.
155. Numerous sources from personal interviews.
156. Personal interview with Jeff Reardon.

CHAPTER 7

1. *The Gazette*, October 5, 1981.
2. *The Sporting News*, September 19, 1981.
3. Numerous sources from Montreal dailies.
4. *The Gazette*, October 7, 1981.
5. www.retrosheet.org.
6. *La Presse*, October 10, 1981.
7. www.retrosheet.org.
8. Personal interview with Steve Rogers.

9. Personal interview with Bill Stoneman.
10. Personal interview with Steve Rogers.
11. *Chicago Tribune*, October 7, 1981.
12. Hal Bodley, *The Team That Wouldn't Die*.
13. Personal interview with Steve Rogers.
14. Personal interview with Steve Rogers and author's recollection.
15. *The Sporting News Baseball Guide*, 1982.
16. Personal interview with Steve Rogers.
17. *The Sporting News Baseball Guide*, 1982.
18. www.baseball-reference.com.
19. www.retrosheet.org.
20. Numerous sources from Montreal dailies.
21. Personal interview with Ray Burris.
22. *Los Angeles Herald*, October 16, 1981.
23. *The Sporting News*, October 31, 1981.
24. Personal interview with Jerry White.
25. www.retrosheet.org.
26. Steve Garvey and Skip Rozin, *Garvey*.
27. *The Gazette*, October 19, 1981.
28. Personal interview with Larry Parrish.
29. Andre Dawson and Tom Bird, *Hawk*.
30. Personal interviews with Steve Rogers and Jeff Reardon.
31. Personal interview with Jeff Reardon.
32. *The Sporting News Baseball Guide*, 1981.
33. Author's recollection.
34. Personal interview with Larry Parrish.
35. Personal interview with Jerry White.
36. Personal interview with Jerry White.
37. Personal interview with Steve Rogers.
38. Personal interview with Steve Rogers.
39. Personal interview with Jeff Reardon.
40. Personal interview with Pierre Ladouceur.
41. Personal interview with Jim Fanning.
42. Personal interview with Ray Burris.
43. Personal interviews with Norm Sherry and Larry Parrish.
44. Personal interview with Larry Parrish.
45. *The Gazette*, October 20, 1981.
46. Personal interview with Scott Sanderson.
47. Brodie Snyder, *The Year the Expos Finally Won Something*.
48. *The Sporting News*, September 19, 1981.
49. *Journal de Montreal*, September 15, 1981.
50. *The Gazette*, November 12, 1981.
51. Personal interview with John McHale.
52. *La Presse*, November 11, 1981.
53. *Journal de Montreal*, October 21, 1981.
54. *La Presse*, October 14, 1981.
55. *The Gazette*, October 21, 1981.
56. *The Gazette*, October 21, 1981.
57. *Journal de Montreal*, November 13, 1981.
58. *Sportmania*, December 1981.
59. *Journal de Montreal*, December 12, 1981.
60. *La Presse*, December 12, 1981.
61. *La Presse*, January 7, 1982.
62. *La Presse*, December 12, 1981.
63. *Journal de Montreal*, December 12, 1981.
64. *La Presse*, December 22, 1981.
65. *Journal de Montreal*, December 9, 1981.

CHAPTER 8

1. *Journal de Montréal*, January 7, 1982.
2. Andre Dawson and Tom Bird, *Hawk*.
3. *Journal de Montréal*, January 13, 1982.
4. *The Gazette*, January 9, 1982.
5. *The Sporting News*, January 16, 1982.
6. *La Presse*, January 13, 1982.
7. *La Presse*, January 15, 1982.
8. Multiple sources from Montreal dailies.
9. *Journal de Montréal*, January 30, 1982.
10. Multiple sources from Montreal dailies.
11. *The Gazette*, February 16, 1982.
12. *La Presse*, January 30, 1982.
13. *Journal de Montréal*, February 21, 1982.
14. *The Gazette*, February 23, 1982.
15. *Journal de Montréal*, March 6, 1982.
16. *Journal de Montréal*, March 4, 1982.
17. *Journal de Montréal*, March 16, 1982.
18. *La Presse*, March 22, 1982.
19. *La Presse*, March 24, 1982.
20. *La Presse*, March 24, 1982.
21. *Journal de Montréal*, March 20, 1982.
22. *La Presse*, March 17, 1982.
23. *Journal de Montréal*, March 12, 1982.
24. *La Presse*, March 25, 1982.
25. Personal interview with Larry Parrish.
26. Personal interview with Eddie Robinson.
27. *The Gazette*, April 1, 1982.
28. Multiple sources from Montreal dailies.
29. *Journal de Montréal*, April 1, 1982.
30. *Journal de Montréal*, March 2, 1982.
31. Personal interview with Elias Sosa.
32. *Journal de Montréal*, April 7, 1982.
33. *Journal de Montréal*, April 12, 1982.
34. *Journal de Montréal*, April 14, 1982.
35. *The Gazette*, April 17, 1982.
36. www.retrosheet.org.
37. *Journal de Montréal*, May 1, 1982.
38. Personal interview with Wallace Johnson.
39. Bill Lee and Dick Lally, *The Wrong Stuff*.
40. *Journal de Montréal*, May 9, 1982.
41. Bill Lee and Dick Lally, *The Wrong Stuff*, and multiple sources from Montreal dailies.
42. Multiple sources from Montreal dailies.
43. *La Presse*, May 11, 1982.
44. *La Presse*, May 10, 1982.
45. *La Presse*, May 11, 1982.
46. *La Presse*, May 11, 1982.
47. Personal interview with Ray Burris and www.retrosheet.org.
48. *Journal de Montréal*, May 19, 1982.
49. *Journal de Montréal*, May 20, 1982.
50. *La Presse*, May 21, 1982.
51. *La Presse*, May 20, 1982.
52. *The Gazette*, May 26, 1982.

53. *The Sporting News*, September 12, 1981.
54. *Journal de Montréal*, June 17, 1982.
55. Personal interview with Dan Schatzeder.
56. *Journal de Montréal*, June 19, 1982.
57. *Journal de Montréal*, June 19, 1982.
58. *La Presse*, June 6, 1982.
59. *Journal de Montréal*, June 30 and July 1, 1982.
60. *Journal de Montréal*, July 2, 1982.
61. *Dimanche-Matin*, July 4, 1982.
62. *Journal de Montréal*, July 7, 1982.
63. *La Presse*, July 8, 1982.
64. *Journal de Montréal*, July 12, 1982.
65. *La Presse*, July 9, 1982.
66. *La Presse*, July 15, 1982.
67. *The Gazette*, July 14, 1982.
68. *The Gazette*, July 15, 1982.
69. Personal interview with René Guimond.
70. Personal interview with René Guimond.
71. Personal interview with Roger D. Landry.
72. Personal interview with Roger D. Landry.
73. Author's recollection from multiple visits to Baseball Hall of Fame.
74. Personal interview with René Guimond.
75. *Journal de Montréal*, July 20, 1982.
76. *La Presse*, July 20, 1982.
77. *Journal de Montréal*, July 9, 1982.
78. Personal interview with Jeff Reardon.
79. *Journal de Montréal*, August 3, 1982.
80. *The Gazette*, March 21, 1983.
81. *The Gazette*, October 21, 1981.
82. *La Presse*, May 14, 1982.
83. *La Presse*, August 4, 1982.
84. www.retrosheet.org.
85. *The Gazette*, November 4, 1981 and *La Presse*, November 13, 1982.
86. *The Gazette*, August 11, 1982.
87. *The Gazette*, August 12, 1982.
88. Personal interview with David Palmer.
89. Personal interview with Ian MacDonald.
90. Multiple sources from Montreal dailies.
91. Multiple sources from Montreal dailies.
92. *Journal de Montréal*, August 17, 1982.
93. *La Presse*, August 16 and 17, 1982.
94. *La Presse*, August 16, 1982.
95. *The Gazette*, August 16, 1982.
96. Personal interview with Steve Rogers.
97. Personal interview with Jim Fanning.
98. *La Presse*, August 31, 1982.
99. *Journal de Montréal*, September 3, 1982.
100. *Journal de Montréal*, September 16, 1982.
101. *Toronto Star*, September 16, 1982.
102. *The Gazette*, September 16, 1992.
103. Personal interview with Michael Farber.
104. *The Gazette*, December 11, 1982.
105. Personal interview with Jim Bay.
106. Personal interview with Dave Van Horne.
107. *The Gazette*, December 11, 1982.
108. Personal interview with Jim Bay.

109. Personal interview with John McHale.
110. Personal interview with John McHale.
111. Dick Williams and Bill Plaschke, *No More Mr. Nice Guy*.
112. *Cleveland Plain Dealer*, September 3, 1980.
113. *The Sporting News*, November 28, 1983.
114. Multiple sources, including Keith Hernandez and Mike Bryan, *If at First*.
115. Multiple sources, including Whitey Herzog and Kevin Horrigan, *White Rat*.
116. Confidential source who asked to remain unnamed.
117. *La Presse*, September 17, 1982.
118. *The Gazette*, September 20, 1982.
119. *Toronto Star*, September 18, 1982.
120. *La Presse*, September 27, 1982.
121. Personal interview with Jim Fanning.
122. www.baseball-reference.com.
123. Multiple sources from Montreal dailies.
124. *Toronto Star*, September 18, 1982.
125. Personal interview with Jim Fanning.
126. *The Gazette*, September 25, 1982; *Journal de Montréal*, October 1, 1982; *La Presse*, October 2, 1982.
127. Personal interview with Bill Beacon.
128. *Journal de Montréal*, October 1, 1982.
129. Personal interview with Steve Rogers.
130. Personal interview with Dave Van Horne.
131. Personal interview with Serge Touchette.
132. Personal interview with Larry Parrish.
133. Personal interview with Bill Gullickson.
134. Personal interview with Bill Lee.
135. Personal interview with Rodney Scott.
136. Bill Lee and Dick Lally, *The Wrong Stuff*.
137. Personal interview with Jim Fanning.
138. Personal interview with John McHale.
139. Personal interview with Al Oliver.
140. Personal interview with Steve Rogers.
141. Multiple sources from Montreal dailies.
142. *La Presse*, October 7, 1982.
143. Several interviews with former players.
144. *La Presse*, October 13, 1982.
145. *The Gazette*, November 4, 1982.
146. *Journal de Montréal*, March 1, 1982.
147. *The Gazette*, October 30, 1982.
148. *Journal de Montréal*, January 9 1893.
149. *The Gazette*, November 6, 1982.
150. *La Presse*, January 18, 1983.
151. *Montreal-Matin*, October 19–22, 1976.

Chapter 9

1. *La Presse*, February 19, 1983.
2. *Journal de Montréal*, February 26, 1983.
3. *Journal de Montréal*, February 26, 1983.
4. *La Presse*, February 23, 1983.
5. *Journal de Montréal*, February 19, 1983.

6. Personal interview with Jeff Reardon.
7. *The Sporting News*, March 5, 1984.
8. *La Presse*, February 10, 1983.
9. Multiple sources from Montreal dailies.
10. *Journal de Montréal*, February 20, 1983.
11. *La Presse*, February 23, 1983.
12. *The Gazette*, February 26, 1983.
13. *La Presse*, March 8, 1983.
14. *La Presse*, March 3, 1983.
15. *The Gazette*, February 25, 1983.
16. *La Presse*, March 9, 1983.
17. *The Sporting News*, November 1, 1983.
18. *La Presse*, March 2, 1983.
19. *Journal de Montréal*, March 8, 1983.
20. *Journal de Montréal*, March 10, 1983.
21. *Journal de Montréal*, March 15, 1983.
22. *Journal de Montréal*, March 16, 1983.
23. *La Presse*, March 18 and 22, 1983.
24. *La Presse*, April 5, 1983.
25. *The Sporting News*, April 11, 1983.
26. *Journal de Montréal*, March 26, 1983.
27. *Journal de Montréal*, April 1, 1983.
28. Multiple sources from Montreal dailies.
29. *Journal de Montréal*, April 4, 1983.
30. *La Presse*, April 15, 1983.
31. *Journal de Montréal*, April 13, 1983.
32. *Journal de Montréal*, April 27, 1983.
33. *The Gazette*, April 21, 1983.
34. *Journal de Montréal*, April 28, 1983.
35. *Journal de Montréal*, May 2, 1983.
36. *The Sporting News*, May 1983.
37. *The Gazette*, May 11, 1983.
38. *The Gazette*, May 4, 1983.
39. *La Presse*, May 11, 1983.
40. *La Presse*, May 6, 1983.
41. *The Gazette*, May 9, 1983.
42. *La Presse*, May 6, 1983.
43. *La Presse* May 13, 1983.
44. *The Gazette*, May 14, 1983.
45. *The Gazette*, May 18, 1983.
46. *The Gazette*, May 18, 1983.
47. *Journal de Montréal*, March 3, 1983.
48. *The Gazette*, May 19, 1983.
49. *La Presse*, June 1, 1983.
50. *La Presse*, May 30, 1983.
51. *The Sporting News*, June 13, 1983.
52. *La Presse*, June 1, 1983.
53. *La Presse*, June 3, 1983.
54. *La Presse*, June 10, 1983.
55. *Journal de Montréal*, June 23, 1983.
56. *The Gazette*, June 17, 1983.
57. *The Gazette*, June 18, 1983.
58. *La Presse*, June 20, 1983.
59. *La Presse*, June 17, 1983.
60. *Journal de Montréal*, June 16, 1983.
61. *La Presse*, June 27, 1983.
62. *The Gazette*, June 28, 1983.
63. www.retrosheet.org.
64. *Journal de Montréal*, July 9, 1983.
65. *The Gazette*, July 14, 1983.
66. *The Gazette*, July 5, 1983.
67. *The Gazette*, July 2, 1983.
68. *The Gazette*, July 6, 1983.
69. *New York Times*, July 4, 1983.
70. *Journal de Montréal*, July 12, 1983.
71. Personal interview with Jerry White.
72. *La Presse*, July 13, 1983.
73. *The Gazette*, July 18, 1983.
74. *Journal de Montréal*, July 17, 1983.
75. *La Presse*, August 31, 1978.
76. Personal interview with Warren Cromartie.
77. *La Presse*, July 12, 1983.
78. *Dimanche-Matin*, July 17, 24, 31 and August 7 and 14, 1983.
79. *The Gazette*, July 21, 1983.
80. *Journal de Montréal*, July 21, 1983.
81. *The Gazette*, July 28, 1983.
82. Personal interview with Jeff Reardon.
83. *La Presse*, July 29 and 30, 1983.
84. *The Gazette*, July 30, 1983.
85. *Journal de Montréal*, August 3, 1983.
86. *The Gazette*, August 2, 1983.
87. *The Gazette*, August 3, 1983.
88. Multiple sources from Montreal dailies.
89. *The Gazette*, August 15, 1983.
90. *Journal de Montréal*, September 12, 1983.
91. *The Sporting News*, several dates, and Bowie Kuhn and Marty Appel, *Hardball*.
92. *The Gazette*, August 29, 1983.
93. *La Presse*, August 24 or 25, 1983.
94. *The Sporting News*, January 24, 1983.
95. *The Gazette*, April 22, 1983.
96. *The Sporting News*, January 31, 1983.
97. *Journal de Montréal*, August 16, 1983.
98. *Journal de Montréal*, August 23, 1983.
99. *La Presse*, August 19, 1983.
100. *La Presse*, August 19, 1983.
101. *La Presse*, August 24, 1983.
102. *La Presse*, August 25, 1983.
103. *La Presse*, September 7, 1983.
104. *La Presse*, September 16, 1983.
105. Personal interview with Bob James.
106. Personal interview with Serge Touchette.
107. Personal interview with Bob James.
108. Personal interview with Bob James.
109. *The Gazette*, September 22, 1983.
110. Multiple sources from Montreal dailies.
111. *The Gazette*, September 23, 1983 and personal interview with Tim Burke.
112. *Journal de Montréal*, September 23, 1983.
113. *Dimanche-Matin*, September 25, 1983.
114. *The Gazette*, September 26, 1983.
115. *La Presse*, September 30, 1983.
116. Warren Cromartie and Robert Whiting, *Slugging It Out in Japan*.
117. *La Presse*, September 2, 1983.
118. *La Presse*, May 13, 1983.
119. *The Sporting News*, August 9, 1982 and multiple sources from Montreal dailies.

120. Personal interview with Harry Renaud.
121. Personal recollection from Gary Carter.
122. *Sports Illustrated*, June 14, 1976.
123. *Journal de Montréal*, September 25, 1983.
124. *The Gazette*, September 8, 1983.
125. *Journal de Montréal*, September 26, 1983.
126. *Journal de Montréal*, October 3, 1983.
127. *Journal de Montréal*, October 1, 1983.
128. *La Presse*, December 16, 1983.
129. *Boston Globe*, September 21, 1983.
130. *Journal de Montréal*, December 20, 1983.
131. *The Gazette*, November 12, 1983.
132. Personal interview with Reuven Katz.
133. Multiple sources from Montreal dailies.
134. *The Gazette*, January 7, 1983.
135. *The Gazette*, January 21, 1983.

CHAPTER 10

1. Gary Carter and Ken Abraham, *The Gamer*.
2. *The Gazette*, January 31 and February 1 and 11, 1984.
3. *The Gazette*, February 20, 1983.
4. *The Gazette*, February 20, 1984.
5. *Journal de Montréal*, August 11, 1983.
6. *La Presse*, February 20, 1984.
7. *La Presse*, March 2, 1984.
8. *La Presse*, February 25, 1984.
9. Personal interview with Bob Elliott.
10. *Journal de Montréal*, February 28, 1984.
11. *The Gazette*, February 28, 1984.
12. *The Gazette*, February 29, 1984.
13. *La Presse*, May 6, 1983.
14. *Journal de Montréal*, March 1, 1984.
15. *Journal de Montréal*, May 9, 1982.
16. Al Oliver and Andrew O'Toole, *Baseball's Best Kept Secret*.
17. *The Gazette*, February 27, 1984.
18. *La Presse*, February 20, 1984.
19. Personal interview with Steve Rogers.
20. *La Presse*, March 3, 1984.
21. *The Gazette*, March 12, 1984.
22. *Journal de Montréal*, February 28, 1984.
23. *Inside Sports*, April 1984.
24. *New York Post*, March 19, 1984.
25. Multiple interviews with teammates and opponents.
26. *The Gazette*, March 19, 1984.
27. *La Presse*, March 31, 1984.
28. *La Presse*, April 1, 1984.
29. *La Presse*, February 22, 1984.
30. *La Presse*, April 1, 1984.
31. *La Presse*, April 2, 1984.
32. *La Presse*, April 2, 1984.
33. *The Gazette*, April 12, 1984.
34. *La Presse*, April 13, 1984.
35. *La Presse*, April 21, 1984.
36. Multiple sources from Monteal dailies.
37. *The Gazette*, April 10, 1984.
38. *La Presse*, April 29, 1984.
39. *Sports Illustrated*, May 7, 1984.
40. Personal interview with Jacques Doucet.
41. *La Presse*, May 15, 1984.
42. Personal interview with Pierre Rinfret.
43. *La Presse*, May 15, 1984.
44. *The Gazette*, March 12, 1981.
45. Multiple sources from Montreal dailies and author's recollection.
46. *Journal de Montréal*, May 6, 1983.
47. *Journal de Montréal*, June 30 and April 3, 1978.
48. Personal interview with Darren Dilks.
49. *The Gazette*, May 22, 1984.
50. *Globe and Mail*, May 26, 1984.
51. *The Gazette*, May 30, 1984.
52. *La Presse*, June 4, 1984.
53. www.baseball-reference.com.
54. *Journal de Montréal*, June 15, 1984.
55. *La Presse*, June 5, 1984.
56. *The Gazette*, June 16, 1984.
57. Personal interview with Jeff Rimer.
58. Personal interview with Jeff Rimer.
59. *La Presse*, June 17, 1984.
60. Personal interview with Jeff Rimer.
61. *La Presse*, June 17, 1984.
62. *Journal de Montréal*, June 28, 1984.
63. *Journal de Montréal*, June 28, 1984.
64. *La Presse*, August 3, 1984.
65. Multiple sources from Montreal dailies.
66. Personal interview with Bill Virdon.
67. Personal interview with John McHale.
68. *La Presse*, August 17, 1984.
69. *The Gazette*, August 16, 1984.
70. *La Presse*, August 17, 1984.
71. *Journal de Montréal*, August 18, 1984.
72. Personal interview with John McHale.
73. Personal interview with Jim Fanning.
74. Multiple sources from Montreal dailies.
75. Multiple sources from personal interviews.
76. *La Presse*, February 22, 1983.
77. *Journal de Montréal*, December 11, 1981.
78. *The Gazette*, October 9, 1984.
79. Personal interview with Jim Fanning.
80. Personal interview with Dave Van Horne.
81. *The Gazette*, Octrober 3, 1984.
82. Personal interview with Bill Virdon.
83. *La Presse*, December 4, 1984.
84. *Journal de Montréal*, August 31, 1984.
85. *Journal de Montréal*, August 31, 1984.
86. *Journal de Montréal*, August 31, 1984.
87. *Journal de Montréal*, August 31, 1984.
88. Multiple sources from Montreal dailies.
89. Personal interview with John McHale.
90. *New York Times*, April 10, 1984.
91. *Globe and Mail*, September 12, 1984.
92. Jean-Paul Sarault, *Les Expos, Cinq Ans Après*.
93. *Journal de Montréal*, September 28, 1978.

94. *Journal de Montréal*, April 4, 1979.
95. Andre Dawson and Tom Bird, *Hawk*.
96. *Journal de Montréal*, February 21, 1984.
97. *Globe and Mail*, September 12, 1984.
98. *The Gazette*, October 3, 1984.
99. www.baseball-reference.com.
100. *The Gazette*, October 12, 1984.
101. *The Gazette*, October 17, 1984.
102. *The Gazette*, October 10, 1984.
103. *The Gazette*, October 4, 1984.
104. *The Gazette*, November 22, 1984.
105. Gary Carter and Ken Abraham, *The Gamer*.
106. *The Gazette*, December 4, 1984.
107. *The Gazette*, December 7, 1984.
108. *La Presse*, December 12, 1984.
109. *La Presse*, December 12, 1984.
110. Personal interview with Bob Elliott.
111. Personal interview with Galen Cisco.
112. Personal interview with René Guimond.
113. Personal interview with John McHale.
114. Personal interview with John McHale.
115. Personal interview with René Guimond.
116. *Journal de Montréal*, September 26, 1983.
117. *The Gazette*, January 15, 1985.
118. *La Presse*, January 31, 1986.
119. *La Presse*, January 31, 1986.
120. Interviews with executives who wanted to remain anonymous.
121. Personal interview with John McHale.
122. Personal interview with Bob Bailey.
123. Personal interviews with John McHale and Charles Bronfman.

Bibliography

BOOKS

Allen, Maury. *Mr. October: The Reggie Jackson Story*. New York: Times, 1981.

Alou, Felipe, with Herm Weiskopf. *My Life and Baseball*. Waco: Word, 1967.

Armour, Mark, and Daniel Levitt. *Paths to Glory*. Washington: Brassey's, 2003.

Bavasi, Buzzie, with John Strege. *Off the Record*. Chicago: Contemporary, 1987.

Bench, Johnny, with William Brashler. *Catch You Later*. New York: Harper & Row, 1979.

Bodley, Hal. *The Team That Wouldn't Die: The Philadelphia Phillies, World Champions, 1980*. Wilmington: Serendipity, 1981.

Bowa, Larry, with Barry Bloom. *Bleep!* Chicago: Bonus, 1988.

_____. *I Still Hate to Lose*. Champaign, IL: Sports Publishing, 2004.

Burke, Tim, with Gregg Lewis. *Major League Dad*. Colorado Springs: Focus on the Family, 1994.

Carter, Gary, with Ken Abraham. *The Gamer*. Waco: Word, 1993.

Carter, Gary, with John Hough, Jr. *A Dream Season*. Orlando: Harcourt Brace Jovanovich, 1987.

Carter, Gary, with Phil Pepe. *Still a Kid at Heart*. Chicago: Triumph, 2008.

Caza, Daniel and Denis Brodeur. *Les Expos: Du Parc Jarry au Stade Olympique*. Montreal: Les Éditions de l'Homme, 1996.

Cohen, Stanley. *Dodgers! The First 100 Years*. New York: Birch Lane, 1990.

Cromartie, Warren, with Robert Whiting. *Slugging It Out in Japan*. New York: Kodansha International, 1991.

Dawson, Andre, with Tom Bird. *Hawk*. Grand Rapids: Zondervan, 1994.

Drysdale, Don, with Bob Verdi. *Once a Bum, Always a Dodger*. New York: St. Martin, 1990.

Fitzpatrick, Frank. *You Can't Lose Them All: The Year the Phillies Finally Won the World Series*. Dallas: Taylor, 2001.

Gagnon-Torres, Danielle, with Ken Lizotte. *High Inside*. New York: G.P. Putnam's Sons, 1983.

Gallagher, Danny. *You Don't Forget Homers Like That: Memories of Strawberry, Cosby and the Expos*. Toronto: Scoop, 1997.

Garvey, Cynthia, with Andy Meisler. *The Secret Life of Cindy Garvey*. New York: Doubleday, 1989.

Garvey, Steve, with Skip Rozin. *Garvey*. New York: Times, 1986.

Gold, Eddie, and Art Ahrens. *The New Era Cubs, 1941–1985*. Chicago: Bonus, 1985.

Golenbock, Peter. *The Spirit of St. Louis: A History of the Cardinals and Browns*. New York: Avion, 2000.

_____. *Wrigleyville: A Magical History Tour of the Chicago Cubs*. New York: St. Martin's, 1996.

Gooden, Dwight, with Bob Klapisch. *Heat: My Life on and off the Diamond*. New York: William Morrow, 1999.

Gooden, Dwight, with Richard Woodley. *Dr K.* New York: Dell, 1986.

Gossage, Rich, with Russ Pate. *The Goose Is Loose.* New York: Ballantine, 2000.

Hernandez, Keith, with Mike Bryan. *If at First.* New York: Penguin, 1987.

Herzog, Whitey, with Kevin Horrigan. *White Rat.* New York: Harper & Row, 1987.

Herzog, Whitey, with Jonathan Pitts. *You're Missin' a Great Game: From Casey to Ozzie, the Magic of Baseball and How to Get It Back.* New York: Simon & Schuster, 1999.

Howe, Steve, with Jim Greenfield. *Between the Lines.* Grand Rapids: Masters, 1989.

Hudon, François. *Le Parc Jarry de Montréal.* Montréal: Logiques, 2001.

Hunter, Jim, with Armen Keteyian. *Catfish.* New York: McGraw-Hill, 1988.

Jackson, Reggie, with Mike Lupica. *Reggie: The Autobiography.* New York: Villa, 1984.

John, Tommy, and Sally John. *The Sally and Tommy John Story.* New York: Macmillan, 1983.

John, Tommy, with Dan Valenti. *T.J., My 26 years in Baseball.* New York: Bantam, 1991.

Johnstone, Jay, with Rick Talley. *Over the Edge.* Chicago: Contemporary, 1987.

_____. *Temporary Insanity: The Uncensored Adventures of Baseball's Craziest Player.* Chicago: Contemporary, 1985.

Kaat, Jim, with Phil Pepe. *Still Pitching.* Chicago: Triumph, 2003.

Kuhn, Bowie, with Martin Appel. *Hardball.* New York: Times, 1987.

Lasorda, Tom, with David Fisher. *The Artful Dodger.* New York: Arbor House, 1985.

Lasorda, Tom, with Bill Plaschke. *I Live for This! Baseball's Last Believer.* Boston: Houghton Mifflin, 2007.

Lee, Bill, with Richard Lally. *The Wrong Stuff.* New York: Viking, 1984.

LeFlore, Ron, with Jim Hawkins. *One in a Million: The Ron LeFlore Story.* New York: Warner, 1978.

Libby, Bill. *Catfish: The Three Million Dollar Pitcher.* New York: Coward, McCann & Geoghegan, 1976.

Litwin, Mike. *Fernando!* New York: Bantam, 1981.

Marshall, Nancy, and Bobbie Bouton. *Home Games: Two Baseball Wives Speak Out.* New York: St. Martin's, 1983.

Matthews, Gary, with Fred Mitchell. *They Call Me Sarge: An Intimate Look at the Personal and Professional Gary Matthews.* Chicago: Bonus, 1985.

McCarver, Tim, with Ray Robinson. *Oh Baby, I love it!* New York: Villard, 1987.

McCollister, John. *The Bucs! The Story of the Pittsburgh Pirates.* Lenexa, KS: Addax, 1998.

McGraw, Tug, with Don Yaeger. *Ya Gotta Believe! My Roller-Coaster Life as a Screwball Pitcher and Part-Time Father, and My Hope-Filled Fight Against Brain Cancer.* New York: New American Library, 2004.

McKeon, Jack, with Tom Friend. *Jack of All Trades.* Chicago: Contemporary, 1988.

McKeon, Jack, with Kevin Kernan. *I'm Just Getting Started: Baseball's Best Storyteller on Old School Baseball, Defying Odds, and Good Cigars.* Chicago: Triumph, 2005.

Miller, Marvin. *A Whole Different Ball Game: The Sport and Business of Baseball.* New York: Birch Lane, 1991.

Moore, Joseph Thomas. *Pride Against Prejudice: The Biography of Larry Doby.* New York: Praeger, 1988.

Morgan, Joe, with David Falkner. *Joe Morgan, A Life in Baseball.* New York: W.W. Norton, 1993.

Morgan, Joe, and Richard Lally. *Long Balls, No Strikes: What Baseball Must Do to Keep the Good Times Rolling.* New York: Crown, 1999.

Murff, Red, with Mike Capps. *The Scout.* Dallas: Word, 1996.

Nettles, Graig, with Peter Golenbock. *Balls.* New York: G.P. Putnam's Sons, 1984.

Nathanson, Mitchell. *The Fall of the 1977 Phillies: How a Baseball Team's Collapse Sank a City's Spirit.* Jefferson, NC: McFarland, 2008.

Niekro, Phil, with Tom Bird. *Knuckle Balls.* New York: Freundlich, 1986.

Oliver, Al, and Andre O'Toole. *Baseball's Best Kept Secret: Al Oliver and His Time in Baseball.* Pittsburgh: City of Champions, 1997.

Porter, Darrell, with William Deerfield. *Snap Me Perfect: The Darrell Porter Story*. Nashville: Thomas Nelson, 1984.

Ranier, Bill, and David Finoli. *When the Bucs Won It All: The 1979 World Champion Pittsburgh Pirates*. Jefferson, NC: McFarland, 2005.

Raymond, Claude, with Marcel Gaudette. *Le Troisième Retrait*. Ottawa: Les Éditions de l'Homme, 1973.

Reston, James, Jr. *Collision at Home Plate: The Lives of Pete Rose and Bart Giamatti*. New York: HarperCollins, 1991.

Robertson, John. *Le Grand Orange des Expos*. Scarborough, ON: Prentice-Hall, 1971.

Robitaille, Marc. *Une Vue du Champ Gauche*. Montréal: Les 400 Coups, 2003.

Rose, Pete, with Rick Hill. *My Prison Without Bars*. Emmaus, PA: Rodale, 2004.

Rose, Pete, with Roger Kahn. *Pete Rose: My Story*. New York: Macmillan, 1989.

Russo, Jim, and Bob Hammel. *Super Scout: Thirty-Five Years of Major League Scouting*. Chicago: Bonus, 1992.

Ryan, Nolan, with Harvey Frommer. *Throwing Heat: The Autobiography of Nolan Ryan*. New York: Avon, 1990.

Ryan, Nolan, with Jerry Jenkins. *Miracle Man*. Dallas: Word, 1992.

Sahadi, Lou. *The Pirates*. New York: Times, 1980.

Sarault, Jean-Paul. *Les Expos, Cinq Ans Après*. Montréal: Éditions de l'Homme, 1974.

_____. *Gary "le Kid" Carter*. Montreal: Quebecor, 1983.

_____. *Pete Rose, Sa Vie Sa Carrière*. Montreal: Quebecor, 1984.

Schmidt, Mike, with Glen Waggoner. *Clearing the Bases: Juiced Players, Monster Salaries, Sham Records, and a Hall of Famer's Search for the Soul of Baseball*. New York: HarperCollins, 2006.

Schoor, Gene. *Seaver: A Biography*. Chicago: Contemporary, 1986.

Smith, Ozzie, with Rob Rains. *Wizard*. Chicago: Contemporary, 1988.

Snyder, Brodie. *The Year the Expos Almost Won the Pennant*. Toronto: Virgo, 1979.

_____. *The Year the Expos Finally Won Something*. Toronto: Checkmark, 1981.

Sokolove, Michael. *Hustle: The Myth, Life, and Lies of Pete Rose*. New York: Simon & Schuster, 1990.

Stargell, Willie, with Tom Bird. *Willie Stargell: An Autobiography*. New York: Harper & Row, 1984.

Thornton, Andre, with Al Janssen. *Triumph Born of Tragedy*. Eugene, OR: Harvest House, 1983.

Torre, Joe, with Henry Dreher. *Joe Torre's Ground Rules for Winners: 12 Keys to Managing Team Players, Tough Bosses, Setbacks and Success*. New York: Hyperion, 1999.

Torre, Joe, with Tom Verducci. *Chasing the Dream: My Lifelong Journey to the World Series*. New York: Bantam, 1997.

Turner, Dan. *Les Expos, Nos Amours*. Montréal: France-Amérique, 1983.

Ward, Martha Eads. *Steve Carlton, Star Southpaw*. New York: G.P. Putnam's Sons, 1975.

Welch, Bob, with George Vecsey. *Five O'Clock Comes Early: A Cy Young Award Winner Recounts His Greatest Victory*. New York: Fireside, 1991.

Williams, Dick, with Bill Plaschke. *No More Mr. Nice Guy*. San Diego: Harcourt Brace Jovanovich, 1990.

Wills, Maury, with Mike Celizic. *On the Run: The Never Dull and Often Shocking Life of Maury Wills*. New York: Carroll and Graff, 1991.

Winfield, Dave, with Tom Parker. *Winfield: A Player's Life*. New York: W.W. Norton, 1988.

Wittingham, Richard. *The Los Angeles Dodgers: An Illustrated History*. New York: Harper & Row, 1982.

Wright, Jim. *Mike Schmidt, Baseball's Young Lion*. New York: G.P. Putnam's Sons, 1979.

Zimmer, Don, with Bill Madden. *The Zen of Zim: Baseballs, Beanballs, and Bosses*. New York: Thomas Dunne, 2004.

_____. *Zim, a Baseball Life*. Kingston, NY: Total Sports, 2001.

Personal Interviews

Arsenault, Paul
Bailey, Bob
Bay, Jim
Beacon, Bill
Beaudry, Richard
Blanchard, Michael
Boire, Joseph
Boone, Mike
Bouchard, Serge
Bristol, Dave
Bronfman, Charles
Burke, Tim
Burris, Ray
Carter, Gary
Cash, Dave
Cisco, Galen
Cromartie, Warren
DeMars, Billy
Didier, Mel
Dilks, Darren
Doucet, Jacques
Dunn, Bob
Durivage, Pierre
Durocher, Pierre
Elliott, Bob
Fanning, Jim
Farber, Michael
Fryman, Woodie

Fuentes, Mike
Giroux, Monique
Green, Dallas
Grimsley, Ross
Guimond, Rene
Gullickson, Bill
Holt, Larry
Hriniak, Walt
Hutton, Tommy
James, Bob
Johnson, Wallace
Knowles, Darold
Ladouceur, Pierre
Lajeunesse, Michel
Landry, Roger D.
Lavigueur, Rene
Lea, Charlie
LeFlore, Ron
Marshall, Mike
McDonald, Ian
McHale, John
Milo, Richard
Murray, Dale
Nichols, Lance
Palmer, David
Parrish, Larry
Parrish, Wayne
Perez, Tony

Raymond, Claude
Reardon, Jeff
Renaud, Harry
Reusch, Ron
Rimer, Jeff
Rinfret, Pierre
Rogers, Steve
Sanderson, Scott
Sarault, Jean-Paul
Schatzeder, Dan
Scott, Rodney
Sherry, Norm
Smith, Bryn
Sosa, Elias
Speier, Chris
Stanhouse, Don
Stoneman, Bill
Strachan, Al
Touchette, Serge
Tremblay, Rejean
Twitchell, Wayne
Vaillancourt, Serge
Valentine, Ellis
Van Horne, Dave
Virdon, Bill
White, Jerry
Wulff, Steve

Periodicals

Boston Globe
Chicago Tribune
Cleveland Plain Dealer
Dimanche-Matin
The Gazette
Globe and Mail
Houston Post
Inside Sport

Journal de Montreal
Los Angeles Herald
Los Angeles Times
Montreal-Matin
Montreal Star
New York Times
Ottawa Citizen
Pittsburgh Post-Gazette

La Presse
Sport
The Sporting News
Sportsmania
Sports Illustrated
Toronto Star

Index

Numbers in **_bold italics_** indicate pages with photographs.